THE CREATION OF TOMORROW

THE CREATION

Paul A. Carter

OF TOMORROW

Fifty Years of Magazine Science Fiction

New York   Columbia University Press

Paul A. Carter is Professor of History, University of Arizona, Tucson

Library of Congress Cataloging in Publication Data

Carter, Paul Allen, 1926–
    The creation of tomorrow.

    Bibliography: p.
    1. Science fiction—History and criticism.   2. Science
fiction—Periodicals—History.   3. American periodicals
—History.   4. Literature and society.   5. Literature
and technology.   I. Title.
PN3448.S45C36   813'.0876   77–5606
ISBN 0–231–04210-8

Columbia University Press
New York   Guildford, Surrey

To Mr. and Mrs. Sam Raffety

Contents

Genealogy of the Magazines Cited

In Order of Establishment

WEIRD TALES. 1923–1954, and four issues in 1974.

AMAZING STORIES (in this book abbreviated as *Amazing*). 1926–1976. Changed name in 1972 to *Amazing Science Fiction.* Companion magazines: *Amazing Stories Quarterly; Amazing Stories Annual* (1927 only); *Fantastic Adventures,* 1939–53; *Fantastic,* 1952–76. The last two mentioned are separate titles and should not be confused.

SCIENCE WONDER STORIES (in this book abbreviated as *Wonder*). 1929–1955. Changed name in 1930 to *Wonder Stories;* in 1936, to *Thrilling Wonder Stories.* Companion magazines: *Air Wonder Stories,* 1929–30; *Science Wonder Quarterly,* afterward *Wonder Stories Quarterly,* 1929–33; *Startling Stories,* 1939–55; *Captain Future,* 1940–44.

ASTOUNDING STORIES OF SUPER SCIENCE (in this book abbreviated as *Astounding* or *ASF*). 1930–1976. Changed name in 1933 to *Astounding Stories;* in 1938 to *Astounding Science-Fiction;* in 1960 to *Analog Science Fiction/Science Fact* (in this book abbreviated as *Analog*). Companion magazine: *Unknown,* afterward *Unknown Worlds,* 1939–43.

MARVEL SCIENCE STORIES. 1938–1941; revived 1951–52. For three issues (1939–40) this was known as *Marvel Tales.* Companion magazine: *Dynamic Science Stories,* 1939 and 1952–54.

SCIENCE FICTION. 1939, 1943. Companion magazines: *Future Fiction,* later *Future* combined with *Science Fiction,* afterward *Future Fantasy and Science Fiction,* 1939–51; *Science Fiction Quarterly,* 1940–43 (reprinted book-length novels from the old *Wonder Stories Quarterly,* cited above, together with new short stories).

FAMOUS FANTASTIC MYSTERIES. 1939–1953. Reprinted stories from the files of general (non-sf) pulps such as *Argosy* and *All-Story,* usually with one new short story per issue. Companion magazine: *Fantastic Novels,* 1940–51.

PLANET STORIES (in this book abbreviated as *Planet*). 1940–1955.

ASTONISHING STORIES (not to be confused with *Astounding*). 1940–1943. Companion magazine: *Super Science Stories,* 1940–51. Editor Frederik Pohl afterward edited *Galaxy,* cited below.

COMET. Five issues, 1940–1941. Editor F. Orlin Tremaine had formerly edited *Astounding Stories,* cited above.

STIRRING SCIENCE STORIES. Four issues, 1941–1942. Companion magazine: *Cosmic Stories,* three issues, 1941. Editor Donald A. Wollheim now directs the sf paperback publishing house DAW Books.

THE MAGAZINE OF FANTASY. 1949–1976. With its second issue this became *The Magazine of Fantasy and Science Fiction* (in this book abbreviated as *Fantasy and Science Fiction* or *F & SF*).

GALAXY SCIENCE FICTION (in this book abbreviated as *Galaxy*). 1950–1976. Companion magazine: *If: Worlds of Science Fiction,* afterward *Worlds of If,* 1951–74.

OTHER WORLDS. 1949–1957. Changed name in 1957 to *Flying Saucers from Other Worlds,* and thereupon ceased to be a science fiction magazine.

VERTEX. 1973–75. Not to be confused with *Vortex Science Fiction* and other similarly titled magazines.

A note on the word "science fiction". For much of the field's history this term was spelled with a hyphen—*science-fiction. Astounding Science-Fiction* dropped the hyphen from the title on the magazine's spine in 1951, following a general typographic trend. For consistency's sake in this book the term is set as two words, thus: *science fiction.* It may be abbreviated as *sf* or *stf* or *S-F*—but never, NEVER as "sci-fi"!

THE CREATION OF TOMORROW

Chapter 1

Extravagant Fiction Today
Cold Fact Tomorrow

No one man is going to discover the secret of atomic power. . . . But you can be fairly certain of this: the discoverer of the secret of atomic power is alive on Earth today. His papers and researches are appearing regularly; his name is known.

John W. Campbell, Jr., "Fantastic Fiction," an
editorial in *Astounding Science-Fiction*, 21 (June
1938)

Atom Explosion Frees 200,000,000 Volts; New Physics Phenomenon Credited to Hahn

New York Times, January 29, 1939

Vision Earth Rocked by Isotope Blast Scientists Say Bit of Uranium Could Wreck New York

New York Times, April 30, 1939

1

Artist: Frank R. Paul.

"Only hunting and nomad people could sustain life there. Northern cities of once great importance were deserted. The population streamed southward."

"The Cosmic Cloud," by Bruno H. Burgel. *Wonder Stories Quarterly*, **3 (Fall, 1931), p. 6.**

SCIENCE FICTION IN RECENT YEARS has suffered a fall into respectability. Its new status was dramatized the morning after the moon landing of Apollo 11 (July 1969) when CBS interviewed several science fiction writers—Ray Bradbury, Arthur Clarke, Robert Heinlein—and listened to them with the same respect accorded by television that day to Henry Steele Commager, Norman Mailer, and sundry scientists, military men, and theologians. For writers like these, such deference was a new experience. At that time many followers of this field could still remember the days when they furtively purchased science fiction magazines and hid under jackets or sweaters their garishly colored covers, adorned with bug-eyed monsters in pursuit of not-quite-dressed girls. "A funny thing happened to me today in school," young Edmund Murman wrote toward the end of 1940, and he proceeded to tell the editors of *Amazing Stories* how his teacher had caught him reading their magazine in study hall and promptly confiscated it. (His letter was published in *Amazing* for January 1941, with a cautionary editorial caption: "During Study? Tush, Edmund.") In 1944, a Methodist minister in Idaho sold a story to one of the more lurid-looking pulps; when it appeared on the newsstands in the small town where he lived, he went out and bought every copy he could lay hands on lest his parishioners learn of his indiscretion.

Inevitably, skirmishes and harassments of this kind found their way into the stories themselves. Robert Heinlein, in his third published story, "Requiem" (*Astounding Science-Fiction: 24*, January 1940), made his hero at one point endure a conversational admonition Heinlein surely had not had to invent: "The trouble with you is, you read too many of those trashy magazines. Now, I caught my boy reading one of 'em just last week and dressed him down proper. Your folks should have done you the same favor." Was it the trash contained in the magazines (and much of it *was* trash, as even the most dedicated science fiction enthusiasts now admit) that prompted such putdowns? Or was it science fiction's shocking insistence that the world of the future may really be *different* from the known, and therefore acceptable, world of the present? Not just bigger and faster, but different? Fear of that unknown "differentness" continues to haunt people's imaginations today, inclining them to describe anything shockingly new as "like science fiction"—which tranquilizes their souls with the assurance that no matter how tangible an effect it is already having on their lives, the new phenomenon is, after all, fantastic and untrue.

Science fiction is an imaginative extrapolation from the known into the unknown. In a technological era, future technology becomes one of the more spectacular unknowns. Thus technological extrapolation was a major theme for Hugo Gernsback, who in 1926 founded *Amazing Stories,* the first periodical in the world devoted solely to science fiction, and thereby became the progenitor of all "those trashy magazines." "It is most unwise in this age to declare anything impossible," Gernsback affirmed in the June 1926 *Amazing,* "because you may never be sure but that even while you are talking it has already become a reality." "If only five hundred years ago (or little more than ten generations), which is not a long time as human progress goes," he wrote a month later, "anyone had come along with a story wherein radio telephone, steamships, airplanes, electricity, painless surgery, the phonograph, and a few other modern marvels were described, he would probably have been promptly flung into a dungeon. . . . There are few things written by our scientifiction writers, frankly impossible today, that may not become a reality tomorrow."

This theme of prophecy disguised as fiction was stated in Gernsback's maiden editorial for *Amazing Stories* (April 1926), and it was an argument to which the crusading editor returned again and again. From the magazine's first issue onward, Gernsback's editorials, strategically visible to the reader on an odd-numbered page facing the table of contents, proudly carried the slogan "Extravagant Fiction Today—Cold Fact Tomorrow." Science fiction was not only legitimate as extrapolation, Gernsback suggested; it might even become a positive incentive to discovery, inspiring some engineer or inventor to develop in the laboratory an idea he had first read about in one of the stories. Furthermore, the stories were a comparatively painless way of imparting today's scientific and technical lore: "They supply knowledge that we might not otherwise obtain—and they supply it in a very palatable form."

The founder of *Amazing Stories* never recanted his faith. For the magazine's thirty-fifth anniversary issue (*Amazing:* 35, April 1961), Gernsback contributed a guest editorial: "As we look back over the vista of modern science fiction, we are struck by the fact that the outstanding stories in the field—the ones that endure—are those that almost invariably have as their wonder ingredient true or prophetic science." Nowadays, many readers, writers, and critics of science fiction would dispute that claim. As Brian Aldiss put it in his historical study *Billion Year Spree* (1973), "Science fiction is no more written for scientists than ghost stories are written for ghosts."

However, we should resist the temptation to condescend. Although his editorial style at times irritatingly blended the note of Chautauqua uplift with that of the hard sell, Hugo Gernsback does seem quite sincerely to have conceived his mission as a species of popular education, in an age when a college degree was not yet the expected goal of most young Americans. And his readers and writers quickly picked up their editor's thesis that science fiction was also a means for learning science. "Print all scientific facts as related in the stories, in italics," one eager reader of *Amazing Stories* suggested (May 1926). The magazine's compositors did not take that advice literally, but many an author did provide brief cram courses in the requisite science or engineering, sometimes more than the story really required. L. Taylor Hansen, for example, describing a tunnel under the ocean through which trains would be propelled by compressed air ("The Undersea Tube," in vol. 4, November 1929), vivified that brainchild by including with the text two cross-sectional drawings of the device. Most writers did not go quite so far, but they hardly needed to, with artist Frank R. Paul to fill the generously large pages of *Amazing Stories* (and its companions, *Amazing Stories Quarterly* and a short-lived *Amazing Stories Annual*) with imaginative and at the same time faithfully literal pen-and-ink renderings of their fictional technology.

Early in 1929 Gernsback lost control of the new magazines he had founded, in a merciless publishing war with Bernarr Macfadden. But Thomas O'Conor Sloane, his managing editor—a chemistry Ph.D. and the son-in-law of Thomas A. Edison—stayed on under the new owners (Teck Publications), and continued very much in the founder's didactic tradition. "Readers may complain of the wild visions exploited in some science stories, where the authors seem to deal in absurdities," Sloane wrote in an editorial, "The Atom and the Stars" (*Amazing:* 5, November 1930). "Such people should read Eddington's latest paper"—referring to a forecast that well-known physicist had made of a power station operated by the energy contained in a teacup of water—"and see if the wildest imaginings of romancers go much beyond it."

II

Ten years after the birth of *Amazing Stories,* under Sloane's editorship some of the characters in the stories were still lecturing each other as if they were in school classrooms. Gathered around a campfire four days by canoe into the wilds of northern Quebec, in Edmond Hamilton's somewhat crude but chillingly effective story "Devolution" (*Amazing:* 10, December 1936), two of the campers sit digesting their hotcakes and bacon while a third, having finished his evening pipe, fills them in on the theory of evolutionary mutation: "The germ cell of every living thing on earth contains in it a certain number of small, rodlike things which are called chromosomes. These chromosomes are made up of strings of tiny particles which we call genes. . . . " The literary damage that could be done to a work of fiction in this fashion was obvious: "It is as easy to ruin everything by loving science too much as by understanding it too little," Isaac Asimov has written (*Opus 100,* 1969). From the standpoint of literary enjoyment, it is probably just as well that editors Gernsback and Sloane often broke their own rules.

As early as July 1926, for example, *Amazing Stories* reprinted H. G. Wells's "The Man Who Could Work Miracles," a delightful little yarn, but one classifiable as "science fiction" only by stretching that term a good deal. (The story "blurb" printed with Wells's brief opus—very likely written by Gernsback himself—managed tenuously to define the tale as science fiction by calling it an anticipation "of the modern conception of time-space"; surely this was straining at a gnat.) In that same issue in a letter to the editor, the young science fiction writer G. Peyton Wertenbaker warned: "The danger that may lie before *Amazing Stories* is that of becoming too scientific and not sufficiently literary." Having in mind other kinds of fiction that were being published in 1926 (e.g., *The Sun Also Rises*), some outside readers might have considered that Wertenbaker's definition of "literary" did not fill the bill either; for science fiction, Wertenbaker wrote, "is designed to reach those qualities of the mind which are aroused only by things vast, things cataclysmic, and things unfathomably strange."

In September 1927, *Amazing Stories* printed "The Colour Out of Space," by Howard Phillips Lovecraft, a writer whose work indeed dealt with things vast, cataclysmic, and unfathomably strange. A few days after that story's acceptance, Lovecraft wrote to Gernsback's competitor, Farnsworth Wright, the editor of *Weird Tales* (July 5, 1927): "All my tales are based on the fundamental premise that common human laws and interests and emotions have no validity or significance in the vast cosmos-at-large." Any story that ventured very far out into that cosmos must take account of its essential alienness—a long step indeed for readers accustomed to the premise that the proper study of mankind is man. Yet Howard Lovecraft, a serious literary craftsman, anchored many of his own tales in a specific (usually New England) setting for verisimilitude; "The Colour Out of Space," for example, was set in the central Massachusetts region then in the process of being flooded for Quabbin Reservoir. In his letter to Wright, printed in Lovecraft, *Selected Letters*, II (Sauk City, Wisconsin, 1968), Lovecraft argued that even in far-out interplanetary epics "the human scenes and human characters must be handled with unsparing realism."

"Unsparing realism," however, was hardly a hallmark of the work of Howard Phillips Lovecraft, the inventor of a writing technique one science fiction writer-critic has termed "First Person Delirious" (Algis Budrys, "H. P. Lovecraft and Others," *The Magazine of Fantasy and Science Fiction:* 49, September 1975). Nevertheless, that same critic argues, Lovecraft and the younger writers he influenced gave pulp science fiction something it badly needed—"love of language, expressed both as vocabulary and as poetic effect in prose." Hugo Gernsback had, so far as I can tell from reading his magazines, no concern with style whatsoever; the main thing was to make the prophecy and expound the science, no matter how clumsily you told the tale. "But for the heirs of H. P. Lovecraft," Algis Budrys argues, "the humanities were necessarily part of their profession. . . . To be struck in the eye by a word like 'eldritch' is at least to be made aware that there *are* more words than are normally heard in the street or found in school textbooks written down to the level of the uneducated." Lovecraft, Budrys concludes, was a major force in transforming magazine science fiction from the literary mess so much of it was in Gernsback's day into an art form.

At the time *Amazing Stories* published Lovecraft's "The Colour Out of Space," however, that leavening influence was yet a long way off. More immediately important for the development of American science fiction was the influence of H. G. Wells. His literary method was almost the polar opposite of Lovecraft's, but it also represented a corrective on the clunky, marvel-upon-technical-marvel approach favored by Gernsback. Just as Lovecraft advised—but was himself rarely able to achieve—Wells's human scenes and human characters were handled with realism. The effectiveness of many of his novels, as Bernard Bergonzi has shown (*The Early H. G. Wells*, 1962), rests in part on their rootage in a concrete British milieu of hedgerows and crooked streets. Even when the action moves away from this planet, in *The First Men in the Moon*, the fabulous visions are filtered through the eyes of "Mr. Bedford," an archetypically commonplace lower-middle-class Englishman even more prosaic in outlook than an American astronaut. Similarly, Jules Verne's main theme had been man. *From the Earth to the Moon* is memorable not only for the accuracy of some of its predictions (e.g., the lunar missile would be fired from Florida, in fact only about a hundred miles from the actual Apollo launch site), but also for the characters in his imagined "Gun Club of America," who decide upon the moon shot and carry it out, a refreshing collection of eccentrics by comparison with the prim bureaucracy of NASA. Several novels by both Verne and Wells were reprinted in the early years of *Amazing Stories* (it was cheaper to reprint than to buy new); and although the more recent generation of science fiction writers tended to take from the masters more their cosmic inventiveness than their perceptions of human nature, there were some significant exceptions.

One was David H. Keller, a physician from back-country Pennsylvania who differed from most of Gernsback's writers in his almost Thoreaulike aversion to a society based on machine technology. Subordinating the gadget to the gadgeteer, Keller typically described the marvelous inventions in his stories with beguiling imprecision. "All we need is a starter and a stopper," muses the hero of Keller's "The Flying Fool" (*Amazing:* 4, July 1929),

> and of course the stopper would be just a gradual shutting off of the starting force. Then there would have to be something to cause a progressive movement in the air, something like the propeller of an airplane and something more to guide the thing with, and there would have to be a method of obtaining power from the air

—so complete a caricature of the usual Gernsback engineering mystique as to amount to downright sabotage.

Another of Keller's early pieces, "The Revolt of the Pedestrians" (*Amazing:* 2, February 1928), made the Lamarckian forecast that as people continued to use automobiles their legs would atrophy to the point of complete uselessness, and that technology would close the gap by providing all citizens with individual-sized "autocars." (Babies, in this world of the future, go through a phase for a few months of trying to use their legs, but it is something they are expected to get over, like thumb-sucking.) The magazine's heading for the tale was determinedly Gernsbackian: "There is excellent science in this story, and if you do not believe that too much riding in cars is bad for you, just speak to your doctor." But that comment grossly misinterpreted the author's intention. The exact technology of a wholly motorized population *could* have been validly made into science fiction; how, for example, did they manage school attendance, common meals, hospital care? But what intrigued Dr. Keller was the evolution of society itself under such conditions, and the opportunity this afforded for satire—and for the moral judgment that there can be such a thing as too much technology.

Later on, Keller made that judgment explicit in a serial, *The Metal Doom (Amazing:* 7, May, June, July 1932), in which all the metal in the world disappears and humanity perforce has to revert to simpler conditions—improvising log forts, pioneer style, out of the now useless telephone poles. (It was a theme to which science fiction was to return again and again, as will be seen in chapter 9). Cautionary tales like "The Revolt of the Pedestrians" and "The Metal Doom," however, stood in the early days of magazine science fiction as something of a dissenting opinion or minority report, in counterpoint to the prevailing scientism of Hugo Gernsback's editorials. That technical and scientific commitment never wavered, even after Gernsback lost control (as reported in the *New York Times*, February 21 and March 29, 1929) of the pioneering magazines he had founded.

Within weeks after the forced sale of *Amazing Stories,* the vivid primary colors—especially red—that characterized cover paintings by Frank R. Paul were adorning a brace of new monthly publications, *Science Wonder Stories* and *Air Wonder Stories,* together with a *Science Wonder Quarterly* to accommodate the longer stories. Volume One, number one of the first of these (June 1929) was inaugurated with a typical Gernsback editorial: "It is the policy of *Science Wonder Stories* to publish only such stories that have their basis in scientific laws as we know them, or in the logical deduction of new laws from what we know."

This time the magazine's founder buttressed his claim to scientific respectability by enlisting a panel of experts "to pass upon the scientific correctness of such stories." And an impressive panel it was. As listed in the third issue of *Science Wonder Stories* (August 1929), it included two astronomers, an astrophysicist, three botanists, a chemist, an entomologist, three mathematicians, an M.D., a psychologist, and a zoologist. They were affiliated with reputable institutions: Wellesley, Dartmouth, the Armour Institute; one, Clyde Fisher, was curator of the American Museum of Natural History. Listed under "Physics and Radio" was Lee DeForest, inventor of the triode, the audio oscillator, the phonofilm method of sound recording, and much else. The consultant astrophysicist was Donald H. Menzel of the Lick Observatory, whose subsequent publications included *Selected Papers on Physical Processes in Ionized Plasma, Fundamental Formulas of Physics, Principles of Atomic Spectra,* and, significantly, some memorable debunking of the "UFOs" or flying saucers. Nor was this window dressing; Menzel has informed me that Gernsback regularly sent him story manuscripts and took due account of his criticisms.

The hopes Hugo Gernsback expressed for his new venture, in its inaugural editorial, were high indeed. As with *Amazing Stories,* he seems to have aimed at a special-interest audience, not so much the general pulp magazine reader as the zealous amateur chemist, astronomer, or radio experimenter, who might also be reading *Popular Mechanics* or *Scientific American.*

Perhaps especially he appealed to the bright but introverted high schooler destined for Cal Tech or M.I.T., lost in one corner of a prestige world dominated by athletes, cheerleaders, fancy dressers, and good dancers, who in his loneliness would welcome the colorful appearance each month of *Wonder Stories* as the coming of a friend:

> Science fiction, as published in *Science Wonder Stories,* is a tremendous new force in America. They are the stories that are discussed by inventors, by scientists, and in the classroom. Teachers insist that pupils read them, because they widen the young man's horizon, as nothing else can.

Young men who had been dressed down for reading "those trashy magazines" might well have wistfully queried whether the existence of such teachers and classrooms were anything more than just another science wonder story! But in that golden year of 1929 some of their elders were believing in equally extravagant fictions of another sort. It may be worth noting here that the philistine character in Heinlein's story "Requiem," who chastises the hero for reading those magazines and longing for the moon, ends by advising him to "stick to your discounts and commissions; that's where the money is."

III

As on much else in America, the Depression was rough on science fiction. Magazine circulations dwindled; *Amazing Stories* in its prime had had no difficulty in drawing a readership of more than 100,000, but by 1936 Hugo Gernsback doubted that that figure could be met by the combined circulations of all the science fiction magazines. *Air Wonder Stories* discontinued after a run of eleven issues (July 1929–May 1930); *Science Wonder Quarterly* lasted one more year. Their surviving companion, its title bobtailed to *Wonder Stories,* reduced its princely bulk and page size to more menial dimensions, reverted to a rawer grade of pulp paper, went bimonthly, and—frowsiest touch of all—ceased trimming its edges. *Amazing,* under its post-Gernsback management with Dr. Sloane as editor, went through the same process of physical deterioration. Beginning with the June 1938 issue, *Amazing Stories* moved to Chicago under still a third owner, Ziff-Davis, Inc. Its content radically changed in an action-adventure direction. Nevertheless, in a subtitle carried on the front cover for the first year or so under Ziff-Davis, the new management paid a lingering tribute to the Gernsback tradition: "All Stories Scientifically Accurate."

Meanwhile, in a desperate last effort to keep his own magazine afloat, Gernsback proposed to take it off the newsstands and sell it by subscription only (editorial in *Wonder Stories,* April 1936). The gambit failed. Purchased by a pulp adventure magazine chain, *Wonder Stories* with its August 1936 number became *Thrilling Wonder Stories.* Its first editorial paid lip service, at least, to Gernsback's canons of scientific plausibility. But a new slogan run in red letters across the bottom of the cover painting suggested that the latest owners had quite a different perception of their audience: "Stranger Than Truth."

The depth of the Depression saw also the hopeful launching of the third (fourth, if we count *Weird Tales,* to be discussed further below) of the pioneering science fiction magazines. Surviving to our own day under the name *Analog,* this one has acquired a certain dowager gentility. Four and a half decades ago it called itself, with less restraint, *Astounding Stories of Super-Science.* The contrast in tone with Gernsback's *Wonder* and Sloane's *Amazing Stories* was marked. In *Amazing's* more affluent days, around 1927, a strip of type at the bottom of the front cover had listed its companion magazines: *Radio News, Science and Invention, Radio Listener's Guide, Radio Internacional,* and—typically for the period—*Spare-Time Money Making.* By contrast, *Astounding's* first contents page listed among its fellow travelers in the Clayton magazine chain such titles as *Ace-High, Ranch Romances, Cowboy Stories, Clues, All Star Detective Stories, Flyers, Forest and Stream,* and *Miss 1930.* Nevertheless, in a kind of pulp parody of Gernsback, *Astounding*'s editor Harry Bates made the same kind of predictive claim. There had been a time when the idea of circumnavigating the earth or of wireless telegraphy, aircraft, sixty-story buildings, radio, and so on would have seemed fantastic, and "that is the only real difference between the astounding and the commonplace—Time" (editorial, "Introducing Astounding Stories," January 1930). Ordinarily, however, Bates did not even write editorials. He started a letter column, mandatory for science fiction readers by that time; otherwise he let the raw pulp action-adventures brawl on.

Somehow, paradoxically, that period of hard times—economic, scientific, and literary—was quietly incubating the creativity of a coming new generation of science fiction writers. Frederik Pohl, who lived through it all, has said (in *The Early Pohl*, 1976) that it was the discrepancy in the world they lived in, sociopolitically a failure so far as anyone could tell, but technically and mechanically a brilliant success, that turned these kids on to science fiction. Pohl's memoir and others (*The Early Asimov*, 1972; *Early Del Rey*, 1975; and so on) tell with reminiscent fondness of that era, when a ten-cent hot dog was enough to get a schoolboy through lunch and you could go to the movies for a dime—but if you lived in New York you took your stories personally around to the magazines, because the nickel subway fare (or walking) was cheaper than sending the stuff through the mails with return postage at one three-cent stamp every thousand words. In due course these brash youngsters as a result would develop an unusual and highly personal relationship with science fiction's busy editors, who on occasion might reject an author's story and then buy him lunch. But that future was hidden from most of them in the dismal early 1930s.

In 1933 the Clayton chain, which had won the esteem of professional pulp writers by paying as much as three cents a word—princely wages for those times—failed. *Astounding Stories* skipped seven months, and then reappeared under the imprint of another chain publisher, Street and Smith, which had begun life clear back in the Gilded Age as a producer of Western and detective dime novels. Its new editor, F. Orlin Tremaine, promptly began to upgrade the magazine's contents, both scientific and literary. To implement these new policies, the new editor introduced what he called the "thought-variant" story, opening the way to bold if sometimes shaky philosophical speculation and, more cautiously, to the breaking of a few magazine taboos.

Praising him for these innovations, Harold Collender, in a letter to the editor (*Astounding:* 12, January 1934), contrasted the style of the former Clayton pulp *Astounding* with its competitors, *Amazing* and *Wonder.* In so doing, reader Collender acutely analyzed the dilemma for all science fiction editors and writers, of how to deal with science in fiction in such a way that the result was both valid as science and viable as fiction:

> The old *Astounding,* frankly, stood in the main for plain, outright action-adventure stories, such as you may read in any ordinary magazine, but surrounded, to give them a tiny taste of newness, by mechanical gadgets, planets, world-menaces, horrible villains from interstellar space. The joker was that most of its authors, though they could think up these things and make them terribly blood-curdling, couldn't begin to explain them plausibly or indeed intelligently at all. It was all done for the thrill, the kick, the climax, and the happy ending. . . .
>
> Well, the other two magazines *could*—or made out as if they could—explain the machines and the invaders and the funny new diseases. . . . In fact, they explained for pages and pages, and then put on a couple of more pages of footnotes, still doggedly explaining. But in the heat and stress of explanation, they forgot utterly that there is such a thing as literary art.

It was a problem not fully solved under the Tremaine regime, if indeed it is intrinsically soluble at all. Meanwhile, taking a cue from his competitor Dr. Sloane, Tremaine enhanced the scientific credibility of the stories in the new *Astounding* by also running factual articles. By 1937 these had become quite solid expository essays; they included, for example, Willy Ley's "The Dawn of the Conqest of Space" (*Astounding:* 19, March 1937), a sober and informed discussion of the advantages of liquid-fueled over solid-fueled rockets, and R. D. Swisher's "What are Positrons?" (August 1937), an admirable exposition in laymen's language of the Dirac theory. Tremaine encouraged the readers also to address themselves to technical questions. "I have been pleased to see serious discussions of scientific data creeping into Brass Tacks" (the magazine's name for its letter column), Tremaine noted, and in the November 1936 issue, partly on the ground that, by their treatment of stories and artwork in terms of superficial likes and dislikes, the letters to the editor were becoming monotonous, he announced that he was converting the "Brass Tacks" department into "Science Discussions."

Tremaine described this change with an enthusiasm that out-Gernsbacked Gernsback: "There is no reason why *Astounding* should not serve as an exponent of scientific advancement." Out of the readers' bull sessions in "Science Discussions," the editor predicted, could come major scientific breakthroughs: "We must so plan that twenty years hence it will be said that *Astounding Stories* has served as the cradle of modern science." Somehow it did not work out that way. Within the limits of their own scientific competence, some readers sought to comply, submitting letters to "Science Discussions: The Open House of Scientific Controversy" on spectroscopy, rocket engineering, mathematical puzzles, the effect of liquid air on magnetism, or a theory to account for the retrograde motion of Jupiter IX. But they also took up great amounts of space riding hobbyhorses, such as the Atlantis hypothesis, or questioning whether for interplanetary flight the achievement of escape velocity was really necessary. Tremaine's successor as *Astounding*'s editor, John W. Campbell, Jr.—whose scientific credentials were rather more impressive than Tremaine's—quietly reversed the priorities, changing the name of the column (in vol. 22, November 1938) to "Brass Tacks and Science Discussions."

If "Science Discussions" never quite raised *Astounding* into a vest-pocket version of the proceedings of the Royal Society, nevertheless the scientific criticism in these letters from readers did serve to discipline the science served up in the stories. In the *Amazing Stories* "Discussions" column under Sloane and in the "Reader Speaks" department in *Wonder Stories* under Gernsback, vigilant readers had frequently spanked authors for factual errors in their fiction (e.g., providing the moon with an atmosphere), and they continued to do so in *Astounding*'s "Brass Tacks" under Campbell. For example, when Alexander M. Phillips contributed to *Astounding* a story titled "A Chapter From the Beginning," detailing an adventure of a shambling primordial hominid named Nwug (*Astounding:* 25, March 1940), one alert reader (C. S. Gregg, in "Brass Tacks" for May 1940) deduced that the story was supposed to have taken place in North America during the Miocene period, and that the life forms Phillips described as having existed then were, from the standpoint of paleontology, anachronisms; moreover, that a being so relatively advanced as Nwug would definitely not have walked on its knuckles. Some readers went after the artists as well; "the helical sweep of a mammoth's tusk is admittedly not easy to draw," wrote Caleb Northrop (*Astounding:* 24, September 1939), "but it's a shame that Mr. Wesso didn't drop up to the American Museum of Natural History to see how the problem is handled by specialists." The scientific interest of many readers ran ahead of their actual expertise, but enough people with advanced degrees in science or engineering read the magazines and wrote the editors to give these criticisms some show of authority.

In "The Eyrie," as the letter column in *Weird Tales* was called, this kind of criticism was all but nonexistent. Founded three years before *Amazing,* in 1923, *Weird Tales* was not strictly speaking a science fiction magazine. Its editor, Farnsworth Wright, had to steer a course between two opposed categories of readers, one of which enjoyed science fiction, while the other, attuned to Gothic supernaturalism, wanted no science at all in the stories. Arguments among that magazine's readers in the 1930s raged not over the mistakes in the stories, but over the nudes in Margaret Brundage's cover paintings (see chapter 7). To be sure, some *Weird Tales* correspondents, such as Forrest Ackerman and Sam Moskowitz—both of whom remained active into the 1970s—also read the science fiction magazines, and judged the latter by rigorous Gernsbackian standards. Other readers of *Weird Tales,* however, insisted that they did not want science in their fiction. "The hard facts of science, the coldness of time-travel and space-travel," wrote L. A. Petts from Tolworth, England (*Weird Tales:* 31, April 1938), "do not mix . . . with old-age romance and witchery." That sentiment was savagely reciprocated by some on the science fiction side. "Are you in such dire straits that you *must* print this kind of drivel?" asked Cleveland C. Soper when Tremaine ventured to publish a three-part serial by Howard Phillips Lovecraft, which *Weird Tales* had rejected (letter in *Astounding:* 17, June 1936). " . . . This story does not belong in *Astounding Stories,* for there is no science in it at all." Unimpressed by the considerable literary clout Lovecraft had amassed by that time, and apparently unaware that a Lovecraft story had once passed muster with Gernsback, Soper warned: "If such stories as this—of two people scaring themselves half to death by looking at the carvings in some ancient ruins, and being chased by something that even the author can't describe, . . . are what is to constitute the future yarns of Astounding Stories, then heaven help the cause of science-fiction."

                              IV

There were limitations as to how effective this sort of purist scientific discipline could be. Some writers who had themselves started out as science fiction fans, turning out amateur fiction and literary criticism in their mimeographed fan magazines prior to turning professional, eagerly accepted the Gernsback-Sloane-Tremaine-Campbell guidelines. But not all such fan writers conformed. Ray Bradbury, who began to publish professionally in the early 1940s, stated in a 1974 interview (*Arizona Daily Star,* Tucson, September 28, 1974) that in matters of science he was "totally stupid." In fact, he added, "If you're too good a scientist, you're not a good writer." Others, less conscientious than either Bradbury or his more science-oriented fan contemporaries (e.g., Isaac Asimov and James Blish), were simply impatient at the necessity for interrupting their story lines to get the science straightened out. They were, after all, writing for cash for magazines published as men's-adventure pulps in which fast action was the *sine qua non,* and they were not being paid anything extra for doing encyclopedia research.

Such writers quickly found ways of finessing the science fiction editors' and readers' requirements. As one successful practitioner pointed out (Ross Rocklynne, "Science-Fiction Simplified," *Writer's Digest:* 21, October 1941), you could always fake it, either by telling your story from the uncomprehending layman's point of view ("I don't recall everything he said—it was way over my head") or by having the learned professor's explanation interrupted by action such as a woman's scream. At the story's climax, the pulp canons of rugged adventure commonly pushed the gadgets offstage anyhow. "Why does science collapse the minute the hero puts a strain on it?" reader Myrtle Gebhart complained (letter in "Brass Tacks," *Astounding:* 25, June 1940): "Most of the s-f writers build up their backgrounds beautifully. Then, at the crucial moment, ye hero's atom gun doesn't work, or something goes wrong with the cyclotrons, or his ray beam, or his field of force—so he goes to it with his fists. . . . It's such a let-down, makes one wonder: when such improvements come—problematical, but possible—won't science be able to hold its own?"

Some of the authors contrived to create superscientific marvels by the simple expedient of coining words. Many readers eventually developed an indulgent affection for this kind of foolishness, in which (to quote a letter to the editor by Charles W. Jarvis in *Astounding:* 24, December 1939) "Buck Rogers chases Killer Kane through Martian skies with a flying belt and Jack Williamson uses his famous geo . . . s—supply your own endings, they all sound good—to send the villain to perdition in the vastness of inter-universal space." As a matter of fact, the editors themselves, even men so conscientious as John W. Campbell and T. O'Conor Sloane, occasionally sabotaged the effort at scientific exactness in the interest of telling a good story. Sloane, for example, did not personally believe in the possibility of interplanetary travel. But he justified publishing stories on that theme nevertheless, "since our readers like inter-planetary stories; since they unceasingly ask for them in letters to us, and since there is any amount of science . . . to be gleaned therefrom" (*Amazing:* 4, November 1929). As for John Campbell, when chided by several readers for having accepted and published one story based upon an astronomical impossibility, he replied (*Astounding:* 29, May 1942) that the basic idea was "interesting enough to make the flaw forgiveable." Years afterward, in an article "Science Fiction We Can Buy" (*The Writer:* 81, September 1968), Campbell made this policy quite explicit: "Minor goofs in science— provided they're not crucial to the theme of the story—can be forgiven."

Nevertheless, he warned prospective writers for his magazine, the manuscripts he most frequently rejected were written by "people who don't know the difference between science fiction and fantasy." Campbell and his competitors—Gernsback and Sloane in the early years, and later Horace Gold and Anthony Boucher—violated their self-imposed rules sparingly, in the same way that a detective story writer is allowed an occasional false clue or improperly planted suspect in the interest of telling a good story, provided he or she ordinarily plays fair with the reader. This principle of fair play adds a dimension to science fiction criticism that the critic of other kinds of fiction does not usually have to consider.

People unaware of this dimension in science fiction quite commonly don't know what to make of the beast. Take, for example, the second sentence of A. E. Van Vogt's first published story, "Black Destroyer" (*Astounding:* 23, July 1939):

"The black, moonless, almost starless night yielded reluctantly before a grim reddish dawn that crept up from his left." In an English Lit classroom a teacher would probably discuss this passage in terms of its imagery, showing how the author used color words—black, reddish, and so on—to establish a mood. The teacher might consider the passage overwritten, pointing out that nights are not "reluctant" nor dawns "grim," save as we perceive them so. If he took this line of argument, however, he would miss the point that this particular fictional night is moonless and almost starless for a scientifically necessary reason. The action in the story takes place on the only planet of a solar system nine hundred light years distant from any other star, and its night sky *would,* in fact, be blacker than the one we are accustomed to. With no worlds near enough to reach by simple rocket propulsion, the highly intelligent race that inhabits the planet has never had the incentive nor the ability to travel through space—*and in the story that fact is crucial.* Van Vogt's sentence rightly read, therefore, tersely and economically conveys a great deal of information, but the reader who knows little and cares less about science will miss the message entirely. To attempt to *teach* science fiction, as has been much in vogue in recent years, without awareness of this dimension of the subject can be disastrous.

Even with the population explosion of new science fiction magazines around 1939 (*Science Fiction* and *Future Fiction, Startling Stories, Planet Stories, Comet, Stirring Science Stories, Dynamic Science Stories, Super Science Stories,* and all the rest), the effort to safeguard the integrity of the science in science fiction continued. Nothing infuriated regular readers more than to have an "outsider" patronize their field by asserting, as Phil Stong did in the foreword to his hardcover anthology from the pulps, titled *The Other Worlds* (New York: Funk and Wagnalls, 1941), that "the first requirement of a good fantastic story—and half the magazines who specialize on these things neglect the fact—is that it should not be even remotely possible." Reviewing Stong's book for one of the newer magazines (*Astonishing Stories:* 3, September 1941), science fiction fan, author, and editor Donald A. Wollheim indignantly declared: "No self-respecting editor (even of a fantasy magazine) or writer goes on such a basis."

Amazing Stories under its Chicago management, together with its new companion, *Fantastic Adventures,* was frequently condemned by fans for straying away from the canons of "good" science fiction; yet it was the assistant editor of those magazines, Jerry K. Westerfield, who testified ("The Sky's No Limit," *Writer's Digest:* 20, January 1940) that "most of our regular authors"—young men between twenty and thirty years old, who made between $1,200 and $2,400 a year from their writing—*"take their work very seriously."* They believed that space travel to Mars and suspended animation for thousands of years and other technical marvels "are definitely coming in the near future."

There was, of course, the embarrassing possibility that even when the science in the stories was accurate, as far as anyone could tell at the time they were written, the scientists themselves might one day change their minds. But that, veteran science fictionist Isaac Asimov insists, is not quite the point. In one of his regular "Science" columns for *Fantasy and Science Fiction* (vol. 47, October 1974), Asimov has argued that, yes, science fiction extrapolates from the known to the unknown— but not to the point of on-the-hour forecasting of tomorrow's weather or the next day's Dow Jones closing averages: "With fortune-telling the science fiction technique has little to do."

Horace Gold, the able editor of *Galaxy Science Fiction* (founded in 1950), concurred (editorial in *Galaxy:* 3, November 1951): "What science fiction must present entertainingly is speculation. Not prophecy, but fictional surmises based on present factors, scientific, social, political, cultural, or whatever. When a story hits a future development on the head, it should be considered a minor accident; its main job was not to *predict,* but to *conjecture* what might happen if certain circumstances followed certain lines of development."

Moreover—and this is crucial—there are other kinds of implausibilities besides the purely scientific. "You haven't a single author on your payroll who displays any real social insight," complained J. E. Enever, one British reader of *Astounding*, in a letter to the editor early in 1940. "Briefly, you can do with some H. G. Wellses or Olaf Stapledons to supplement your army of Vernes" (vol. 25, March 1940, p. 151). The charge was not quite fair; there had been through the 1930s an occasional Nathan Schachner, David H. Keller, or Miles J. Breuer who had engaged, sometimes clumsily, in social criticism. On the whole, however, Enever's charge was just, and it is a criticism of science fiction that continues to be made, especially by people who have not read very much science fiction. By 1940, however, the situation had changed. Ironically, on the page just previous to Enever's highly critical letter were printed the closing paragraphs of a two-part serial, Robert Heinlein's "If This Goes On——," which seriously tried to apply the insights of the social rather than the natural sciences; and the very next issue of *Astounding* carried the first installment of L. Ron Hubbard's "Final Blackout," a somber forecast—with no technological gimmickry whatsoever—of one possible outcome of the then-raging Second World War.

V

Even on that score, the magazines in a sense had the last word. Future war—including future nuclear war—had been fictionally forecast for a quarter of a century, most notably by H. G. Wells in *The War in the Air* (1908) and *The World Set Free* (1914). It was in continuity with science fiction's own traditions, therefore, that the October 1939 number of *Amazing Stories*, which appeared on the newsstands in the month of August, should carry a grim tale of a renewed outbreak of war in Europe. Titled "Judson's Annihilator," it was based on the major premise that "the scientists' brains have built the twentieth century; their morals will blow it to bits." In the story, an aerial invasion of England is thwarted when the fleet of enemy warplanes is warped into another era by time machine. But this is no conventional evil-Nazis-versus-pure-Englishmen epic; for the English hero enters that future time only to discover, as have the German fliers who preceded him, that regardless of which side "wins" the present war, the world will become a savage ruin. "When I began to plan this story," its British author, John Beynon Harris, explained, "I found that there was no need to use that hoary old standby the mad scientist . . . when the reputedly sane scientists are quite efficiently getting on with the job of world destruction before our eyes" (comment in "Meet the Author," *Amazing:* 13, October 1939). And the brief essay describing the magazine's back cover for that month, a painting of an atomic power plant, noted that atomic energy also could be employed in war, releasing "power so terrible that entire cities might be blasted away."

On August 6, 1945, over a crowded city in Japan, the extravagant fiction of today became the cold fact of tomorrow. Many science fiction writers during the war suspected in general what was going on; a few of them worked on secret military research; one wrote a story close enough to the actual technology of the yet-unbuilt American atomic weapon that when *Astounding*'s editor John Campbell published it the FBI came calling ("Deadline," by Cleve Cartmill, *Astounding:* 33, March 1944). Interestingly, one regular reader found that story scientifically implausible! "Deadline," whose plot turned upon two subcritical masses of U-235 being brought together to cause a nuclear chain-reaction explosion, according to M. Eneman (letter in "Brass Tacks," *ASF:* 33, July 1944), was "mediocre fantasy."

As a group, these authors "had been living very close to atomic power for a long time," Theodore Sturgeon testified in a story published not long after Hiroshima ("Memorial," *ASF:* 37, April 1946). "All of them were quite aware of the terrible potentialities of nuclear energy," said Sturgeon. "Practically all of them were scared silly of the whole idea." Their fear, however, prior to Hiroshima, was for humanity in general; for themselves, "except in a delicious drawing room sort of way," most of them were not afraid, "because they couldn't conceive of this Buck Rogers event happening to anything but posterity."

But it had, and it threw the science fictionists into a moral dilemma Hugo Gernsback had probably never anticipated. "A mother can tell her child exactly what will happen if he sticks his hand in the fire; that doesn't mean she *wants* it to happen," John Campbell defensively explained ("Science-Fiction and the Opinion of the Universe," *Saturday Review,* May 12, 1956). Less loftily, Isaac Asimov, on behalf of his colleagues, made what amounted to an act of contrition. "Well, the atomic bomb came, and it finally made science fiction 'respectable,'" Asimov wrote (in *Opus 100,* 1969): "For the first time, science-fiction writers appeared to the world in general to be something more than a bunch of nuts; we were suddenly Cassandras whom the world ought to have believed. But I tell you, I would far rather have lived and died a nut in the eyes of all the world than to have been salvaged into respectability at the price of nuclear war hanging like a sword of Damocles over the world forever."

Prophecy was indeed, as Asimov elsewhere noted, something different from fortune-telling.

But if the recoil from the extravagant fact of today could be so strong, how deeply rooted had been the Gernsbackian commitment to cold reality in the fiction of tomorrow? Had most science fiction readers experienced merely a *frisson* from the stories, of the kind a hardheaded skeptic might get from a ghost story well-enough told to convince him or her momentarily that "this could be true"? The question is not entirely rhetorical; early in 1939 Campbell launched a companion magazine to *Astounding* called *Unknown.* Although the new publication dealt not in rocket ships and ray guns, but in elves and witches and vampires, it was quickly apparent that the two magazines had heavily overlapping constituencies. The paradox was not lost on alert readers (and writers): "The Jekyll-science-fictionist stands for experimental truth, for logic, for *proof.* The Hyde-nocturnal-seeker exists in frank fear of the dark, in the world of dreams, . . . of witches'-brew, of curses, of Kismet. Fantasy fiction," concluded Seymour Kapetansky, "has bred the most illogical double-track mind in history," able to enjoy both the brisk technocratic forecasts of *Astounding* and the sinister revenants in *Unknown* (letter in *Astounding:* 24, October 1939).

However, the paradox may be more apparent than real. The fact of today may have become so extravagant that no mere fiction could cope with it. Back in Gernsback's heyday, Clarence E. Ayers (in *Science: The False Messiah,* 1927) had compared the findings of modern science with the messages of ancient Israel's prophets, and found both equally fabulous:

> These men tell tales of the creation of all living things from primordial ooze, of the origin of the earth from spouts of incandescent gas from the sun, of rays that penetrate the solidest-seeming stuff. . . . They sing of matter which is not matter but energy . . . which changes places from moment to moment, and of different moments which are simultaneous in different locations. These are the real marvels of the age of science. We must not dismiss them lightly because we believe that they are true. . . .
>
> To be sure, science does not represent itself as folklore. . . . Folklore never does. We must not imagine Moses coming down from Mount Sinai and urging Joshua and Aaron to bear in mind that his various narratives are folklore. It was enough that they were marvelous. . . . But it should also be a mistake to suppose that the Israelites were as surprised by Moses' story as we should be, or as surprised as they would have been to hear him say that he had been borne through the clouds at one hundred twenty miles to the hour and accompanied by the sound of an awful roaring. Sufficient unto the day is the folklore thereof.

Some readers and writers of *Weird Tales* had always understood this point. "We live in a weird universe, whose surface we have barely scratched," one such author declared—in an early letter-column debate over the inclusion of more science fiction alongside the magazine's usual supernatural lore, published an entire year before Gernsback founded *Amazing*

(Norman Elwood Hammerstrom in "The Eyrie," *Weird Tales:* 5, January 1925, 181). "The wildest miracles are perfectly possible. As people learn more and more, such stories as mine [a science fiction thriller titled "The Brain in the Jar"] will seem more plausible." Thumbing through the crumbling pulp pages of *Amazing, Astounding,* and *Wonder,* it is possible to find stories, putatively science fiction by Gernsback's or Campbell's definition, which at deeper evocative levels yield quite a different meaning. The nightmare world depicted by Jack Williamson in "Through the Purple Cloud," to take one early example (*Wonder Stories:* 2, May 1931), a crater-enclosed black landscape under an empty red sky from which fall football-sized drops of viscid rain, is a long psychic voyage away from Hugo Gernsback's "cold fact of tomorrow." Gernsback himself noted that the scene might well have been imagined by Poe.

Unknown was a casualty of the austerities of wartime publishing. *Weird Tales* folded in the general collapse of the pulps in 1954. Of the four pioneer magazines in the science fiction field, the two that have survived, *Astounding* (now *Analog*) and *Amazing Stories* (now *Amazing Science Fiction*), were also two that had ordinarily eschewed ghost stories and other forms of supernaturalism. Always, states Greg Benford (*Amazing:* 49, September 1975), the fantastic happening in science fiction "is rendered credible by the concrete underpinning of scientific fact. Without this hard basis, science fiction becomes science fantasy."

Amazing's pages in recent years, however, have also contained numerous tales classifiable as borderline cases; for example, the story "Lord of Rays" by Robert F. Young (*Amazing:* 49, July 1975), in which a conventionally equipped astronaut in orbit around the sun encounters an Egyptian mummy, laid out in an oar-propelled sun boat as described in the *Book of the Dead.* Even the more hardnosed, engineering-oriented *Analog,* in the second installment of a serial "Cemetery World," by Clifford D. Simak (*Analog:* 90, November, December 1972; January 1973), introduced the readers to a band of ghosts led by a garrulous shade named Ramsay O'Gillicuddy.

(Their ghosthood is scientifically verified, more or less, but the explanation in essence comes down to the old "psychic residue" theory, set forth in Latin as long ago as the first century A.D. in a haunted house story by Pliny the Younger.) Moreover, in the postwar years nonscientific or supernatural fantasy has made its own magazine comeback, both in its own right (*Fantastic,* founded 1952) and in a periodical devoted to both genres (*The Magazine of Fantasy and Science Fiction,* 1949). During the new vogue for the occult in the early 1970s— *Rosemary's Baby, The Exorcist,* and so on—there was even a brief but heroic attempt to revive the twenty-years-defunct *Weird Tales.*

In short, the "illogical double-tracked mind" first noted in 1939, living simultaneously in a brightly lighted technological wonderland and in the darkness of graveyards and dreams, is still very much with us. But perhaps the science fiction/fantasy writer and reader is only giving voice to the present-day experience of Everyman—who also, in a rapidly changing world, whether or not he wants to, must make his own extrapolations from the known into the unknown.

Chapter 2

What's It Like Out There?
Rockets to the Moon, 1919–1944

Over-enthusiastic speculation and 'fictionizing' . . . have thrown the whole subject [of space travel] into the domain of the fantastic so far as most people are concerned. . . . Down the ages drift echoes of the disgusted grunts of the adventurous caveman's mates as he lashes his log contraption together; the contemptuous head-tappings as Columbus' three caravels stand out to the west; the merciless witticisms as Langley and the Wrights tinker with their queer machines. . . .
As a matter of course money has little taste for such projects as these; for they are profoundly impractical—as impractical as a work of great music, or as Columbus's first voyage across the western ocean. Society can get along perfectly well, in a material sense, without such gestures. It is, perhaps justly, hard to interest capital in making them; and rocket experiments are quite expensive gestures. . . .
But the work goes on.

—Peter Van Dresser, "The Conquest of Outer Space," *Harper's Magazine,* 171 (September 1935).

Artist: Frank R. Paul.

An unusual mode of spacecraft propulsion: acceleration through a succession of magnetized rings. "The Moon Conquerors," by R. H. Romans. *Science Wonder Quarterly*, 1 (Winter, 1930), p. 168.

IF SCIENCE FICTION IS AN EXTRAPOLATION from the known into the unknown, then the *Odyssey* of Homer is science fiction. Until somebody came back from the western Mediterranean with an accurate map, no one knew for certain that the strait of Messina wasn't guarded on one side by a whirlpool and on the other by a many-headed monster. As known geography rolled back the unknown frontiers, science fiction (as thus defined) moved with them. Centuries after Homer's time, around 160 A.D., the satirist Lucian of Samosata composed a "true history" *(Vera Historia)* to supply an adventure purportedly missing from the *Odyssey,* in which the voyagers are caught up in a waterspout and transported to the moon. Out of Lucian grew a long tradition of literary trips to Luna, nourished especially by the astronomy of the seventeenth-century *savants* and by the aeronautics of the later eighteenth-century balloonists, until the genre took its modern form in the writings of Verne and Wells.

By that time, the factual frontiers were ready to move out again. "The earth is the cradle of humanity, but man will not stay in the cradle forever," wrote the Russian seer Konstantin Tsiolkovski in 1903. But after centuries of treating space travel as fantastic fiction, many Earthmen balked at the idea of actually doing it. Some national cultures seem to have been more receptive to the idea than others. Tsiolkovski, who as early as 1895 proposed a satellite station much like the actual *Soyuz 2*, remains a prophet with honor in his own country; the Soviet regime in the 1920s reprinted his pre-Revolutionary writings (including a science fiction novel), and a vast crater on the far side of the moon now bears his name. However, when the American experimenter Robert H. Goddard proposed the use of rocket propulsion as a method of reaching extreme altitudes, in a modest Smithsonian monograph published in 1919, he was spanked by the heavy hand of the *New York Times.*

Goddard's entire proposal, climaxed by calculations as to how much flash powder the rocket would need to carry to be visible by telescope as it hit the dark new moon, was "A Severe

Strain on Credulity," the *Times* declared (January 13, 1920). Exasperatingly, even that literate newspaper committed a scientific blunder of a popular kind that hampered all rocket experimentation in the next two decades: this editorial stated that in the vacuum beyond Earth's atmosphere a rocket could not function because it would have nothing "against which to react." So little had the elementary axioms of modern science penetrated even the educated lay consciousness in the two centuries since Newton! But the newspaper insisted that it was Goddard, not the *Time*'s editorial writer, who "seem[ed] to lack the knowledge ladled out daily in high schools." And of course the professor really knew better: "There are such things as intentional mistakes or oversights," forgivable as poetic license in the writings of a Jules Verne or an H. G. Wells, but "not so easily explained when made by a savant who isn't writing a novel of adventure." The Smithsonian, the *Times* hinted darkly, was being defrauded.

By taking the trouble to fire a revolver in a vacuum, and showing that the weapon recoiled even though the exhaust gases had nothing to "push against," Goddard presumably proved his theoretical point (*Scientific American:* 132, January 1925). But his troubles were not yet over. In the summer of 1929 the explosion of one of his experimental rockets some ninety feet above Auburn, Massachusetts, "sent Worcester ambulance and police hunting for tragedy" (*Time,* July 29, 1929), and public indignation forced Goddard to move his work to New Mexico, a state, as J. N. Leonard was later to write (*Flight Into Space,* 1957), "whose empty stretches, so much like the surface of the moon, seem to attract the rocket men."

Urban crowding was not the only reason Goddard was driven away, for similar accidents happened in 1931 and 1932 on the *Raketenflügplatz* in suburban Berlin, where German rocket enthusiasts regularly launched their liquid-fueled cylinders; yet the Society for Space Travel (*Verein für Raumschiffahrt*) and the municipal authorities were able somehow to compose their differences. To be sure, the historical context was entirely different. In 1932 the *VfR* lost the services of its most promising young member, a brilliant nineteen-year-old named Wernher von Braun, to the secret Army Weapons Department, which was interested in rocket research in a thoroughly mundane way. Willy Ley, the *VfR's* vice-president, reported many years afterward (in "V-2: Rocket Cargo Ship," *Astounding:* 35, May 1945) a conversation he had had in 1929 with Hermann Oberth, who ranks with Tsiolkovski and Goddard among the fathers of space travel. "Do you think, Herr Professor, that there will be a need for rockets carrying a load of mail over five hundred kilometers?" Ley asked. "Oberth looked at me with the smile which old-fashioned pedagogues reserve for people whom they call 'my dear young friend' and said after awhile: 'There will be need for rockets which carry a thousand pounds of dynamite over five hundred kilometers.'"

Lacking such obviously utilitarian motives, private American rocket investigators were easily victimized by public opinion. Robert Goddard "early discovered what most rocket experimenters find out sooner or later—that next to an injurious explosion, publicity is the worst possible disaster," wrote his fellow experimenter, G. Edwards Pendray (*Scientific American:* 167, May 1938). Understandably bitter at the press, which had "branded him 'Moon Man' and hinted that he was a crackpot after the Worcester interlude" (*Newsweek:* 6, October 5, 1935), Goddard kept reporters two hundred yards off while he squired Harry Guggenheim and Charles Lindbergh around the premises of his New Mexico retreat in 1935. According to *Time* for March 2, 1936, "Dr. Goddard hates to stir up gaudy talks of moon flights"—and small wonder. Occasionally a leading magazine in the interwar years would publish an article such as James R. Randolph's "Can We Go To Mars?" (*Scientific American:* 139, August 1928) and would editorially conclude that "the plan is theoretically sound"; but the answering voices of negation were vigorous and dogmatic. Significantly, the editors of *Scientific American* first submitted Randolph's article to several laymen for their opinion; they voted against it. Then it was sent to several physicists, who favored publication. Even that early, the natural sciences and "the humanities" may have been crystallizing into the mutual incomprehension and hostility of which Sir Charles Snow was to write in *The Two Cultures* (1959).

However, many scientists in America were also skeptical. Interviewing one prominent American astronomer in 1927 for a mass-circulation magazine, George W. Gray reported: "Professor [William H.] Pickering is of the opinion that the only feasible method of getting to the moon is visually through the eyepiece of a good telescope" ("Marvels of the Moon," *American Magazine:* 104, August 1927). Forest Ray Moulton, coauthor of a then widely accepted theory of the solar system's origin, was even more emphatic: "There is not the slightest possibility of such a journey," he declared (in *Consider the Heavens*, 1935):

> There is not in sight any source of energy that would be a fair start toward that which would be necessary to get us beyond the gravitational control of the earth. There is no theory that could guide us through interplanetary space to another world even if we could control our departure from the earth; there is no means of carrying the large amount of oxygen, water and food that would be necessary for such a long journey, and there is no known way of easing our . . . ship down on the surface of another world, if we could get there.

"And," retorted Willy Ley in *Rockets: The Future of Travel Beyond the Stratosphere* (1944), "there is no reason to make any of these statements!"

When Orson Welles panicked the nation with his famous "invasion from Mars" radio broadcast in 1938, Science Service, a strong voice for the scientific establishment itself, reassuringly announced that interplanetary travel is impossible; to reach escape velocity, even from the lighter gravity of Mars, would require more fuel than a rocket could theoretically carry ("'Monsters' to Mars," *Scientific Monthly:* 47, December 1938). By then, however, Major-General Walter Dornberger and Wernher von Braun were hard at work on that very problem, in a region of "dunes and marshland overgrown with ancient oaks and pines, nestling in untroubled solitude" (Dornberger, *V-2,* 1954) only four hours by train north of Berlin; a place with the Wagnerian-sounding name of Peenemünde. It was not quite so ideal for the purpose as Goddard's New Mexico, but it would do.

In that same autumn of the Orson Welles Mars scare—and of the Munich crisis—astronauticist Peter Van Dresser published in *Astounding* (vol. 22, October 1938) an article called "Why Rockets Don't Fly." His conclusion was simple: money. All of Robert Goddard's initial pioneering work had been financed by a grant of only $11,000, and Weimar Germany's civilian *VfR* spent no more than $20,000 in its most prosperous year. But, as Arthur C. Clarke of the British Interplanetary Society later pointed out (in *The Exploration of Space,* 1959), the German War Department sank £ 35,000,000 into the building of Peenemünde. "The parallel with the history of nuclear physics is as striking as it is depressing." Even at Peenemünde, however, more than sheer militarism was involved. "Our aim from the beginning was to reach infinite space," General Dornberger afterward wrote. Indeed, according to Nazi leader Albert Speer's personal memoir, *Inside the Third Reich,* von Braun himself was denounced to the Gestapo during the war—and briefly arrested—for dreaming about orbiting spaceships, flights to the moon, and atomic energy for voyages to the stars when he was supposed to be concentrating on the immediate necessities of the Third Reich.

II

Whether performed on a shoestring by the amateurs of the *Verein für Raumschiffahrt* or carried out with the backing of the mighty *Wehrmacht,* rocket investigation in Germany was hampered—and, on several occasions, all but destroyed—by skeptics within the Nazi government. But skepticism in America, as in pre-Hitler Germany, was less efficiently organized. If rocket experimenters faced the opposition of sensation-hungry newsmen, they received at the same time some news media endorsements and, in Goddard's case, a Guggenheim grant. They could also count on one staunch, if at that time less reputable, ally in the science fiction magazines, which catered to a readership that also dreamed of orbiting spaceships, flights to the moon, and atomic energy for voyages to the stars.

Hermann Oberth himself, who would live long enough to be feted at one *Apollo 11* prelaunch party as the man who had started it all, served in 1929 as the scientific adviser to Fritz Lang's science fiction motion picture *The Girl in the Moon (Frau im Mond)*. The plan was that the UFA Film Company would finance the building of one of Oberth's rockets, which in turn would be launched in time to serve as publicity for the picture's première. (By an irony, Oberth's preferred location for this public relations action was a spot on the Baltic coast not far from Peenemünde.) Max Valier, a young German popular science writer and lecturer, who had spent much of the 1920s in fruitless efforts to develop a rocket-powered automobile for the German motor tycoon Fritz von Opel, was killed by the explosion of an oxygen tank during a rocket experiment in 1930; a year later, the American science fiction magazine *Wonder Stories* editorially hailed him as "the first man to give his life to rocketry," in a biographical sketch accompanying the English translation of Valier's short story "A Daring Trip to Mars" (*Wonder Stories:* 3, July 1931).

In the 1930s, the alliance between fact and fiction in rocket experimentation became even more substantial. The founding of the *Verein für Raumschiffahrt* in Germany in 1927 was followed by the establishment of an American Interplanetary Society in 1930 (rechristened the American Rocket Society in 1934); by a British Interplanetary Society in 1933; and by Soviet, French, and Austrian organizations. These informal clubs have been credited, in a standard work on space science first published in the USSR, with a major influence upon the development of astronautics (Ari Shternfeld, *Soviet Space Sci-*

ence, 2nd rev. ed., 1959). Robert Goddard, for many years a member of the American Rocket Society and eventually elected to its board of directors, commonly was silent on the subject of space travel because of the unkind treatment he had received from the press. But alongside him in the quest for space were others who held office in these national rocket societies and also wrote science fiction for the American pulp magazines.

Willy Ley, for example, as a German refugee in America after 1934, published not only articles on rocketry and on zoology—the latter in such eminently reputable outlets as *Natural History* and *La Nature*—but also, under the pseudonym Robert Willey, a number of carefully researched science fiction stories. To be sure, his characters face and solve variations on the customary pulp story problems of adventure and intrigue: they escape from "Novaya Respublika," a Soviet colony on Mars complete with a five-year plan and cities having names like "Planetogorsk" ("At the Perihelion," *Astounding Stories:* 18, February 1937), or they thwart a Japanese bid for the conquest of space ("Orbit XXIII-H," *Astounding:* 22, September 1938). But they also wrestle, in highly convincing fashion, with such purely technical difficulties as mass-ratios, refueling in space, and the choice of the proper "Hohmann orbits" for traveling between the planets—named after the city architect of Essen-on-the-Ruhr, Walter Hohmann, who during the 1920s had actually calculated just such trajectories.

Several of Ley's British and American equivalents led the same kind of literary double life. G. Edwards Pendray, science editor of the *Literary Digest,* president of the American Rocket Society, and designer of the first liquid-fueled rocket engine used in that society's experiments, wrote three longish science fiction yarns for *Wonder Stories* in 1930 and 1931 under the pseudonym Gawain Edwards. P. E. Cleator, president of the British Interplanetary Society, ordinarily wrote factual rather than fictional predictions of space flight, such as his book

Rockets Through Space (1936), but he also committed to paper for *Wonder Stories* (5, March 1934) a tale of "Martian Madness." Laurence Manning, a founder of the American Rocket Society, editor of its journal *Astronautics,* and codesigner of one of its rockets, wrote a dozen stories that appeared in *Wonder,* including his jaunty satire "Seeds From Space" (vol. 7, June 1935), and two others with Fletcher Pratt's collaboration. Nathan Schachner, another founder and an early president of the American Rocket Society, who suffered injury in one rocket engine experiment, wrote his first science fiction "on a bet," as he afterward testified, "and much to my surprise it was accepted" (autobiographical sketch in *Fantastic Adventures:* 1, September 1939). In addition to writing some sixty science fiction stories, Schachner also managed to bridge the "two cultures" chasm successfully; he published articles on history for the *American Mercury,* historical novels, a book on the medieval universities, and biographies of Thomas Jefferson, Alexander Hamilton, and Aaron Burr. Somehow he also found the time to practice law.

Stories by writers like Ley, Pendray, Cleator, Manning, and Schachner were usually far from being literary masterpieces. But they did provide a kind of yardstick by which the engineering plausibility of other fictional trips to the moon could be measured. Max Valier, in "A Daring Trip to Mars," took time out from his narrative to discuss the errors committed by "previous novelists," most notably their description of the phenomenon of weightlessness. (The occupants of the spaceship would not "feel lighter and lighter from hour to hour" as they moved farther away from the earth, Valier correctly pointed out; rather, they would experience null-gravity conditions "at that moment, a slight distance above the earth, when the rocket is shut off.") Otto Willi Gail's "The Shot Into Infinity," which appeared in *Wonder Stories Quarterly* (Fall 1929) following prior book publication in Germany, contains far too much "schmaltz" and Teutonic nationalism for today's reader; its heroine dies in space and is carried out of the ship at the story's end to the funeral strains of *Deutschland über Alles*. But Gail's moonship *Geryon,* which the author credited conceptually to Goddard and Oberth, was a well-thought-out, three-stage rocket. The launch technique was different, but its ascent compares—roughly but plausibly—with that of *Apollo 11:* ninety-eight seconds to burnout of the first stage, as against three minutes for *Apollo;* five minutes into the flight for ejection of the second stage at an elevation of 700 kilometers (426 miles), as compared with nine minutes and twelve seconds, downrange 883 miles at an altitude of 100 miles for *Apollo.* Once the *Geryon* is well under way its occupants engage in a space walk: "The sunlit helmets and suits gleamed in the absolute darkness with an unearthly phosphorescence," the novelist wrote. "Day and night had joined in a seemingly impossible union"—language not unfamiliar to any reader of *Life* or the *National Geographic* in the 1960s.

Shots as close to the mark as that one were accompanied, however, by other stories that make one understand why the science fiction magazines were so often dismissed as "pseudo-science" (a term that used to infuriate science fiction fans). A prime example is Harl Vincent's "The Explorers of Callisto" (*Amazing Stories:* 4, February 1930). Unlike the monstrous tower of a Saturn-Apollo stack, the rocket ship in this tale is only forty feet long; in fact, it is a rebuilt airplane, lacking only struts and guy wires. In addition to rocket-firing cylinders, it has conventional landing gear and tail structure, a 15-cylinder, 600 horsepower radial engine for getting through Earth's atmosphere, and a propeller. After the proud inventor, Ray Parsons, has shown his handiwork *for the first time* to his friends Gary Walton and Eddie Dowling, one of them asks, "When do we go?" The hero replies, "Can you make it the day after tomorrow?" It is conceivable that a spaceship built by a civilization less cumbersome than ours might have successfully taken off without its inmates being first subjected to NASA's relentless "simulation" exercises, but this author seems to have gone to the opposite extreme. And, unfortunately, he helped to establish a hack literary tradition that is alive yet. Writing as recently as 1973 (from Houston, home of NASA's famed Mission Control), reader Larry Carroll complained in a magazine letter column (*Fantastic:* 22, September 1973): "I can no longer enjoy stories based on the premise that this galaxy will be colonized by white male Anglo-Europeans clad in diving suits and riding poorly-disguised versions of the V2 rocket, whose primary vices are alcohol, cigarettes, and a compulsion to explain familiar details to each other," in the same fashion that Ray had explained his moon rocket to Gary and Eddie back in 1930.

After takeoff—barely clearing a board fence and the tops of some trees, in the fashion not of a rocket, but of a heavily loaded small airplane of the period—the good ship *Meteor* duly proceeds to the moon; the flight itself is somewhat more plausibly presented, although the dialogue is pure Batman-and-Robin. On the moon's far side the three adventurers encounter space-suited soldiers pursuing a fugitive across the lunar surface. Rescuing their intended victim, our hero looks through the space suit's faceplate: "Christopher!" he exclaimed. "It's a girl! And a peach!" Her name is Lola, and she turns out to be the daughter of the king and queen of Callisto, fifth of the Jovian satellites; with scarcely another look at Earth's moon, the action moves forthwith out to a moon of Jupiter's. Perhaps it is no cause for wonder that although T. O'Conor Sloane, editor of *Amazing Stories* in the early 1930s, published many stories of interplanetary travel, he personally and editorially denied its possibility.

III

Sloane's skepticism, however, was based not upon the *New York Times*'s fatuous reasoning, but upon the more plausible ground that the acceleration necessary to attain escape velocity would crush the pilot—a question that was, in fact, not resolved until the high altitude test-piloting and centrifuge experiments of the late 1950s. Science fiction writers some-times sought to meet this objection by positing "acceleration compensators" (as in John Beynon Harris, "The Moon Devils," *Wonder Stories:* 5, April 1934) or—a less question-begging response—by assuming that the astronaut would black out during liftoff: "Within the compact control room at the heart of the great space-ship, its solitary occupant lay unconscious in the straps and paddings of his seat, as the vast cylinder roared skyward" (Richard Vaughan, "The Exile of the Skies," Part I, *Wonder:* 5, June 1934).

As replies to his editorials made evident, not all of Sloane's readers agreed with his negative verdict on space travel. And the skepticism of Dr. Sloane was more than overmatched by the enthusiasm of Hugo Gernsback, his predecessor as editor of *Amazing Stories* and his competitor as editor of *Wonder.* In support of his more favorable judgment, Gernsback in the second issue of *Science Wonder Stories* (June 1929) began serial publication of a translated nonfiction popular science essay, "The Problems of Space Flying," by the Austrian writer Hermann Noordung, which dealt with such topics—now familiar, but then startling—as the influence of weightlessness upon the human system, the problems of cooking and eating under such conditions, and the space-station technique for space travel.

Understandably, Hugo Gernsback approved of Robert Goddard. In an editorial during his tenure at *Amazing Stories* (1, February 1927), Gernsback hailed Goddard for having routed his critics on the question of rocket flight in a vacuum, commenting that "just as the heavier than-air machine was pooh-poohed by scientists of repute, space flying is being pooh-poohed today by the same class of scientists." But the harassed American rocket experimenter was also singled out for specific vindication in at least one story published in *Amazing* under the regime of the more mistrustful Sloane: "Now that the Goddard rocket has at last made a fair hit on the moon," says one character in a story published in 1929 but presumably taking place a few years in the future, it behooves men to work out the technical details of a practicable space suit. Therefore, in a fictional world far more cozy than that of V-2 and *Apollo 11,* "a little social club of amateur astronomers, . . . mostly engineers or manufacturers from New York or Boston," builds the suits, while (in poetic justice to Goddard) the Smithsonian Institution on a readily granted government appropriation builds the rocket (J. Rogers Ullrich, "The Moon Strollers," *Amazing:* 4, May 1929). In this instance, the implausibilities were not technological but social.

Like Hugo Gernsback, F. Orlin Tremaine, after he became editor of *Astounding Stories* in 1933, dissented from the skepticism of their competitor, T. O'Conor Sloane. In an *Astounding* editorial, "Blazing New Trails" (vol. 17, August 1936), prompted by the publication of P. E. Cleator's *Rockets Through Space* with its prediction that "a trip to the moon is actually possible to-day," Tremaine declared: "Perhaps we dream— but we do so logically, and science follows in the footsteps of our dreams." However, the *Literary Digest* for May 16, 1936, also taking as its point of departure the publication of Cleator's book, ran an article on the American Rocket Society, "Hopping Off to a Dance on the Moon," which—as that title suggests—detailed the rocket experimenters' continuing difficulties with "the ridicule of the public." So far as the man in the street who did not read science fiction was concerned, dreams about trips to the moon were still just dreams.

Meanwhile, at least a few of the science fiction writers had begun to sense that dreams which come true sometimes yield only disenchantment. In "Magician of Dream Valley" (*Astounding:* 22, October 1938), Raymond Z. Gallun pictured "Imbrium City," the first human colony on the moon, as a place of "vast slag heaps," lighted by "the greenly phosphorescent pall of radioactive waste-vapors ejected from the chimneys of the plant." Man is building not a lunar utopia, but an industrial wasteland to match the moon's own natural bleakness:

Artist: Frank R. Paul

"Rockets flamed and roared from the soaring nose of the great cylinder, and simultaneously, the space-ship rocked upward in a tormented frenzy of flight."

Note the *Jaws*-like zoömorphism of this particular spacecraft. Such
animation is not typical; spaceships pictured in the 1930s more
commonly appeared as cigars or spheres. "The Exile of the Skies,"
by Richard Vaughan, *Wonder Stories*, 5 (Jan. '34), 550.

Sweeping around the ugly and eternally threatening squatness
of the rocket fuel plant . . . were the gray plains of a "sea"
which, on the quick-cooling Moon, had never contained water
in any appreciable quantity. The aspect of those gently
undulating expanses of billion-year-old lava was too awesome
now, under the grimly factual stars, for any preconceived idea
of romance in connection with them to overbalance their
depressing suggestion of eternal death.

The only redeeming feature in this dreadful landscape
consists of winking, mysterious "Hexagon Lights," which turn
out to be sentient creatures of pure energy—and the radioactive waste-vapors from the fuel plant are poisoning them to
death. In a desperate effort at self-preservation, the Hexagon
Lights seek to destroy the factory. The hero, as he usually
does in such tales, thwarts them; but at the very end, like the
paleface Americans after their subjugation of the Indian, he is
caught up in sympathy and regret for this beautiful life-form
that has fallen victim to technological pollution.

Many critics of science fiction have seen in the field a
positivistic and optimistic bias, which indeed it had. But even
in the preatomic 1930s, minority reports like Gallun's continued to offer a more somber theme. It was foreseen in the pulp
magazines, for example, that the conquest of space could have
an appalling cost in human life. Manly Wade Wellman's "Men
Against the Stars" (*Astounding:* 21, June 1938) is told from the
viewpoint of John Tallentyre, a vexed executive at a spaceport
on the moon, who sends men out on missions farther into
space although he knows that almost all the ships carrying
them will explode. "Five days out in space, Mars-bound," we
are shown the crew of Ship Number Fifty-Nine grousing at
their moon-bound superiors, whom the ship's engineer
regards as "straw-stuffed uniforms [who] sit back there with
their feet on desks, while we're gunnin' out here, out where
the danger and the work is." A spacehand comes to the
executives' defense, arguing that "they've probably got worries of their own":

"Worries of their own?" echoed the engineer. "On that buttonpusher's work? Say, if either of them worried a day of his life, I hope this ship blows apart right no——"

Number Fifty-Nine was rose-red flame and sparklets of incandescent metal in that instant.

Number Fifty-Nine was one of Tallentyre's worries.

Tallentyre has previously been shown gunning down a would-be mutineer; for the man in command in this imagined Mission Control, the job is worth doing, at whatever cost. For some fictional heroes, however, it was not. The protagonist in Edmond Hamilton's "What's It Like Out There?"—written in 1933, but (significantly) not published for another two decades (*Thrilling Wonder Stories:* 41, December 1952)— receives an astronaut's welcome from his own hometown, and tactfully makes the modest little speech that has been expected of this kind of hero ever since Lindbergh. Afterward, however,

I wanted to go on and add, "And it wasn't worth it! It wasn't worth all those guys, all the hell we went through, just to get cheap atomic power so you people can run more electric washers and television sets and toasters!"

But how are you going to stand up and say things like that to people you know, people who like you? And who was I to decide?

After World War II, this kind of disenchantment was to become almost a literary convention. "There are no adventures in space," says a character in Bryce Walton's short story "Design for Doomsday" (*Planet Stories:* 3, Spring 1948). "Either a space-flight is safe monotony, or quick death." Once the exploratory phase was over, actual daily life and work on another planet might resemble not the adventures of Odysseus, but rather such earthly occupations as coal mining; and mine accidents are not commonly romanticized as "adventures." Drawing not on previous science fiction, but on a tough, realistic fictional tradition of the 1930s that documented the work lives of sandhogs and construction workers—the tradition of Pietro di Donato's terrible *Christ in Concrete*—Walter M. Miller wrote (in *Fantasy and Science Fiction: 13*, August 1957) of "The Lineman," who is one member of a work gang running high voltage cable from the crater Copernicus across the moon. Theirs is a world of drab pain and sudden ugly death, of brutal beatings and hasty commercial sex—and then, at the end, the romance of lunar voyaging breaks through in spite of it all:

> Relke started cranking again, rocking his body to the rhythm
> of the jack, to the rhythm of echoes of thought. Got to build the
> line. Damn it, build the line. . . . The line was part of a living
> thing that had to grow. The line was yet another creeping of
> life across a barrier, a lungfish flopping from pool to pool, an
> ape trying to walk erect across still another treeless space. Got
> to build the line. Even when it kills you, got to build the
> line. . . . The lineman labored on in silence. The men were
> rather quiet that shift.

Or, conceivably, "what it's like out there" may be neither romantically dangerous nor realistically lethal, but merely dull. As early as 1939, when most lunar fiction was still geared to pulp canons of fast action, a character in one story by Paul Ernst is portrayed as putting in his time on the moon only as the necessary prerequisite to a better paying Earthside post. He has a rousing encounter with an invisible rock-eating monster just landed from a meteorite, but he decides not to report the episode lest he be deemed mentally unbalanced and lose his job! After all, he and the bureaucracy of the "Spaceways Corporation" know well that "Nothing Happens on the Moon" (*Astounding: 22*, February 1939).

IV

In the real world, meanwhile, at places like Peenemünde, a great deal was happening. American science fiction writers did not know what von Braun and Dornberger were doing, but they understandably took a dim view of the prospect of space flight being achieved in Hitler's Germany. In the fading peacetime months of 1939, Robert Moore Williams published the tale of "Lundstret's Invention" (*Amazing Stories:* 13, June 1939) in which a dying refugee scientist shoots his rocket uselessly out into space to keep it from falling into Nazi hands. In his last words, Lundstret admonishes young American scientist Martin Langley to carry on his work after the present international crisis is over: "Perhaps—by that time—science will be ruling the world—instead of the hoodlums. . . ." Hitler's fictional successor as leader of Germany is not a hoodlum in Henry Gade's "Pioneer—1957!" (*Fantastic Adventures:* 1, November 1939), but Kurt Roedler, the dashing and personable young Führer in that story, has plans as grandiose as those of his scruffy predecessor. It is all right for men to venture into space, Roedler tells an American rocket experimenter, provided first that a world state be set up under German rule, so that space travel may be developed with proper efficiency. In the tale that aim is thwarted, but nonviolently. Since this Nazi is (in the author's words) "a nice guy," the story's American hero kidnaps him for his own good, and they and their girl friends (Roedler's is English) blast off by spaceship for other worlds, leaving the job of rocket development on earth to be done not by the militaristic Germans, but by the "business-minded" Americans. "With the last Dictator threat of war gone (you were that, you know)," he admonishes Roedler, the American scientists will "find a way to put the secret of my ship to practical application."

In the future anticipated in "Pioneer—1957!" (an unusually early date for the fictional achievement of space flight, by the way), Americans, Englishmen, and Germans all agree that, regardless of who sponsors it, space travel would be a good thing to do. Rare indeed, in those days, was the writer who foresaw that society might reject the whole idea. "It may not be mechanical faults that stop men from reaching the skies—it may be human trends," said the editor's introduction to one of Isaac Asimov's first published stories, "Trends" (*Astounding:* 23, July 1939). Written while its eighteen-year-old author was

on a $15-a-month National Youth Administration job
intended to help him get through college—and influenced by
the manuscript typing that job required, for a sociologist who
was writing a book on social resistance to technological innova-
tion—"Trends" was set in a "Neo-Victorian Age" in the mid-
1970s. A massive religious revival puts a halt to all attempts to
reach the moon, judging them to be impious defiance of the
Almighty. A disastrous rocket explosion, deliberately set off
by a convert to give such ventures a bad image, triggers the
passage of an act of Congress in 1973 that outlaws all research
on space travel, and sets up a Federal Scientific Research
Investigatory Bureau to pass upon the legality of all scientific
experimentation. (The Supreme Court upholds this "Stonely-
Carter Act" by a 5 to 4 decision in "*Westly* v. *Simmons.*") With
such substitution of political for engineering verisimilitude,
magazine science fiction had begun to enter upon a new
phase.

The politics of the late 1930s subtly colored science fiction's
technological forecasts in various ways. Even though rockets
in science fiction had long been used in sanguinary wars, both
on Earth and in interplanetary (and interstellar) space, occasionally they figured in a defense of American isolationism
verging on outright pacifism. In "Fugitives From Earth," by
Nelson S. Bond (*Amazing Stories:* 13, December 1939), World
War II has been raging for three years. American rocket
experimenters under the leadership of Frazier Wrenn, hiding
out in the Arizona desert from government bombing planes
and from "ruthless, sweeping 'drafts' which have bled the
country of its finest young manhood," are building a spaceship in which to escape this wartorn world. German rocket
experimenters led by Erik von Adlund are doing likewise,
hoodwinking their government, which believes Adlund "is
creating a new weapon with which to carry on the war."
(Impudently, they use the *Raketenflügplatz,* where the *VfR* in
peacetime innocence had launched its actual missiles, in the
very shadow of their nation's capital.) Americans and Germans share their engineering secrets, trading America's "per-

malloy" for Germany's "sur-atomic power"; as Frazier Wrenn
explains to his associates, "There is one thing we must leave
behind us when we make attempt to escape our doomed Earth
in this rocket-ship. That thing is—national pride." At the
appointed time, with a success that at least in this one instance
convicts both the Gestapo and the FBI of monumental ineffi-
ciency, the spaceships *Goddard* and *Oberth* lift off.

Hard-pressed Britons in 1939 did not feel they had the
option of renouncing national pride. Yet Arthur C. Clarke,
noting that the British Interplanetary Society had "now been
carefully packed up in cold storage for the duration," its
officers "scattered to the four winds or called up," permitted
himself a moment of ironic detachment before plunging into
the Battle of Britain. "Obviously," he wrote to *Astounding*'s
editor John Campbell (25, March 1940, p. 156), "a slight
disturbance like the present civil war cannot be permitted to
upset the conquest of space!" For the time being, in Britain
and America as in Germany, the dream of conquering space
had to yield to the reality of conquering national enemies, and
the very instrument that had been scorned when men aimed it
at the moon was praised now that they were aiming it at each
other. Rockets reappeared in U.S. newspaper headlines, no
longer as the insane creations of "moon men" but as sober
instruments for the massive support of infantry. "From the
frozen steppe of Russia to Libya's burning sands," declared
Carter Sprague in a factual article, "The Rocket's Red Glare"
(*Startling Stories:* 9, June 1943), "the weapon of the future is
already exacting its terrible toll."

More was to come. On October 3, 1942, a tense countdown
of the kind the world would later come to know at Cape
Kennedy took place at Peenemünde, with scientists, military
men, and anonymous employees anxiously watching their
handiwork on a TV monitor, provided by the Siemens Electrical Corporation (Walter Dornberger, *V-2*, 1954). The tension
of those long, drawn-out "Peenemünde minutes," as they
called them, broke as the "slender, perfect body of the rocket,
lacquered black and white," rose out of the evergreen forest

into the sky to a height of sixty miles, breaking the altitude record set in World War I by Big Bertha. "We have invaded space with our rocket," General Dornberger exultingly told his co-workers, "and . . . have proved rocket propulsion practicable for space travel." Meanwhile, however, he acknowledged, there was a war to be won. The Allies concurred; in August of 1943 the RAF blasted Peenemünde with a massive thousand-plane raid.

Yet there remained islands of calm even in the hurricane years of war. In October of 1942 the cover painting for *Astounding,* in serene contrast to the bug-eyed monsters and screaming maidens who were staple fare on other magazine covers at that time, depicted in subdued hues the now classic image of a rocket standing on the silent lunar surface, while Earth glows overhead out of a dark sky. Although the cover story, Lester del Rey's "Lunar Landing," was hastily written to meet an editorial deadline, it showed nonetheless the mastery of plausible detail that was becoming increasingly common in the magazines:

> With the loose easiness of motion necessary here, he reached up and unfastened the zipper above him, then wriggled out of his sleeping sack, and pulled himself down to the floor by means of the ropes that were laced along the walls for handholds. . . . Grey took the coffee gratefully, drinking slowly through one straw; cups would have been worse than useless out here, since liquids refused to pour, but chose to coalesce into rounded blobs, held in shape by surface tension.

The passage strikingly anticipates a description by cosmonauts Yuri Gagarin and Vladimir Lebedev of what happened to free-floating food particles aboard *Vostok 2* in their memoir published in English as *Survival in Space* (1969). But del Rey's emphasis was no longer, as in earlier stories, primarily upon the plausibility of his gadgets. Grey turns out to be an eighty-pound, four-foot-ten-inch midget, and much of the story probes the psychology of his relationship with a normal-sized female member of the crew. The technological reasons for this plot situation are perfectly sound: the solution of the old mass-ratio problem dictates that rocket ships carry the lightest payloads possible, and one logical inference might be that the ship's crews should consist of women and/or small men. In practice it has not worked out that way; or, rather, this supposedly technical and engineering question has been answered in a nonscientific if not *un*scientific way. In 1963 the USSR's Valentina Tereshkova orbited the earth; from the standpoint of women's liberation in the West the shame of the USA's program was not so much that a woman pilot did not duplicate the feat as that our society did not feel that such a step was even imaginable. This specific kind of social history was something the magazine science fiction of the 1930s and 1940s rarely, if ever, foresaw.

V

On September 8, 1944, the first V-2's fell on London. Jerry Shelton, a young science fiction writer in the American army that invaded Europe, described those tense September days in a letter to science fiction editor John W. Campbell, Jr. ("Eyewitness Report," *Astounding:* 36, October 1945). Fighting on German soil in the vicinity of Aachen, Shelton had seen and heard what he believed was a V-2 in flight; he and other Americans under fire also encountered the militarily far more dangerous V-1's (explosives-laden, radio-controlled drone planes). Because of censorship, he was permitted to describe neither phenomenon to anyone back home. As he recalled, "It was nerve-wracking to be constantly saying to yourself: 'How about this? Here I am running around in a sweat trying to dodge something all us science-fiction guys have been writing and dreaming of—it's actually a reality—and I'm on the wrong end, and I can't write and tell Campbell that somebody is really on the way to space!'"

Men older than Shelton, like the British Interplanetary Society's Arthur Clarke and German refugee rocket experimenter Willy Ley, were torn between their hostility to the foundering Nazi regime and an exultant sense that their own previous work had been vindicated. "Yes, we might as well admit it, V-2 is the first spaceship," Ley declared ("V-2: Rocket Cargo Ship," *Astounding:* 35, May 1945). "The re-creation of these things can be undertaken with confidence after the war, because Peenemünde proved that it can be done." Even after this convincing vindication of rocket propulsion, however, to many earthbound humans the thought of flight into space remained not quite proper. "The subject of projection from the earth, and especially a mention of the moon, must still be avoided in dignified scientific and engineering circles," wrote Robert Goddard on May 1, 1945 (one week before Germany's surrender), "even though projection over long distances on the earth's surface no longer calls for quite so high an elevation of eyebrows" (Foreword to Goddard, *Rockets* [1946], p. x). Neil Armstrong himself, the first human actually to leave a boot-print in the dust of the moon, recalled (in *First on the Moon,* 1970) that even a decade after the successful achievement of rocket flight, his own decision to go into high-altitude test flying and research after graduation from college was still considered questionable: "In those days—1955—space travel was almost a dirty expression."

It was becoming a dirty expression for new reasons, quite the opposite of the kind Goddard had had to contend with. The moon men of the 1930s were criticized on the ground that what they proposed to do was *not* possible; the moon men of the 1960s were criticized on the ground that it was. The argument was no longer that it can't be done, but that other things more urgently need doing; the moon can wait. (So one can imagine a humane critic in 1493 urging the Spanish government not to squander any more public funds on New World exploration on the grounds that Madrid badly needed urban renewal.) Within two years after V-2, one science fiction writer, Ray Bradbury, foresaw and captured this change of mood also. "Why, *why* this rocket?" asks the hero of Bradbury's story "Rocket Summer," as he watches the crowd surging beyond the barrier while the first spaceship prepares to blast off (*Planet Stories:* 3, December–February 1946–47). "*Look* at them. Their sex still a mixture of Victorian voodoo and clabbered Freud. With education needing reorientation, with wars threatening, with religion and philosophy confused, you want to jump off into space." As he looks up at the towering rocket, this story's protagonist is lured in spite of himself by the dream that drew Tsiolkovski and Jules Verne, Robert Goddard and H. G. Wells, Neil Armstrong and Willy Ley; but he consciously, and regretfully, says "No":

> If for one moment you let yourself think of [the rocket], you loved it, too, for even though it symbolized wars and destruction, you had to admire its balance and slenderness of structure. With it, you could rub away the fog cosmetic of Venus, re-delineate its prehistorically shy face. And there was Mars, too. Man had been imprisoned a million years. Why not freedom now, at last?
>
> Then he labeled all these fantasies by their correct name, ESCAPE.

A grumpy Freudian might have said that the pleasure principle was now being displaced by the reality principle. Just as the actual Strait of Messina bore little resemblance to the snarling Scylla and foaming Charybdis imagined by Homer, so the actual conquest of space inevitably destroyed part of what had made it seem attractive in the first place. When, in 1946, man reached out and for the first time lightly touched the moon, by means of a radar pulse bounced off the lunar surface from the U.S. Army Signal Corps' laboratory in Belmar, New Jersey, a distinguished American scholar, who had chronicled the classic literary lunar voyages from Lucian's time onward, lamented that all the charming fantasy and fun that had formerly accompanied such voyaging was gone. "In our modern imaginary journeys to the planets men sail in great space ships constructed upon sound technological principles," Marjorie Nicolson wrote (*Voyages to the Moon,* 1948). "They have gained verisimilitude, but they have lost the excitement of breathless discovery. The poetry of true belief is mute." Perhaps, indeed, if fantasy is fun, then true belief is boring; some members of the generation following Neil Armstrong's greeted his achievement with a disconcerting "So what?" As one such child of the 1960s wrote at the end of the lunar landing year 1969 (quoted in Frederick Gentles and Melvin Steinfeld, *Dream On, America,* 1971), "I once dreamed of man touching the moon. Now I saw it. And I didn't care."

Marjorie Nicolson's remark that the poetry of true belief is mute was to be borne out by many an astronaut or cosmonaut; as a species they are notoriously tongue-tied in their efforts to describe for their fellow Earth people "what it's like out there." However, it would be a bit unfair to the men and one woman of the first generation in space to say with Nicolson that they had lost the excitement of breathless discovery. On the contrary, their responses to space ranged from deeply felt religious acts to exuberant expressions of physical joy. With a bemused expression on his distinguished features, the veteran newscaster Eric Sevareid commented over CBS on the morning after the first moon walk: "They said it was *pretty.*" That lunar voyagers could seriously employ such a word to describe the moon's ultimate desolation may have come as a surprise to some of their earthbound fellows, but any long-term reader of science fiction understood at once what was meant.

American science fiction readers and writers, moreover, have strenuously protested their nation's apparent abandonment of space as a frontier, once the motive of getting there ahead of the Russians was gone and the last of the spectacular Apollo launches, space walks, and splashdowns was over. Only one side of Ray Bradbury's complicated response to space was expressed in the story "Rocket Summer"; the opposite side appears in such early Bradbury tales as "King of the Gray Spaces" (*Famous Fantastic Mysteries:* 5, December 1943), which forecast a time when kids would go down to the Los Angeles Rocket Port to watch a liftoff, in the same spirit that other youths in nineteenth-century America had gone down to the depot to cheer the trains:

It was a hundred years of dreaming all sorted out and chosen and put together to make the hardest, prettiest, swiftest dream of all. Every line was like perfect steel muscles sleeping there in the middle of the field, ready to wake up with a roar, jump and hit its silver head against the Milky Way's ceiling, and make the stars fall down like frightened confetti. You felt it could do that, kick the Universe right in its belly and tell it to get out of the way.

The magazine gave the story an appropriate illustration of a daydreaming lad with his books, his compasses, and his globe, dreaming of one day becoming an astronaut. Three decades later, as the Apollo mission drew closer, Bradbury wrote of it in a tone of exultant fulfillment ("An Impatient Gulliver Over Our Roofs," *Life*, November 24, 1967), and when it was all over he was regretful if not bitter. "It's been a lonely business, mine, to speak for space travel the past 35 years," he confided to the unlikely pages of *Playboy* (December 1972). "I felt little or no company when I was 17, in my last year at high school, writing my first stories about landing on the moon. I don't feel much more company surrounding me today."

Some commentators not generally known as science fiction fans agreed with Bradbury. Two decades into the Space Age, charged Melvin Maddocks in the *Saturday Review* (February 24, 1973), "we are all, in one way or another, trying to evade that overwhelming fact." Instead, "with do-it-yourself diagrams and layman's explanations, we turn each Apollo rocket into a kind of nationally shared erector set." But, in spite of television's untiring effort to cut it down to suitably trivial size, the fact remained overwhelming. Even though at Cape Canaveral "a shiny monument for the original seven astronauts now stands surrounded by tall weeds," wrote Jack Haldeman in an article, "Space Through My Fingers" (*Amazing Science Fiction:* 48, October 1974), "things *happened* here and you can't carry away their effect on the future course of mankind and sell it for scrap."

From science fiction's point of view, the proper metaphoric comparison of Armstrong's long step down upon the gritty lunar soil is not with Columbus's crew setting foot on San Salvador; rather, it must be compared with the supreme effort of that anonymous lungfish which first slopped up on the beach to stay. It is a migration into a new medium, as terrifyingly different from life's previous environs as the new, windy, sunblazing medium that life entered in the Paleozoic Age differed from the familiar cool depths of the sea. "A world such as this calls as imperiously for exploration as an unknown continent," Peter Van Dresser wrote more than forty years ago (*Harper's*, September 1935): "It possesses the quality of *endlessness*, that feeling of receding vistas that has attracted the Western mind across oceans, above the clouds, into the depths of space and matter. . . . We must bring into hard reality the promise of this vision."

But suppose the Western mind no longer hungers for endlessness? As early as the eighteenth century, one luminous Western mind, Voltaire, urged in *Candide* that man cease chasing after El Dorado and settle down to cultivate his own garden. Suppose the lungfish decides it honestly prefers the opulent baths of ocean to a stinking tidal mud flat? But that is not the way to look at the matter, the science fictionists reply. In due course, if not sooner, the ocean will become as polluted as that mud flat. The only way man can insure himself against some of his other follies—most notably self-annihilation in war—is to seed himself out among the stars. Scrapping the space program, Bradbury wrote in his *Playboy* article ("From Stonehenge to Tranquillity Base"), is equivalent to "riding the machine back into the swamp, there to drown and die."

Later in the essay, its author acknowledged a debt to Arnold Toynbee, and Bradbury's argument does have the ring of Toynbee's "challenge-and-response" thesis, with its celebrated metaphor of the cliff-climbing civilizations: "Sometimes mankind reminds me of a creature that has taken a billion years to climb a million-mile-high cliff. And here he is, putting his arm up over the edge, and almost making it. Then, at the last moment, he leaps up, tromps upon his own fingers—and plunges screaming back into the abyss."

It would not have occurred to such a writer to say that we must choose environmental balance, or nuclear disarmament, or the relief of poverty *instead* of space travel. When that kind of conflict was acted out politically, as in "Star Probe," by Joseph Green (*Analog:* 95, October, November, December 1975), whose hero is a rocket company executive and whose heroine is a flaming Berkeley-style antiestablishment radical, the rocketeers win hands down. Ordinarily, however, science fictionists saw such an issue as a false choice. On the contrary, some of them argued, the achievement of space travel and the solution of the ecology/energy crisis are, in fact, linked and inseparable. "The next few decades are the critical decision-making time for the human race," wrote Ben Bova, successor to John Campbell as editor of the magazine that used to be called *Astounding* (editorial, *Analog:* 94, December 1974): "either we grow up and reach out into the Solar System, or we collapse from lack of resources and energy and revert to the Middle Ages."

As the last of NASA's Apollo hardware was used up in the joint Russo-American space mission of 1975, *Analog* celebrated the event with a cover painting by a Soviet cosmonaut, Andrei Sokolov—"a science fiction fan since childhood," Bova assured his readers (*Analog:* 95, July 1975, p. 177). Isaac Asimov's early story "Trends" reminds us that historical tendencies can and do change. Most Russians seem not to share most Americans' current rejection of the space frontier. One day, reflecting upon our own restless and migratory past, we also may change our national mind about space. In that event, the garish pulp magazines of half a century ago may then be accorded a place of honor; prophets in their own time have often seemed somewhat unkempt and disreputable characters. In the meantime, just in case, the International Astronomical Union has prepared for that day by quietly giving three of the recently discovered craters on Mars the names of Campbell, Weinbaum, and Wells.

Chapter 3

Under the Moons of Mars
The Interplanetary Pastoral

*Whenever I see a frog's eye low in the water warily ogling the shoreward
landscape, I always think inconsequentially of those twiddling mechanical eyes
that mankind manipulates nightly from a thousand observatories. . . .
Shape of sea water and carbon rings, yet simultaneously a perplexed professor
on a village street, I look up across the moon and Venus—outward, outward
into that blue-white glitter beyond the galaxy. And as I look and shiver I feel the
voice in every fiber of my being: Have we come from elsewhere? By these our
instruments shall we go home?*

—Loren Eiseley, *The Immense Journey* (1956)

59

D RAWN WITH THE SUDDENNESS OF THOUGHT through the trackless immensity of space" and dumped, naked, "upon a bed of yellowish, moss-like vegetation," Edgar Rice Burroughs's fictional John Carter begins the first of his many adventures on Mars. Combining elements of Owen Wister's *The Virginian* with qualities of that other archetypal Burroughs hero, Tarzan, John Carter is a Western story figure who somehow strayed across the border into science fiction. He bears a proud old Southern name, he has fought for the Confederacy, and after the War Between the States—like the heroes of countless other, nonscience fiction, novels and films—he has wandered out to Arizona Territory to prospect

Raven-haired Firebird in her scarlet chain mail can outdraw any male gunfighter on wild western Mars, including the hero. Nevertheless, when she tries to buy a round of drinks in a wild spacemen's saloon, one of its regular patrons puts her in her place: "We don't let women buy our drinks," he says, and turns back to his cards. Raymond F. Jones, "The Seven Jewels of Chamar." *Planet Stories*, 3 (Winter 1946), pp. 90–91

for gold. There, hostile Indians have killed his partner and chased him into a cave. From thence, outrageously finessing the intricate engineering detail favored by "hard" science fictionists such as Jules Verne, Hugo Gernsback, or John W. Campbell, John Carter is whisked skyward. Mere seconds later, it seems, he opens his eyes "upon a strange and weird landscape." He knows, without doubt, that he is on Mars ("Under the Moons of Mars," *The All-Story Magazine:* February 1912; book version, retitled *A Princess of Mars,* 1917).

As this transplanted hero looks more closely at that strange and weird landscape, it takes on familiarity. "I seemed to be lying in a deep, circular basin, along the outer verge of which I could distinguish the irregularities of low hills." It is high noon, and the dry solar heat on his nude body reminds him of the Arizona desert he has so abruptly left. "Here and there were slight outcroppings of quartz-bearing rock which glistened in the sunlight." As he begins to explore, moving awkwardly in the lighter Martian gravity, the environment again becomes strange. But John Carter's initial impression—that Mars is a place not so very different from Arizona—has decisively influenced all subsequent interplanetary fiction. When Americans land on another world, it seems, they expect it to resemble the American West.

This Western Mars, with its thin (but more often than not breatheable) atmosphere, its dry climate, and its desert landscape, was to reappear again and again in pulp science fiction. John Campbell's *Astounding,* conscious of its scientifically more finicky readers, did not publish so many of these "Martian Westerns"; in an *Astounding* story if you went out for a stroll on Mars, you suited up and carried an oxygen tank, and against the high-pressure, high-gravity, methane–ammonia environment of Jupiter, you probably didn't go out at all. But Campbell, with the sound editor's instinct for a readable story that has made him hard for logical academic critics to classify, knew when to bend or even break his own rules. Alongside the newer, more urbane kind of science fiction associated with Robert Heinlein and Isaac Asimov, he ran for variety an occasional piece like Clifford Simak's "Hermit of Mars" (*Astounding:* 23, June 1939).

"The sun plunged over the western rim of Skeleton Canal and instantly it was night," Simak's story began. "Outside the tiny quartz 'igloo' the night wind keened among the pinnacles and buttresses and wind-eroded formations of the canal. On the wings of the wind . . . came the mournful howling of the Hounds"—in Western terms, supercoyotes, even if they are heavily furred against temperatures down to −50° C. By daylight the landscape is "a riot of red," just like southern Utah. Along the canals, or canyons, trappers from Earth hunt the elusive Martian beaver, selling the pelts at the Red Rock trading post. In a small frontier town "a fellow dealing a stud poker hand" tells a tall tale, like the ones about Paul Bunyan or Pecos Bill. And so on. Simak's Mars is a far more dangerous place than that of Edgar Rice Burroughs; John Carter in the buff would have died instantly in its rarefied air. It has other life-forms far more bizarre than the Hounds; silica-armored Eaters, for example, which love to chomp on human bones to get the phosphorus for their own weird body chemistry. But the migrating herds of Eaters sometimes stampede. "Hear those hoofs!" the hero exclaims, again reminding the reader of the Red Planet's kinship with the Old West.

Astounding's competitors were less inhibited about presenting this kind of material. *Planet Stories,* which flourished throughout the 1940s, offered the interplanetary Western as its staple fare. And, dedicated though they were to mile-a-minute action, *Planet*'s authors quite often were willing to stop the show to let their characters admire the view, much in the manner of the Western writer Zane Grey, who died in 1939 just as the great pulp population explosion began. (In fact, the Death Valley setting used in *Wanderer of the Wasteland,* one of the most popular of Grey's stories, is otherworldly enough that with minor changes it could serve as the scene of an interplanetary tale.) Here, for example, is Mars as portrayed by Erik Fennel, in a story titled "Beneath the Red Planet's Crust" (*Planet Stories:* 3, Fall 1947):

It took their eyes a minute to adjust to the slanting afternoon
sunlight. . . . The rocky backbone of the planet pierced the red
sands here, and through the ages the wind-driven sand had
carved the outcropping into caves and spires and overhanging
ledges and gaunt pockmarked cliffs. . . . The tunnel mouth was
merely a black hole, almost indistinguishable from a multitude
of shadowed cavities where sand-laden storm winds had found
soft spots in the stone.

The Earthman who wanders across this wasteland succeeds in
kicking a drug habit before the story is over; the wide-open
spaces of Mars, like those of the fictional West, can be a force
for moral regeneration.

If the Mars imagined in science fiction was old, cold, and
dry, the Venus described by the writers was commonly young,
hot, and wet—a reasonable enough inference from what little
was then known. Earth's cloud-shrouded sister, writers specu-
lated, might be at an evolutionary stage corresponding to our
own planet's Carboniferous period, or—more dramatically—
to the age of dinosaurs, with the addition perhaps of grey- or
green-skinned lizard-men. Or, the cloud cover might enclose
a wetness so profound as to give Venus a world-girdling
ocean, as in the British lay theologian C. S. Lewis's delightful
allegory *Perelandra* (1944). Often the Venutian landscape was
a riot of dripping vegetation and horrendously toothed beast-
things; more rarely, as in C. L. Moore's memorable "There
Shall Be Darkness" (*Astounding:* 28, February 1942), the
watery scene was still and even cool: "The forest filled a valley
between peaks veined with waterfalls whose music tinkled all
around the canyon. It was half swamp, half lake of clear dark
water out of which gigantic mangroves rose in arches and
columns and long green aisles. . . . The glassy surfaces gave
back such faithful reflections that the forest seemed double,
suspended in green space."

Whether withered and dry or fresh and wet, a fictitious
planetary landscape was supposed to be consistent with what
was actually known. Edgar Rice Burroughs had gotten his
Mars-scape not out of his own unconscious, but from the

popular science writings of American astronomer Percival
Lowell; similarly, the leafy Venus-scape of pulp fiction
derived from a speculation by Swedish astronomer Svante
Arrhenius. But this meant that in successive stories the setting
must be constantly changing, as the content of astronomical
knowledge changed. Burroughs's Mars became less and less
acceptable as the actually measured Martian atmosphere
became thinner and thinner. As early as 1941, in a factual
article, "Dead—and Embalmed," by "Arthur McCann," one of
editor John Campbell's pseudonyms (*Astounding:* 26, January
1941), authors were warned that the steaming, vine-choked
Venus that had figured in so many of their stories was hence-
forth out of the question. Those mysterious, surface-hiding
clouds were not composed of water vapor, and "no planet with
that much carbon dioxide in its atmosphere can have any
extensive plant growth." Some writers, conscientiously working in the Gernsback-Sloane-Campbell tradition, reluctantly
abandoned their livable Martian deserts and their wet Venutian jungles. Clifford Simak, for example, who had modified
the "old" Martian climate considerably for his story "Hermit
of Mars," also wrote an effective tale set on the "new" Venus,
titled "Tools" (*Astounding:* 29, July 1942). But it was a step
taken with obvious regret, and some writers refused to take it
at all.

Mars as nineteenth-century frontier America and Venus as
nineteenth-century frontier Africa had a mythic appeal that
pushed aside all demands of scientific exactitude. Oceanic or
jungled Venuses therefore continued regularly to appear in
pulp fiction, as for example in "The Rocketeers Have Shaggy
Ears," by Keith Bennett (*Planet Stories:* 4, Spring 1950), whose
heroes march out of their wrecked spaceship "into damp
gloom between gargantuan trunks that rose smoothly out of
sight into darkness," enduring "mud and steamy heat, with
punctually once every sixteen hours a breathtaking, pounding
torrent of rain." And in the stories that got Ray Bradbury out
of science fiction's pulp ghetto and brought him to the attention of literary critics, collected in 1950 as *The Martian Chroni-*

cles, the Mars of Edgar Rice Burroughs—old, silent, and dry, but humanly habitable without special equipment—was still taken for granted. When Earthmen land upon a "dried-up sea of Mars," in Bradbury's haunting story "—And the Moon Be Still As Bright" (*Thrilling Wonder Stories:* 32, June 1948), a poetic-minded member of the crew—unmindful that the all-but-oxygenless air of the known Mars will not support combustion—begins the action with a gesture straight out of Zane Grey: "It was so cold that when they first came from the ship into the night, Spender began to gather the dry Martian wood and build a small fire."

II

You can't have a Western without Indians, says literary critic Leslie A. Fiedler in *The Return of the Vanishing American* (1968). "Unless 'stern and imperturbable' Martians await us . . . whom we can assimilate to our old myths of the Indian, Outer Space will not seem an extension of our original America, the America which shocked and changed Europe, but a second, a meta-America, which may shock and change us." Edgar Rice Burroughs did not have to face the prospect of that self-changing shock. John Carter finds his Indians quickly enough, and a fearsome lot they are—fifteen feet tall, green-skinned, red-eyed, and tusked. They ride the mossy Martian plains on eight-legged, pad-footed "horses," armed both with lances and with high-powered rifles. They are nomads; they are chaste; and "their chief form of commonest amusement is to inflict death on their prisoners of war in various ingenious and horrible ways." Shortly after meeting them we see them ambush a wagon train, or rather a convoy of dirigible airships, one of which they shoot down to plunder its cargo. From it the hero rescues a fair young woman, who belongs to a more advanced civilization that also exists on Mars. Apart from exotic detail—both races of Martians, for example, lay eggs—this story is one we have heard many, many times before.

The "higher" Martian civilization, however, is a good deal

"lower" than that of H. G. Wells's Mars—or indeed than that of Wells's and Burroughs's Earth. Quite unlike the shuddersome "intelligences, vast, cool and unsympathetic," which assault our planet with fantastically advanced weaponry in *The War of the Worlds,* Burroughs's civilized Martians commonly settle their personal differences with swords. Hereditary clanship is the height of their politics, and the Bronze Age city-state is the sum of their social structure. From time to time Burroughs bowed to the Wells tradition, creating for example a Martian mad scientist character who conjures up horrid synthetic creatures in his laboratory, in *The Master Mind of Mars* (Gernsback picked that one up for reprinting in his short-lived *Amazing Stories Annual,* 1927). But John Carter's Martian adventures far more typically take place not in a futuristic setting, but in one of great antiquity. The pulp science fiction of the 1930s and 1940s, paying Burroughs the compliment of imitation, repeated not only his Western scenery but also his cultural archaism. Martians, when not organized into Indian tribes, were governed by feudal monarchies, and individually they often had inappropriate Terrestrial-sounding names; "an Indo-Germanic '—a' name for the Princess," as H. P. Lovecraft once put it, "and something disagreeable and Semitic for the villain" (letter to Farnsworth Wright, July 5, 1927, in Lovecraft, *Selected Letters:* 2, 1968). Paradoxically, in interplanetary stories, science fiction's bold voyage to the future has often turned into a nostalgia trip to the past.

Despite his own strong antiquarian leanings, Lovecraft wanted science fiction to break with the Burroughs themes. "We should have . . . no participation in the affairs of pseudo-human kingdoms, or in conventional wars between factions of inhabitants; no weddings with beautiful anthropomorphic princesses; . . . no peril from hairy ape-men of the polar caps," he wrote in a fan magazine essay in 1935, "Some Notes on Interplanetary Fiction" (posthumously reprinted in Lovecraft, *Marginalia,* 1944). "What must always be present in superlative degree is a deep, pervasive sense of *strangeness*—the utter, incomprehensible *strangeness* of a world holding nothing in

common with ours." But few even of Lovecraft's own protégés
took this advice. With one important exception, to be discussed, the science fiction writers of the pre-World War II era
translated the strangeness Lovecraft longed for into mere
exoticism.

They ranged away from Burroughs's Indians-versus-settlers
confrontations, to be sure. One favorite model for their older-
than-Earth Martian civilizations, for example, was the ancient,
but comparatively static, culture of prerevolutionary China.
Done well, this kind of science fiction can be very effective, as
when Leigh Brackett's archetypal hero, Eric John Stark, in
"Queen of the Martian Catacombs" (*Planet Stories:* 4, Summer
1949), wanders through a vividly realized medieval central
Asian world. But Brackett's City of Valkis, with its narrow,
twisting streets, its air "heavy with the smell of wine and
burning pitch and incense," its slave market and auction
block, its soldiers carrying two-handed broadswords, and its
caravans "coming in with a jangling of bronze bangles and a
great hissing and stamping in the dust," is not at all what
Hugo Gernsback envisioned when he declared that the
extravagant fiction of today was destined to become the cold
fact of tomorrow.

Lifting elements "from every sort of adventure fiction—
Spanish Main, Western, Oriental soldier-of-fortune, South
Sea beachcomber, French Foreign Legion, and California and
Alaskan Gold Rush," as Alexei and Cory Panshin sum up in a
significant critical essay, "Masters of Space and Time, 1926–
1935" (*Fantastic:* 21, August 1972), the writers proceeded to
"fill in the map behind the explorers"—taming, as it were, the
strangeness of space into the familiarity of the frontier.
Dreadful, hackneyed pulp stories appeared, purportedly taking place near spaceports on Mercury or Jupiter or Mars,
which could just as well have been set in Asian port cities like
Shanghai or Singapore or Saigon. And the authors clung to
these Arab and Indian and Chinese "interplanetary" settings
as long as they could. Ray Bradbury was able to use his
Burroughs-derived ancient Mars locale, with Earth people

putt-putting through the canals in a motorboat and picnicking in the ruins, in a story "The Lost City of Mars," which appeared in Bradbury's hard-cover collection *I Sing The Body Electric,* published in 1969—the year of man's actual first landing on another world.

But all good things must come to an end. NASA's Mariner and Viking probes have apparently put a stop to all those lost cities, mounted warriors, comely princesses, and bronze-bangling caravans. Regretfully, *Astounding*'s John Campbell wrote a farewell editorial, "Goodbye to Barsoom" (*Analog:* 85, March 1970)—"Barsoom" being the Burroughs Martians' own name for Mars. The "Western" landscape remains; more spectacular than ever, in fact, with its towering volcanoes, its massive dunes, and its vast canyons, as revealed by *Mariner 9.* But the life-forms that peopled Mars through so many decades of science fiction are gone. For an issue of *Analog* devoted to the "new" Mariner-revealed Mars, Richard Hoagland contributed an article explaining "Why We *Won't* Find Life on Mars" (*Analog:* 94, December 1974). Predictably, the magazine ten months later ran a rebuttal, "Why We *Will* Find Life on Mars" by Bob Buckley (*Analog:* 95, October 1975). But the Martian life Buckley expected to find was modeled on existing Earth organisms that the author considered potentially Mars-viable, such as anaerobic bacteria, mushrooms, molds, and perhaps beetles—a far cry from Burroughs's princesses or Wells's big brains. The Viking Mars landing in the summer of 1976 still further diluted the Martian life processes; the most that some NASA scientists would concede from *Viking 1*'s findings was a chemically hyper-active soil. "From this point on there is life on Mars—an extension of our sensibilities," Ray Bradbury proclaimed by way of consolation (*Time,* August 2, 1976). "Man is reaching across space and touching Mars. Our life is on Mars now."

Venus has received even rougher treatment from American and Soviet space explorers. So hot that the probing instruments on Russia's *Venera 8* had to be frozen while in orbit, lest they melt at the planet's surface before they could take and send back their readings, and so deep-atmosphered that an earlier rocket may simply have collapsed from the pressure, Earth's sister planet seems blessed also with furious, dust-laden, probably corrosive winds. In the understatement of the decade, one hopeful science fictionist conceded: "It would be hard to imagine a more demanding place for life to arise" (Greg Benson, "Life on Venus?", *Amazing Science Fiction:* 49, November 1975). As for the other Solar System planets— never very hopeful candidates in the first place—they have suffered similarly discouraging revelations. Science fiction writer Poul Anderson, attending a symposium on the planets at the 1974 meeting of the American Association for the Advancement of Science, heard reports on the *Pioneer 10* flight past Jupiter and realized at once that this hard news from space had scuttled beyond salvage all his favorite Jupiter science fiction stories.

A flicker of hope continues to ride with *Pioneer 11,* which is scheduled to cross Saturn's orbit in 1979; not the planet itself, but its largest satellite, Titan, is believed by the exobiologist Carl Sagan to possess the necessary conditions for "prebiotic molecules," at least, if not for life itself. But that is, of course, by no means the bottom of science fiction's barrel. If you can't find life within our solar system, go beyond it to the stars. E. E. "Doc" Smith showed the way as long ago as August 1928, when the first installment of the "The Skylark of Space" appeared in *Amazing.* By faster-than-light drive—or by sub-lightspeed travel under cryogenic suspension, if the author still considers Einstein's speed limit inviolable—the explorers of space may make landfall on the planets circling other suns, and if the biochemical conditions are suitable, these may turn out to harbor their own princesses and Indians.

"Take a Barsoomian planet," Poul Anderson told a college audience in February 1975, "and move it to the Ginger Star"—a reference to the setting of Mars-wanderer Eric John Stark's latest adventure, a planet "somewhere at the back of beyond, out in the Orion Spur, a newly discovered, newly opened world called Skaith that hardly anyone had ever heard of" (Leigh Brackett, "Ginger Star," *Worlds of If:* 22, February, April 1974). With no violation of scientific plausibility, Stark might then tramp across the wastes of Skaith as he had formerly roamed the deserts of Mars.

Leigh Brackett, Stark's creator, sitting at the same table with Anderson, mildly demurred. Skaith, she pointed out, does not have the same ecology as the "old" pre-Mariner Mars.

"Yes, but the mood is the same" as that of the Burroughs and Bradbury Mars stories, Poul Anderson persisted.

"Only because it's also a dying planet," Brackett replied— tacitly conceding the main point.

Anderson himself, as a matter of fact, was capable of the same kind of transfer of setting and mood. In the same year with Brackett's *Ginger Star* (1974), Anderson published *A Knight of Ghosts and Shadows,* whose climactic scene takes place on a planet of a far-off sun—bigger and duller than Sol, to be sure, but illuminating a planetscape that turns out to be yet another Arizona:

> A breeze whispered, blade-sharp with cold and dryness. It bore
> an iron tang off uncounted leagues of sand and dust. . . .
> Shadows were long and purple over the dunes which rolled
> cinnabar and ocher to the near horizon. Here and there stood
> the gnawed stump of a pinnacle, livid with mineral hues, or a
> ravine clove a bluff which might once have been a mountain.
> The farther desert seemed utterly dead.

Presently, in that galactically remote setting, we enter a Brad- bury-style Lost City of Mars.

But the authors who create such desert or pastoral planet- scapes have become far more careful than were the writers of the pulp era, whose characters romped across the dead sea bottoms of Barsoom. They may take more time with a slide rule, working out the meteorology and geochemistry of an imagined world, than they do at the typewriter actually telling the story of what happens there (see Poul Anderson, "The Creation of Imaginary Worlds" and Hal Clement, "The Crea- tion of Imaginary Beings," in R. Bretnor, ed., *Science Fiction, Today and Tomorrow,* 1974).

When introducing Poul Anderson to a student and fan audience at the University of Arizona, in February of 1975, I quoted as a sample of his work the opening paragraph of his Nebula Award-winning novelette "The Queen of Air and Darkness" (*Fantasy and Science Fiction:* 40, April, 1971)—language that is rich, colorful, poetic, or in the literary sense "romantic." However, when Anderson responded to a question from the floor as to how he came to write that story, he said: "I started out by calculating the orbit of the planet." To the delight of science fictionists—and to the disdain of some "liberal arts"-minded persons, who take positive pride in their own ignorance of such vulgar matters as mathematics— Anderson in his best work brilliantly fuses vivid romanticism with hard-headed realism. It is a synthesis most science fiction writers even today are unable to bring off; most come down off this fence either on the "romantic" or on the "hard" side.

III

The one great exception to the general archaizing and Westernizing of the space frontier, in the pulp science fiction of the Depression years, was the work begun by Stanley G. Weinbaum. His very first tale, "A Martian Odyssey" (*Wonder Stories:* 6, July 1934), is the only short story dating from so early in the 1930s to have been voted into the Science Fiction Hall of Fame by the medium's own professional guild, the Science Fiction Writers of America; and of the fifteen most popular stories in that balloting, "A Martian Odyssey" finished in second place (Introduction to Robert Silverberg, ed., *Science Fiction Hall of Fame,* 1970). The nonreader of science fiction, or the younger reader accustomed to more literary polish, may be at a loss to understand why. Weinbaum's style and characterization, although bright and fresh when compared with the wooden-faced plodding so painfully typical in Gernsback's *Wonder Stories,* seem a bit sophomoric today. Nor is Weinbaum's Mars, with its dry gulches and its varicolored deserts, physically very different from the Mars of Edgar Rice

Burroughs. The crucial difference is in the Martian biology and culture.

Until Weinbaum's time, the reader's choice in extraterrestrial life-forms was usually between human beings (some of whom were very, very good) and monsters (most of which were very, very bad). Weinbaum, by concocting a wacky Walt Disney ostrich-character named Tweel, who enjoys leaping through the Martian air to land on the point of his beak, but who nevertheless has an intellect at least as good as the hero's own, broke clean away from both the Burroughs and the Wells stereotypes of life on Mars. To have created so amiable a category of sentient being, whom one could like and respect regardless of its bodily form or even its mental processes, in the racist 1930s was no small accomplishment.

Weinbaum went on to people other planets of our solar system with bizarre ecologies and offbeat, nonhuman intelligences, as in his saga of "Oscar," the Venutian plant-philosopher, titled "The Lotus Eaters" (*Astounding:* 15, March 1935). The basic idea caught on, and other writers followed suit, until—as one of them afterward confessed—"everybody was going Weinbaum and the editor was plenty sick." ("Thornton Ayre" [John Russell Fearn], sketch in "Meet the Author," *Amazing Stories:* 13, September 1939). Along with the new breed of intelligent beings went a new range of other flora and fauna. Sometimes, as in "Blue Haze on Pluto" by Raymond Z. Gallun (*Astounding:* 15, June 1935), the landscape itself stirred into action:

> Spiny cactiform crystals, shimmering with an inner
> luminescence of their own, were all about him, breast-high,
> covering the floor of the crevasse like a thicket of grotesque
> jewels. They broke with brittle, tinkling sounds as he forced his
> way through their ranks. Long, slender, furry parts of them
> groped through the gloom, touched him in a way that was half
> hungry, half inquisitive

—so that the reader soon realized, had he had any doubts on the matter, that he was not in Arizona after all.

Stanley Weinbaum died in December 1935, only a year and a half after his stories had begun to appear in magazines— tragically cut off before he could even begin to expand and refine his powers. Pictorially, the Weinbaum Revolution outlived him by several years. *Fantastic Adventures,* an outsized companion to *Amazing Stories* launched in 1939, ran a man from Mars on its first back cover (May 1939) who was as outlandish as veteran science fiction artist Frank R. Paul could paint him. He was followed in subsequent issues by beings from Venus, Mercury, Saturn, Neptune, Jupiter's moon Io, and so on. These were not monster-menaces chasing after shapely young women (as the *front* covers of the same magazine so often depicted), nor were they variations on the cowboys-versus-Indians theme. Rather, these were "first contact" situations, with an Earthman in a space suit being lowered to the planet's surface to offer greetings, or sketching the concentric planetary orbits on the ground and positioning a rock to show the planet from which he has come. For this "Life on Other Worlds" series, climaxing a dozen years of science fiction painting, artist Paul really let himself go; it was quite appropriate that that same year he should be chosen as guest of honor at science fiction fandom's first World Science Fiction Convention.

Over the long run, the Weinbaum influence upon science fiction has been profound. A passage in Weinbaum's "Parasite Planet," for example (*Astounding:* 14, February 1935), in which a pair of Earth people wend their way across the "twilight zone" then assumed to exist on Venus toward the distant Mountains of Eternity, may anticipate a similar adventure toward the end of Brian Aldiss's hauntingly beautiful *The Long Afternoon of Earth,* 1962 (episode separately published as "Timberline," *Fantasy and Science Fiction:* 21, September 1961). Again, the mutually parasitic but perfectly balanced ecology of Weinbaum's Venus may be one intellectual source for the fungoid ecology of the planet Nacre, so brilliantly worked out in Piers Anthony's novel *Omnivore* (1968). In the

Artist: Charles Schneeman.

Natty Bumppo had Chingachgook, Ishmael had Queequeg, and Kimball Kinnison has these even more exotic boon companions.

"Gray Lensman," by E. E. Smith.
Astounding Science-Fiction, **24 (October, 1939), p. 9.**

short run, however, the Weinbaum influence suffered a temporary eclipse.

In the magazines of the early 1940s, Weinbaumish stories continued to appear from time to time—but surprisingly few, considering the initial vogue for them. One reason for this change is that some of the magazine editors no longer wanted alien strangeness in the stories they published. Jerry K. Westerfield, assistant editor of *Amazing Stories* and *Fantastic Adventures,* in a "how-to" article misleadingly titled "The Sky's No Limit" (*Writer's Digest:* 20, January 1940), urged writers for those magazines to take a near-present, Earth-centered, locally focused approach:

> Stories starting in some large U.S. city are better than those starting off in space somewhere. A story starting in the present is better than one starting in the past or the future. . . . A large U.S. city like New York is concrete and real to the minds of our readers; while a city off on Mars somewhere is vague and indefinite. The ideal story starts in the U.S. and later the action moves to Mars.

This advice, taken at face value, would have knocked out not only the Weinbaumian extraterrestrial—who, by this guideline, could only have been introduced into the story too late to have any real impact—but also the Burroughs-Brackett-Bradbury "lost city" setting; Eric John Stark could be permitted to walk the streets of Valkis only if he first traversed those of Chicago. Sensible as it sounded—for Wells and Verne had started their interplanetary stories in just such a fashion—*Amazing*'s "realistic" logic, if followed all the way, would have destroyed much of science fiction's intrinsic appeal. *Amazing*, in fact, over the course of the year 1941, inconsistently published several new John Carter stories by Burroughs himself, and its readers loudly preferred the more romantic and "Barsoomian" of these adventures to the initial, more Earthbound one (see comments in the "Discussions" column).

Giving her own practical counsel to new science fiction writers, in an essay on "The Science-fiction Field" (*Writer's Digest:* 24, July 1944), Leigh Brackett pointedly rebutted all advice such as that of the *Amazing* editor—or of the typical "creative writing" instructor!—as hidebound and unimaginative: "Beginners are forever being told to write about their own back yards. But most young people are bored as hell with their own back yards." If that was true in 1944 it is even more true today, when many more young people are reading (and trying to write) science fiction.

In *Astounding*, and later in the new, postwar-founded magazines, Clifford Simak carried valiantly on in the Weinbaum tradition. From "Archie," the sentient radon-based life form in "Tools" (1942), to the unnamed creature from another star trapped on Earth in "The Thing in the Stone" (*Worlds of If:* 20, March 1970), a parade of interesting and appealing non-humans marches through Simak's stories. The folksy, New England-type cantankerousness of the Earthman character who usually encounters one of them only lends spooky plausibility to their alienness. We are strangers in the universe, says Simak, but we are not alone.

Astounding's John Campbell regularly published Simak's work in the 1940s; he also ran an occasional romantic swashbuckler by Leigh Brackett, although she usually found a more congenial market in *Planet Stories*. However, in the end Campbell cut off the Burroughs romanticism and the Weinbaum alienism just as decisively as did his more crassly commercial competitors at *Amazing*. Campbell, by Isaac Asimov's testimony (in *The Early Asimov*, 1972), "liked stories in which human beings proved themselves superior to other intelligences," and he could not abide the idea of man coming out second best.

It was a projection out upon the universe of Campbell's own American superiority complex. Although not in the conventional sense "racist," Asimov believes, *Astounding*'s editor—the son of a D.A.R.—"did seem to take for granted, somehow, the stereotype of the Nordic white as the true representative of Man the Explorer, Man the Darer, Man the Victor." Therefore, "to avoid a collision with Campbell's views," while nevertheless contriving to write something Campbell would buy (the editor had rejected fifteen of the first sixteen stories the young author had offered him), Isaac Asimov began to people the galaxy with an all-human population, briskly organized into interstellar commonwealths, not "frontier" in character so much as extensions of modern, twentieth-century metroculture—indeed, of Columbia and M.I.T.

Exit, therefore, for reasons having nothing to do with astronomic plausibility, both Burroughs and Weinbaum. Not immediately, and not from all stories published in *Astounding:*

E. E. "Doc" Smith, for example, with a half-dozen book-length "space operas" under his belt, was well enough established to resist the trend. Smith's serials "Gray Lensman" (*Astounding:* 24, October, November, December 1939; January, 1940), "Second-Stage Lensmen" (*ASF:* 28, November, December, 1941; January, February 1942), and "Children of the Lens" (*ASF:* 40, November, December 1947; January, February 1948)—all published under Campbell's regime—abounded in superintelligent nonhumans, friendly as well as otherwise. Ranging from wriggling winged lizards to eyeless, blank-headed, many-legged beings with ESP, to "frigid-blooded poison-breathers," some allied with the evil culture of Boskone and others ranked shoulder to shoulder in defense of galactic Civilization, these bizarre beasts carried worthily on in the Weinbaum tradition. But "Children of the Lens" was the last Smith story to appear in *Astounding,* although he had a dozen writing years yet to go. Asimov's galaxy, not Smith's, represented the wave of science fiction's immediate future. Explorers might still occasionally battle beast-things in out-of-the-way places, in the interplanetary fiction of the 1950s and 1960s—or sell them useful commodities, as in Larry Niven's story "Handicap" (*Galaxy Science Fiction:* 26, December 1967)—but more and more frequently, in the longer stories especially, Man traveled the length and breadth of the universe and found only Man.

IV

Happily, not all science fiction writers have restricted themselves to a humans-only cosmos. Campbell himself did not always hold consistently to the anti-alien bias Asimov attributes to him. The editor collaborated closely with one of his writers, Hal Clement, in the creation of the hooting, pincer-waving eighteen-inch centipede intelligences who inhabit the fried-egg-shaped planet Mesklin ("Hal Clement" [Harry C. Stubbs], "Mission of Gravity" [*Astounding:* 51, April, May, June, July 1953] and "Star Light" [*Analog:* 85, June, July,

August 1970; 86, September 1970].) Other writers, especially in more recent years, have also described a universe more Weinbaumian in character than Asimovian, and it may pardonably be hoped that this trend in science fiction will continue. I only regret that the haunting First Contact scenes in Arthur C. Clarke's *Rendezvous With Rama* (1974)—a novel international enough in appeal to have been chosen for publication in Russian in the U.S.S.R.—could not have been illustrated in gloriously garish color by Frank R. Paul.

What bothers me about even the very good stories in the humans-only category—such as Isaac Asimov's "Nightfall" (*Astounding:* 28, September 1941), which came in *first* in the best-fifteen balloting by his fellow authors in the Science Fiction Writers of America—is that their human, Earthlike realism is all too successful. It is too present-day, like those historical novels set in ancient Rome whose characters talk like Victorian Englishmen, if the novel was written by one, or like New York cocktail party givers, if the tale was composed by a dweller in that milieu. Asimov in "Nightfall" asks us to believe that a culture which has evolved in a far-off star cluster under startlingly different astronomical conditions from ours—conditions necessary to the tale's development and outcome—should, with no contact from Earth, have *exactly* duplicated modern Terrestrial society. As the tale begins, an impatient university bureaucrat is being badgered, American-style, by a newspaperman who speaks in colloquialisms such as "Johnny Public." Some literary translators, of course, believe in just such an idiomatic approach, as in the version of the *Iliad* that described Achilles as a "good man in a scrimmage." But it does deflate, in Asimov's otherwise excellent story, that differentness—that "sense of wonder," as the science fictionists themselves used to call it—which is one of the special attractions in this form of imaginative literature.

A different kind of pitfall awaits the purveyor of space opera, in the mode established by E. E. Smith. The Weinbaumish freshness of Smith's outer-space beasties is more than counterbalanced, unfortunately, by the staleness of his sociopolitical assumptions. "Smith writes superb blood and thunder, and he possesses a fine scientific imagination," conceded J. E. Enever in a letter to "Brass Tacks," written while one of the Smith space operas was running serially (*Astounding:* 25, March 1940). "Yet socially the worlds of 'Galactic Patrol' and 'Gray Lensman' are identical with our own"— technocratic, capitalist, and highly policed. But this, as extrapolation, is implausible; "Smith's interstellar communities could no more use our social forms than we can use those of the Amerindians."

Campbell, exercising his editorial prerogative of the last word, staunchly defended "Doc" Smith: "Our society is in the 'civilize-the-newly-acquired-lands stage.' The civilization of Smith's epic is in the same stage. They would be similar!" But the criticism continued. One reader found in the evolution of Smith's own writing a downward trend: "Gray Lensman," said Lew Cunningham (*Astounding:* 25, June 1940), was a distinct disappointment after "Galactic Patrol," the space opera to which it was the sequel:

> Not enough whole-installment interludes on screwy planets or out-of-the-way, unexplored solar systems. . . . Too much dirty spy work among lowly meteor miners and dope addicts! In the unforgettable "Galactic Patrol" you gave the thoughtful reader an impression of the unimaginably huge size of our galaxy. Then in "Gray Lensman" you proceed to shrivel this monstrous aggregation of stars and dirty it up, so to speak, with swarms of meteor miners, throwbacks to the ancient twentieth-century system. In future, let's have more Trenco [one of the more fantastic of Smith's planets] and less thionite [the narcotic drug-leaf grown thereon]!

But if interstellar communities could no more use twentieth-century social forms than twentieth-century communities could use those of the American Indians, to concoct social forms the latter-day cultures *could* use might turn out to be extraordinarily difficult. The sheer magnitude of a galactic civilization would be politically baffling. Writers, beginning with Asimov, quite commonly have given over the entire surface, and perhaps also the interior, of a large planet to the sole purpose of governing the whole. John Campbell got out pencil and paper and came up with some appalling conclusions in an editorial called "Arithmetic and Empire" (*Astounding:* 32, November 1943): if there were 400 million inhabited planets in this galaxy, even averaging a population of no more than a billion each, at one civil servant per million citizens, there would be 400 billion galactic federal employees! What kind of manageable-sized parliament or congress could be had, if the representative had to speak for literally billions of constituents? "Has anyone any workable suggestion for a galactic government?"

One reader replied that government, in order to rule over many stars, would of necessity become an oligarchy. It would have to be staffed by persons "trained from infancy to become government" (E. L. Cameron in "Brass Tacks," *Astounding:* 33, March 1944). The Jacksonian notion of political careers open to all comers must be abandoned; "No longer can a man become a senator because he has been a good small-town banker, nor a president because he was a good newspaper editor." John Campbell, despite his own admitted bent toward elitism, was not too happy with this solution. He referred that reader to a just published story, "Plague" (*Astounding:* 32, February 1944), by veteran writer "Murray Leinster" (Will F. Jenkins), which pictured a galaxy-wide society sinking helplessly into the sea of red tape that so enormous a bureaucracy would necessarily evolve. Leinster's solution to the problem was one of Utopian desperation: at the tale's end the hero urges that the bureaucratic, by-the-rule-book mentality be biologically bred out of the human race. Nobody seems to have remembered the sage advice proffered by Stanley Weinbaum in his second Mars story, "Valley of Dreams" (*Wonder Stories:* 6, November 1934), namely that a *really* advanced society, in which everyone knew what to do and had the freedom to do it, might not require anything so archaic as "government" at all.

The computer revolution had barely begun when this

debate took place in *Astounding*. Superior processes of information retrieval, combined with sophisticated new modes of
constituency input, in theory might make possible a multistel-
lar government deriving its just powers from the consent of
the governed. Few science fiction writers in the past thirty
years, however, have traveled that hopeful road. Instead, they
have either continued along Doc Smith's well-worn track—in
which the exploration of farthest space is carried on in the
finest tradition of the Navy—or they have created far-flung
authoritarian regimes. In the former case, they commit themselves to endless anachronism; why, to take a minor but all too
typical example, should the engineer of the starship *Enterprise*,
in TV's perennially rerunning science fiction series *Star Trek*,
have had a Scottish accent simply because in English-language
fiction ships' engineers have been typecast as Scots ever since
the days of iron and steam? But the Smith space opera tradition, socially regressive though it was, seems downright
enlightened by comparison with the antiquated political forms
typical of more recent interstellar fiction. Writers—even very
good writers—have seemed unable to conceive of galactic
society except in terms of absolutism and/or feudalism.

"Cordwainer Smith" (Paul Linebarger), for example, whose
work in the 1960s won deservedly high esteem, had his Lords
of the Instrumentality, among whom "Mister and Owner" is a
highly honorific form of address; his arbitrary forms of justice; his "under-people." Even so supposedly advanced a
world as that portrayed in Frank Herbert's *Dune* (1965),
perhaps the single most popular science fiction book of the
past two decades—it won both the "Nebula" award, conferred
by the science fiction writers, and the "Hugo," awarded by the
fans—is a curiously old-fashioned place. The planet exists in a
cosmos of squabbling barons and dukes, while its own native
people resemble the nomads of Arabia Deserta just prior to
the advent of Islam. The career of the novel's hero, heir to
one of the dukedoms, exactly suits that environment; it is
rather as if a medieval European knight had gone out east of
Suez and found himself playing the part of Muhammad. In

such a future universe, starships and lasers do have their place, but upon the world of Dune it is important to be able both to strum a nine-stringed *baliset* and to swing a sword. Perhaps John Carter, certainly Eric John Stark, would have felt right at home.

The chief exception to this cultural and political archaism in interstellar science fiction is the peaceable, high cultured, galactic federation that exists before Earth becomes aware of it. Typically, this interstellar civilization admits Earth to probationary membership, on pain of expulsion if our planet cannot live up to its standards. After patiently observing the gunplay on wicked, economically booming frontier Mars, among characters with names like the Black Warrior and Robert the Dog, in "The Seven Jewels of Chamar," by Raymond F. Jones (*Planet Stories: 3*, Winter 1946), the agent of one such galactic civilization regretfully explains why our solar system has failed to qualify for interstellar foreign aid: "In a world where too many men want to rule all other men, we cannot bring powers that would only be a curse to you." Try us again in another ten thousand years, the nonhuman envoy advises. In the meantime, it implies, don't call us, we'll call you.

When Earthmen colonize the galaxy from their own home solar system, as often as not they botch the job; or, if they succeed, they leave Earth behind to become a stagnant (but perhaps happier) rural backwater. One richly metaphorical future Earth of this type is that described in an early-seventies serial by Clifford Simak, "Cemetery World" (*Analog: 90*, November, December 1972; January 1973). Ten thousand years after Earth's last war, the home planet has become a place to which people who have died elsewhere are shipped for burial, in perpetual-care plots tended by an unctuous and heartless funeral corporation. Beyond the chaste headstones and clipped green lawns cared for by Mother Earth, Inc., however, Earth has reverted to untamed wilderness, with forest clearings here and there inhabited by coon-hunting rural characters with names like Luther and Timothy and Zeke. Escaping the cemetery corporation's mechanized clutches, the hero at the beginning of the second installment is "perched on the top rail of a weathered fence" beside the patriarch of one such clan, enjoying the mellow sunshine:

> We went on sitting and I got to thinking that it had been a good day. We had tramped the fields and had husked some ears out of one of the cornshocks so the old man could show me what fine corn they raised; we had leaned our arms on the pigpen fence and watched the grunting porkers, nosing through the rubble on the feeding floor for a morsel they had missed; we had stood around and watched a man work the forge until a plow blade was glowing red, then take it out with tongs and place it on an anvil, with the sparks flying when he hammered it; we had strolled through the coolness of the barn and listened to the pigeons cooing in the loft above; we had talked lazily, as unhurried men will talk and it had all been very good.

V

J. R. R. Tolkien, in an essay on fantasy writing titled *Tree and Leaf* (1964), accused the science fiction writers of imagining "a world like one big glass-roofed railway station," whose inhabitants' ideals would "hardly reach farther than the splendid notion of building more towns of the same sort on other planets." Actually, almost the opposite generalization is true; the human inhabitants of other planets in modern science fiction are apt to build haciendas or manor halls, fishing villages or cobblestoned medieval towns, rather than automated basement burrows or soaring skyscraper condominiums. Where a more urban polity exists in the future, quite often it is back home on Terra itself; an overcrowded, violent, polluted, neurotic Terra from which one escapes by "going native" somewhere out among the stars. "We live in a charged environment," says a dweller on one such Earth, in Piers Anthony's thought-provoking and rather Weinbaumian novel, *Omnivore* (1968): "So many billions of sentient individuals, such intense war hysteria, cultural unrest, pressure to succeed. Most of the people on this planet are desperate to get away from it all—but there is nowhere to go. Only a few qualify for space. And so they grasp at anything in reach, and pull it down in the belief they are climbing."

The speaker is one of the few who do qualify for space, and in the sequel to *Omnivore,* titled *Orn* (1970, serialized in *Amazing Stories:* 43, July 1970; 44, September 1970), he and two companions share an idyll on a planet teeming with archaic life where man has not yet evolved; its flora, fauna, and climate are those of Earth's Paleocene epoch, except for one enclave that is still in the age of the dinosaurs. Defecting from the regimented Earth government that has sent them there, the characters swim, fish, paint, gather specimens, and play tag with a tyrannosaurus. Eventually, however, man the nature-lover is overtaken by man the omnivore. The superbly efficient, look-alike agents of the Terran authorities catch up with the fugitives, and purge their Eden with fire.

Even more desperate is the outcome of "You Can Never Go Back" by Joe Haldeman (*Amazing Science Fiction:* 49, November 1975), a coda to Haldeman's well-received story cycle, *The Forever War.* Discharged from an endless, pointless, savage conflict out among the stars, hero and heroine (both soldiers) return to an overpopulated Earth at the rationed edge of starvation, where schooling is a bad joke and most young people when they graduate go directly on welfare. On a still day the bottom thirty or forty stories of the buildings on Manhattan are buried in smog. Violence is so omnipresent that even ex-soldiers find it terrifyingly casual. Everyone carries a sidearm, and in that lethal environment street sweeping has become "a very high-risk profession." Out in the country a more decent life is possible, in a food-growing commune on the Dakota prairie—except that the communes are constantly being shot up by truck-driving thieves from the cities, too numerous for the authorities to control. There is no escape into the arts: "Paintings and sculpture were full of torture and dark brooding; movies seemed static and plotless; music was dominated by nostalgic revivals of earlier forms; architecture

was mainly concerned with finding someplace to put everybody; literature was damn near incomprehensible." To their
own discomfiture, for they have no illusions about the Army,
the two veterans fly down to Cape Canaveral and re-enlist.

The hero of *Pilgrim's Progress,* who shakes the dust of the
City of Destruction from his feet and fares forth on the
perilous journey to the Celestial City, has had countless imitators in science fiction. Ray Bradbury in "The Million Year
Picnic," the story that concludes his *Martian Chronicles,* hoped
that fallen man might be born again on Mars. In a scene
deriving from "Earth's Holocaust," by Nathaniel Hawthorne,
the father of a family of refugees from Earth's final, self-
destructive war makes a bonfire of papers—"Government
Bonds; Business Graph, 1999; Religious Prejudice: An Essay;
The Science of Logistics; Problems of the Pan-American
Unity; Stock Report for July 3, 1998; The War Digest"—and
tells his children that he is "burning a way of life. . . . That's
what we ran away from." Then he takes his family over by the
nearest canal, where they can watch their reflections, and tells
them they are the Martians. As Mars ceased to be a suitable
place to build a little house on the prairie, the dream moved
on out through the stars. Somewhere, away in the Greater
Magellanic Cloud or at the Galactic Rim, there may still be
clean air and elbow room—in short, a West.

In one especially significant variation on this theme, it is not
individual pilgrims but cities themselves that flee from the
wrath to come. As Earth's Bureaucratic State takes its final
moribund form, in *A Life for the Stars,* by James Blish (1962),
the whole of Pittsburgh moves to Mars, blast furnaces and all,
to process the abundant iron ore that gives that planet its red
color—a far cry indeed from Barsoom. New York City wanders farther off among the stars, selling its skills and labor—a
migrant community, an "Okie" ("Okie," *Astounding:* 45, April
1950; "Bindlestiff," *ASF:* 46, December 1950; *Earthman Come
Home,* 1955). No longer is New York chronically unable to
cope with its own problems; on the contrary, it cruises the

cosmos solving the problems of others—but always one jump ahead of the Earth Police.

The historical framework of the four books comprising Blish's *Cities in Flight* tetralogy is that of Oswald Spengler (see chapter 8), with its pessimistic dogma that all civilizations must ripen and fall. But through that tragic Spenglerian vision breathes a spirit of the profoundest optimism. "Earth isn't a place. It's an idea," declares "Okie" New York's Mayor John Amalfi (a more intellectual version of Fiorello LaGuardia) at the conclusion of *Earthman Come Home,* and *nothing*—not even the end of the universe itself, which takes place in the last of these stories, *The Triumph of Time* (1957)—can defeat that idea.

It is a brilliant dialectical resolution of the age-old historical conflict between town and country, civilization and wilderness, Jerusalem and Eden. We do not find a West "out there," on the North American frontier, or on Barsoom, or on Skaith; we bring it with us.

"We are going to scatter the West throughout the stars," prophesies Senator Wagoner in the "prequel" Blish wrote to these "Okie" stories, *They Shall Have Stars* (1957); "scatter it with immortal people carrying immortal ideas"—not the "West" of John Carter and Zane Grey, but Western civilization itself, with its rational curiosity and its thirst for freedom. The cities in flight *are* the West, in both senses of the term. Steered from the top of the Empire State Building, New York sails grandly through that most ultimate of deserts—deep space; and it does not matter that in the silent tunnels through its granite keel the subway trains no longer run.

Chapter 4

The Fate Changer

man Destiny and the Time Machine

*History does not have to go logically, and its inevitables are never
really inevitable until after they have happened.*

—Bruce Catton, *Glory Road: The Bloody Route From
Fredericksburg to Gettysburg* (1952)

*"Men's courses will foreshadow certain ends, to which, if persevered in, they
must lead," said Scrooge. "But if the courses be departed from, the ends will
change. Say it is thus with what you show me!"
The Spirit was immovable as ever.*

—Charles Dickens, *A Christmas Carol* (1843)

89

Hand in hand through the Dimension of Unreason. "To Follow Knowledge," by Frank
Belknap Long. *Astounding Science-Fiction*, 30 (December, 1942), p. 87.

THERE WAS A TIME, as Hugo Gernsback never tired of reminding his readers, when skeptics would have hooted at the idea of painless dentistry, motorcycles, or neon signs. Accepting such innovations as commonplace, a new generation in its turn derided such notions as spaceships, organ transplants, and atomic bombs. And so it goes. Yesterday, "There ain't no such animal"; today, "You don't say!"; tomorrow, "So what else is new?"

Not all the gambits of science fiction, however, have gone through this process of acculturation. The time machine was as much a staple of science fiction in the pulp era as the rocket or the ray gun or the robot, and it still is. The rocket now sits in the Smithsonian, the ray gun has evolved into the laser, and the robot has become a sophisticated maze of circuitry able to play winning chess. But the time machine still seems as strange and unlikely to most of our contemporaries as it did to the contemporaries of H. G. Wells. Travel through space, improbable as it seemed to many people as recently as the Eisenhower regime, was at least a logical extrapolation from the history of transportation in general. The like cannot as confidently be said of travel through time.

Scattered evidence exists to the contrary. Two respectable British ladies of the Edwardian era claimed to have stepped from the gardens of modern Versailles into those same gardens at the time of Louis XVI and Marie Antoinette; they deposited signed, sworn statements to that effect in the Bodleian Library at Oxford, where said documents may be consulted to this day (see Alexander M. Phillips, "Time-Travel Happens!" *Unknown:* 2, December 1939). But such accounts do not begin to compare, as experimental evidence, with the solid mathematical calculations of Tsiolkovski or with the stratosphere-probing hardware of Robert Goddard. Fictional time travel did have some theoretical rationale, to be sure; the concept of the "fourth dimension" was already under discussion in English literary circles in the 1880s when H. G. Wells was preparing to write the classic time-travel novel. Nevertheless, the consensus of the scientific community until quite

recently—the glib use of the term "space-time continuum" by
science fiction writers to the contrary notwithstanding—has
been that time travel is impossible.

Only as recently as 1974, in the sober pages of the *Physical
Review,* has a physicist been more bold: "General relativity
suggests that if we construct a sufficiently large rotating cylinder, we create a time machine," Frank J. Tipler asserts
("Rotating Cylinders and the Possibility of Global Causality
Violation," *Physical Review D:* 9, April 15, 1974, p. 2206). For
seventy years in the meantime, however, without waiting for
Professor Tipler to solve his equations and come to that
conclusion, writers had happily helped themselves to Mr.
Wells's invention and sent their characters through time in
every direction, forward, backward, and sideways.

If the scientific basis for time travel until recently was
skimpy, so was its literary heritage—in sharp contrast to fictional space travel, which is deeply rooted in a tradition of
exploration and adventure in far-off lands. (*Moby-Dick* is,
from one point of view, a space opera. On the staging area of
Nantucket Island its crews pack up their vehicles for three
years of self-contained voyaging through a harsh and different environment. They prefer to drink their own Nantucket
water drawn from casks rather than take chances with the
dubious streams that may bubble forth on mysterious other
shores; from time to time they sight and battle alien intelligences from unknown depths.) But it is harder to unearth a
similar early lineage for voyaging through time.

In a sense, Charles Dickens's *A Christmas Carol* might be
read as a time-travel story. When Scrooge asks the Ghost of
Christmas Yet to Come "Are these the shadows of the things
that Will be, or are they shadows of things that May be, only?"
he certainly raises a philosophic and ethical issue that is central
in the literature of time travel. Earlier, Edgar Allan Poe
halfheartedly toyed with the idea in "A Tale of the Ragged
Mountains," whose protagonist walks from the vicinity of
Charlottesville, Virginia, in 1827 into the midst of an insurrec-
tion in Benares in 1780. A much livelier tale than Poe's

appeared in the *Dublin Literary Magazine* in 1838, titled "Missing One's Coach" (reprinted in August Derleth's anthology, *Far Boundaries,* 1951); its hero makes his way from the smoking, sooty Newcastle-on-Tyne of young Queen Victoria's time to a monastery in the thickly forested, thatch-roofed England of the eighth century, where he confronts the Venerable Bede and regales him with the wonders of the nineteenth century— wonders that the learned monk satirically deflates, one by one. But it was not until 1895, with the appearance of *The Time Machine,* by H. G. Wells, that the idea really caught fire.

This was Wells's first book (other than a hack biology textbook written simply to put bread on the table), and it brought the young, struggling writer his first real fame. It was a book for its times; what, it asked, would become of the stagnant, class-divided society of late Victorian England if allowed to evolve along existing lines into the indefinite future? But the story far transcended its topicality. *The Time Machine,* like Mary Shelley's *Frankenstein,* is one of the great parables of Western industrial man. Those who have seen only George Pal's film version, with its made-in-Hollywood happy ending, have entirely missed what Wells was driving at in this poem of cosmic doom. It is the final emphatic denial of Darwinian evolutionary optimism; its real hero is not so much the Time Traveller as the Second Law of Thermodynamics. It is also a formal rebuttal to the Christian epic, as the world ends not with choirs of angels and a new Jerusalem descending but with scuttling crabs on a tideless beach and the quiet falling of the snow.

Since *The Time Machine* there have been hundreds, perhaps thousands, of stories written on its central theme. A writer for the science fiction pulps could confidently assume his readers' familiarity with Wells's classic; not only with its specific time-traveling gadget, which was imitated many times over, but— more important—with its mood and point of view. Wells's *fin-de-siècle* pessimism surely influenced John Campbell's "Twilight," for example (chapter 8). It also touched Howard Phillips Lovecraft, who seized upon the radical shock of mental

displacement that travel to far-off time might entail; a terror
at least as keen as the kind evoked by the yawning graveyards,
sag-roofed farmhouses, and musty genealogy, which were
that writer's usual stock in trade. In his "Commonplace Book"
of notes for stories to be written, Lovecraft jotted down one
truly hair-raising idea: "In an ancient buried city a man finds a
mouldering prehistoric document *in English in his own hand-
writing.*" That sentence grew into one of Lovecraft's longest
and most effective tales, "The Shadow Out of Time," published in *Astounding Stories* (17, June 1936).

If the event in that story really happened, says its narrator,
"then man must be prepared to accept notice of the cosmos,
and of his own place in the seething vortex of time, whose
merest mention is paralyzing." Wrenched back into time by an
ancient prehuman civilization that practices time travel as a
novel method for doing scholarly research, Lovecraft's hero
finds himself among other, similarly kidnapped time travelers
from all eons, past and future. Down among his weird captors'
library stacks, he talks with—to list some of the human examples only—

> the mind of Yiang-Li, a philosopher from the cruel empire of
> Tsan-Chan, which is to come in 5,000 A.D.; with that of a
> general of the great-headed brown people who held South
> Africa in 50,000 B.C.; with that of a twelfth-century Florentine
> monk named Bartolomeo Corsi; . . . with that of a Roman
> named Titus Cempronius Blaesus, who had been a quaestor in
> Sulla's time; with that of Khephnes, an Egyptian of the 14th
> dynasty . . . ; with that of a Suffolk gentleman of Cromwell's
> day, James Woodville; with that of a court astronomer of pre-
> Inca Peru; with that of the Australian physicist Nevil Kingston-
> Brown, who will die in 2,518 A.D.; . . . and with so many others
> that my brain can not hold the shocking secrets and dizzying
> marvels I learned from them.

"To Lovecraft," anthologist Donald Wollheim perceptively
wrote (in *The Portable Novels of Science,* 1945), "the millions of
years gone by and the millions of years to come are sources of
dread, because of his knowledge of the cold cruelty of

nature." Mingled with the dread, however, is that other powerful impulse so often expressed in science fiction: the Faustian urge to know all. As Lovecraft's character converses with all these highly knowledgeable people and Things, his sense of estrangement and horror mutates insensibly into fascination.

"Shocking secrets and dizzying marvels" were a commonplace in the science fiction of the mid-1930s, when Lovecraft's exercise in cosmic terror appeared in *Astounding*. But the focus of science fiction by that time was changing. The question "What's it like out there?" was being rephrased as "What difference does it make to me here?" Ralph Milne Farley, in "The Time-Wise Guy" (*Amazing Stories:* 14, May 1940), sent a time traveler 200 million years into the future, to a landscape straight out of Wells: "The time-machine stood on a rocky spit of land, jutting out into a listless sea. . . . A hollow soundlessness hung over the world. . . . Dark, indistinct clouds gathered, ruddy on one side like the smoke of a train when the fireman opens the door to shovel in coal." But the traveler, a callow Joe College type named George Worthey, couldn't care less. Lacking even a tourist's curiosity, he does not wish so much as "to set foot on this barren land of things to be."

The time machine's inventor, Professor Tyrrell—"Old Tillie" to his students—has warned George not to return from the future at the exact moment when he left. But our hero had had plans for the evening of his departure day, plans interrupted by his impromptu journey to the end of time. If he obeys the professor's warning, George is going to miss out on a fraternity dance! Therefore, disregarding "Old Tillie's" advice, he returns to the present at the very second of his departure.

At that point the story breaks off. What happened next? The editors of *Amazing Stories* offered readers a cash prize for the best answer. So conventional had time travel become in science fiction that several contestants came up with the same conclusion as the author's own: George, coming back to the laboratory at the instant he left it, finds himself once again

going *forward* in time. He is caught in an eternally recurring
loop, and he will travel to and from that rocky spit of land at
the end of time, forever and ever, world without end. The
cosmic vision of *The Time Machine* has become comic anticlimax; the universe after all has outsmarted the wise guy. In
pulp stories like this one, the vast historical and astronomical
panorama of Wells and Lovecraft has receded into the wings.
Time travel has become localized as an individual struggle
against destiny.

II

"If it were possible to discover the hour of death, could that
death be deliberately circumvented?" Two short stories asking
that ultimate question appeared in the pulps in the late summer of 1939, "Life-Line" by Robert A. Heinlein (*Astounding:*
23, August), and "The Fate Changer," by Richard O. Lewis,
which carried the story blurb just quoted (*Amazing Stories:* 13,
September). Of this pair, Heinlein's is the better known; it was
his first published story, and its tone of quiet rationality
sharply contrasted with the furnace-draft pulp style generally
prevailing in 1939. Socially aware as in all his early work,
Heinlein assumed that an invention which could accurately
predict an individual's lifespan would be opposed (logically
enough) by the insurance companies, which would have a
vested interest in their customers' not learning that kind of
intimate specific information. The profit motive figures in
Lewis's tale also, but it is embodied in a much more crass form.
    "The Fate Changer" begins: "Samuel J. Curbul, broker, let
the smoke from his expensive cigar roll upward from his thick
lips to drift lazily about his heavy features and to veil his close-
set, piggish eyes." Samuel J. Curbul, broker, was of a type not
at all unusual in magazine science fiction in that post-Crash,
anti-business era. Walter Hirsch, in an essay called "The
Image of the Scientist in Science-Fiction" (*American Journal of
Sociology:* 63, March 1958) based on random sampling of the
science fiction pulps published between 1926 and 1950, found

that capitalists by and large figured in the stories as disreputable characters: "Scientists comprised the major category of both heroes and villains, but businessmen were, proportionately, more villainous than scientists." But the scientist in "The Fate Changer," given the allegorically apt name of Factsworth, appears neither as hero nor as villain, but as victim. A fast-talking operator named Jamison, armed with a power of attorney, has mortgaged Factsworth's laboratory to buy worthless stocks from broker Curbul. Pressed for margin when the securities collapse, the speculator finds no sympathy in the dealer: "I can't foretell the future of stocks," Curbul curtly informs him. Desperate for cash, Jamison reveals the secret that Factsworth knows how to foretell the future. The broker pays him off, goes to see the scientist, and asks Factsworth what he, Curbul, will be doing for the rest of the present week.

"Knowing your world line will in no way aid you as a businessman," Factsworth warns him, "for you cannot step aside from it or change it in any possible way."

Samuel J. Curbul's answer is in the best tradition of free American enterprise: "I'll take my own chances on changing my world-line. I have a strong will."

So the scientist scans the businessman with his machine, makes notes, and reads them out loud. On the way back from the lab that afternoon, Samuel Curbul, arrested for speeding, will bribe a cop with a $20 bill wrapped around a cigar. Later he will pace the floor of his office (that means the market is going to be bearish, the listening stock broker concludes). Still later he will begin an after-dinner speech—and break down in the middle of it, tearing off his collar and rushing outside the hall. He will buy a newspaper, take a cab to his apartment, look repeatedly at his watch, read something in the paper. And that, at 9:47 P.M. this very evening, Factsworth concludes, will be all. *"Your world line ends there."*

The moving finger writes, and having writ moves on. Can piety or wit—or science—lure it back? Factsworth is willing to try: "It would be interesting to science to see you change your world line." He will bring to Curbul's apartment that evening equipment to generate a field that will distort the space-time continuum at the place and moment when the broker would otherwise die.

They part. Distracted by the cold thought of death, Curbul does indeed run a red light and, as predicted, he does bribe the arresting officer. He does pace the office floor; he does begin, and blow, his after-dinner speech; he does automatically buy the paper a newsboy thrusts at him, and he does find himself in a taxi speeding homeward to doom. The slick manner of Robert Heinlein would have been quite out of place here; Lewis portrayed his character's plight with raw pulp power: "Curbul cringed in the corner of the cab like a frightened animal. A piece of torn collar was still clutched in his hand. Colored neon signs were flashing past, car lights stabbed and darted at the windows in panoramic confusion. He felt that he was going mad, felt that he was being held imprisoned upon a narrow path that was hurling him on— on—on to his destruction."

He gets home. Factsworth is not there. He waits. It is 9:32; still no Factsworth. Then, as also had been foretold, he reads an item in the paper, except that now he knows what it says: "Factsworth taken into custody by the police . . . trying to make away with equipment from his lab . . . attached for debt late this afternoon . . . Factsworth claiming life and death matter"—and the check made out to the scientist, which would have paid off all those debts, rests in Curbul's office, never sent. The businessman had not been able to resist one last fatal impulse to cut a corner on a deal.

We have seen here a fresh variation on one of the most compelling myths of Western man, the myth of the Bad Bargain: Faust sells his soul to the devil in exchange for various good things of this world, but the devil cheats. In this case, Faust cheated himself. From either a Marxist or a Calvinist point of view it is a fitting destiny. Jonathan Edwards himself might have relished such a retribution, in which a man's damnation is totally predestined and yet at the same time morally appropriate. Of course, a typical American executive's hypertension might have done Curbul in anyway. The story ends: "The awful pounding ceased abruptly. The newspaper slipped to the floor from nerveless fingers."

If space-time *is* a continuum, then we have no real control over our future, for what will be is all of one piece with what was. "Choice," explains Norman Spinrad in "Weed of Time" (*Vertex:* 1, August 1973), "is an illusion caused by the fact that future time-loci are hidden from those who advance sequentially along the time-stream one moment after another in blissful ignorance." The age-old philosophical question of determinism versus free will is thus resolved emphatically in favor of determinism. Nor does physical travel in time, as distinguished from mere scanning and prediction, necessarily mean escape from this predetermined fate. Traveling back and forth along the time-dimension, in "The Time Cheaters" by Eando Binder (*Thrilling Wonder Stories:* 15, March 1940), the time travelers learn that the impact of their visits has already been allowed for. If they try to change the course of events, for example by stopping the time machine in a different year from the one the records indicate, they will only confirm destiny's decree; the time machine's calibration will have been just sufficiently inaccurate that, willy-nilly, they will land in the correct year anyway. At the end of this story by Binder, the hero accepts the situation philosophically: "Time," he admitted, "is immutable."

In the course of their journey, Binder's time travelers from the year 1940 have learned of the collapse of Japan's occupation of China in 1942 and of a stalemate along the Maginot and Siegfried lines in 1944, followed, on May 16, 1945, by the ultimate in escalation: an invasion from Mars. War shadowed many of the time-travel stories published in the early 1940s, as it touched so much other science fiction. "Forever Is Not So Long," by F. Anton Reeds, for example (*Astounding:* 29, May 1942), begins at a summer garden party in England in 1931, when "the lights of Europe still burned." Young couples are dancing, while along the sidelines sit the gray-tinged members

of England's "lost generation," spiritual casualties of a previous war. While the party goes on, the hero leaves his fiancée
for a brief visit to her father's laboratory a short distance away.
There he becomes the subject of the first experiment in time.

Going forward ten years, to 1941, he finds that the manor
house behind which he had lately danced has been bombed to
rubble. Captured by a Home Guardsman as an intruder, he is
told: "You look remarkably like a chap I soldiered with in
Flanders. Died the last night of Dunkirk . . . a brilliant fellow.
Scientist of promise, I believe, before the war." That soldier's
widow survives, but is said to have been crippled in an air raid
not long before.

Armed with this kind of knowledge, what does one do?
Accept one's destiny, the author answered. The time traveler
escapes from custody, goes back to 1931, returns to the dance,
and tells his betrothed that from now on he will have time only
for her. Quite unknowing of the future, she replies that they
will be "the happiest people in the world . . . forever." The
story closes on a bittersweet echo from the Jazz Age: "Two
trumpets were taking a hot chorus, unmuted, their notes high
and sharp and quivering. 'Forever,' he said."

III

"A common opinion prevails that the juice has ages ago
been pressed out of the free-will controversy, and that no new
champion can do more than warm up stale arguments which
every one has heard." So said William James, as he lectured
the divinity students at Harvard in 1884 on "The Dilemma of
Determinism," ten years before H. G. Wells wrote *The Time
Machine.* "This is a radical mistake. I know of no subject less
worn out, or in which inventive genius has a better chance of
breaking open new ground." Purists may balk at attributing
inventive genius to writers for the pulp magazines of the
1940s; however, their contribution to the free-will controversy
by way of time-travel stories certainly broke open new ground.

We live in "a world in which we constantly have to make . . .

judgments of regret," James argued. The dilemma is that if whatever will be will be, such judgments are irrational—yet, humanly, we cannot help making them. "Determinism, in denying that anything else can be in its stead, virtually defines the universe as a place in which what ought to be is impossible," James concluded. In an historical period more given to ethical and cultural relativism than the era of William James, the question was bound to arise: ought to be, from whose point of view? My own, or society's? The present generation's, or that of the yet unborn?

Alfred Bester, one of the brilliant cluster of science fictionists who began to write in 1939, explored these and other questions in a story that deserves to be better known, "The Push of a Finger" (*Astounding:* 29, May 1942). Its hero is no formal philosopher; he is that stock pulp adventure figure, the cynical/sentimental newspaperman. His beat is the Prog— short for Prognostication—Building, in which a bureaucratic government dedicated to Stability predicts the future by computer. "Prophecy is far from being a mystical function," Chief Stabilizer Groating explains. "It is a very logical science," just a matter of integrating enough accurate data. Its syntheses do not add up to absolute determinism, however; the Stabilizers, having read their daily printouts, may refrain from following the predicted course of action if they consider it detrimental. And some of New York's alternate futures, as the reporter discovers when he peeps through the Prognosticator, are bizarre indeed:

> I caught fuzzy fragments of a demolished Manhattan City with giant crablike creatures mashing helpless humans, their scarlet chiton glittering. Then an even blurrier series of images. A city of a single stupendous building towering like Babel into the heavens; a catastrophic fire roaring along the Atlantic seaboard; then a sylvan civilization of odd, naked creatures flitting from one giant flower to another. But they were all so far off focus they made my eyes ache. . . .
>
> Groating leaned toward me and whispered: "Merely vague possibilities——"

A placard on a newspaper editor's desk, in this Manhattan of the future, reads: "If you take care of the tomorrows, the todays will take care of themselves." But it is axiomatic from the bureaucracy's point of view that the ordinary person on the street should have no input into the system whatever; the alternative to Stability, it smugly insists, is Chaos. In theological language, foreordination has replaced predestination, and it is doubtless no accident that Chief Stabilizer Groating is nicknamed "Jehovah."

The only flaw in this carefully stabilized utopia is that the massed computers—eight floors of them—in the Prog Building have just predicted the end of the universe. That event is yet a thousand years away, but from a Chief Stabilizer's viewpoint a thousand years (to paraphrase the Psalmist) are but as a watch in the night. Furthermore this particular downfall is man-made, and can therefore—perhaps—be man-prevented. The Prognosticator's viewing screen shows a jerry-built spaceship swarming with outlaw technicians and workmen, about to perform in secret a most illegal experiment. Their intention is to release unlimited energy for the betterment of man. What they accomplish instead is Doomsday. The star their spaceship is circling simply blots out; then the spaceship; then more stars, and more stars, and more stars. "It reminded me of school when we added carbon ink to a drop under the mike just to see how the amoebae would take it," the reporter-hero muses. "I started thinking about those amoebae and feeling sorry for them."

What can the Stabilizers do about it? Unfortunately, their equipment has not the power to isolate out the causal factor from the mass of raw data. Instead, at the reporter's suggestion, they work backward in time from the catastrophe three hundred years closer to their own time, to the debates that result in the outlawing of that particular kind of hazardous scientific research. Briefly, the hero glimpses a lovely young woman of that remote future; a glimpse, as it turns out, that is to seal his destiny.

The scanners now for the first time learn of a mysterious

equation, $i = (b/a)\pi \, i \, e/\mu$, and of its brilliant, controversial author, a scientist named FitzJohn. More backtracking, and the monitor picks up FitzJohn himself, delivering a lecture on his "Tension Energy Dynamics Equations" to a raucous, hostile audience in a great amphitheater at the north end of Central Park (not built yet, Chief Stabilizer Groating remarks; they have plans to erect it about three decades hence). Egged on by other professors hostile to FitzJohn's theories, a host of undergraduates cavort in hilarious carnival, chanting anti-FitzJohn slogans and parodying his equations.

The story's point of view has insensibly shifted. FitzJohn in this scene is not the dangerous crackpot who must be stopped before he wrecks the universe; he is a heroic figure, who stands his ground against the mob and converts their jeers into applause. Silence ensues, and he begins his lecture as if nothing has happened. "No scientist is a lone adventurer, striking out into new fields by himself," FitzJohn modestly points out. "The way is always led by those who precede us, and we who seem to discover all, actually do no more than add our bit to an accumulated knowledge." Even the equation basic to his theory is not his own; fifty years prior to this day, some ten years before his own birth, "in Central Park, on the very site of this amphitheater, my father, suddenly struck with an idea, mentioned an equation to my mother." That equation was none other than the fatal $i = (b/a)\pi \, i \, e/\mu$—and fifty years prior to the day of FitzJohn's lecture brings the prognosticators to *this* evening, of the day the action in the story takes place!

It is winter, and they have only about two hours till dark. No time to computer-scan all the possible ancestors of FitzJohn, who in any case may have blotted out his past and changed his name. A cordon of police swarms around Central Park, to intercept any strolling couple who might unknowingly fall into the fateful conversation. Then down into the park whirrs a copter-load of newspaper reporters. One of them, a rookie just hired by her paper, is a girl (this Stabilized future evidently has no place for "affirmative action" to equalize

employment opportunities; the newspaper business is still
basically a man's world)—and she reminds the hero irresisti-
bly of the woman he has glimpsed six hundred years into the
future. In surprise, and in comic anticlimax, he exclaims, "I'll
be a pie-eyed emu!"—which, suitably garbled into family folklore and inaccurately remembered by a loving son, might well
become identified some day with the disastrous $i = (b/a)\pi\, i\, e/\mu$.

The circle is complete; the Prognosticators' frantic security
precautions have brought on the very encounter they sought
to forestall. Boy has met Girl, and the first step has been taken
that will probably lead, at the next millennium's end, to the
blotting out of the stars. Oddly, "Jehovah" Groating does not
simply have the star-crossed couple executed on the spot in
the name of Stability. Instead, he exiles the hero to the asteroids. And there we leave him, fuming: "To hell with Groating
and to hell with Stability and to hell with a thousand years
from now. I've got to see her again—soon." The strong
implication is that he will.

Here is a philosophic and moral paradox that might baffle
both Jonathan Edwards and William James—or Kant, whose
"categorical imperative" (the doctrine that one ought always to
act as if one's own conduct were to become universal law) does
not even begin to fill this bill. Throughout the story there has
been an implication that the persistence, courage, and imagination—however wrong-headed—of FitzJohn and his adherents have the moral edge over the paternalism, self-righteous-
ness, and stagnation—however prudent and logical—of the
Prognosticators. Ultimately, on this time-track, the existence
of the whole world seems to depend on suppressing the liberty
of one lone individual. From that individual's own point of
view, to assert that there is human free will and that the future
really can be changed is to renounce freedom of choice for
oneself personally; conversely, to deny free will, and do what
one must although the heavens fall, is existentially to affirm it.
Bester's hero could have accepted what Freud once said to his

disciple Theodor Reik, as reported in Reik's *Listening With the Third Ear* (1948):

> When making a decision of minor importance, I have always found it advantageous to consider all the pros and cons. In vital matters, however, such as the choice of a mate or a profession, the decision should come from the unconscious, from somewhere within ourselves. In the important decisions of our personal life, we should be governed, I think, by the deep inner needs of our nature.

The way out of the dilemma posed in "The Push of a Finger" transcends socially defined good and evil, and goes beyond rational self-preservation. In the hard-headed engineers' world of science fiction, it is startling to find the conclusion that, after all, "he that saveth his life shall lose it; and he that loseth his life . . . shall find it."

IV

At the conclusion of Robert Abernathy's time-travel story, "Hostage of Tomorrow" (to be discussed in chapter 5), the characters recognize one of the special hazards inherent in time travel: as they move backward over temporal ground they have covered before, they may meet their own former selves. But "we ought to be able to duck ourselves," they decide. "We know where we were, don't we?" Possible varia tions on the meet-oneself-in-time theme are endless, and this kind of logical paradox has a special attraction for the kind of science fiction reader who enjoys intellectual puzzles; it is akin to the "locked room" theme one finds in detective fiction.

The cross-tie between science fiction and the tale of detection would be worth a separate essay in itself. Isaac Asimov has written many a story involving scientific deduction of the details of a crime, and *Fantasy & Science Fiction* editor Anthony Boucher (writing as H. H. Holmes) once turned out a straightforward murder mystery, *Rocket to the Morgue* (1942), in which

most of the characters were recognizable as actual science
fiction authors and fans (Robert Heinlein becomes Austin
Carter; Edmond Hamilton is renamed Joe Henderson; L.
Ron Hubbard is transformed into D. Vance Wimpole;
Astounding editor John Campbell, as Don Stuart, edits a magazine called *Surprising Stories;* and so on). Irrepressible science
fiction fan Forrest J. Ackerman, as he unraveled these identi-
ties for a fanzine review of Boucher's modest *roman à clef,*
remarked that if science fiction did not exist he would probably read detective stories; both kinds of imaginative writing
presumably call for the same kind of logical, problem-solving
thought processes.

Fictional time travel has its own special connections with the
world of the "whodunit." The locked-room puzzle takes on a
new dimension—the fourth dimension—when a murder suspect can escape into the middle of next week, as in the ironic
little story "Time Locker," by Henry Kuttner (writing as Lewis
Padgett in *Astounding:* 30, January 1943). The time-travel
paradox of meeting oneself in the past is adroitly combined
with a mystery story gambit in "Time Wants a Skeleton," by
Ross Rocklynne (*Astounding:* 27, June 1941). The people in
Rocklynne's suspense thriller find an emerald ring on the
finger of a skeleton in a cave, and then they are all hurled
backward in time—only to find the cave empty. The implication is that one of them was/will be killed, in order that the
skeleton would/will be found in the cave at the proper time.
The situation thus resembles the plot of Agatha Christie's
highly effective stage play and film, *Ten Little Indians,* whose
characters must cope with the unpleasant fact that a murderer
on the loose is one of themselves; similarly, the characters in
"Time Wants a Skeleton" pass that fatal emerald from hand to
hand in a deadly adult version of the game of musical chairs.

That version of the meet-yourself-in-the-past paradox is
basically simple. It can get far more complicated. The unsur-
passed virtuoso performance along this line is "By His Bootstraps," by Robert A. Heinlein (writing as Anson MacDonald
in *Astounding:* 28, October 1941). This ingenious tale opens

with a harassed university student pounding a typewriter, surrounded by coffee grounds and cigarette butts as he struggles to meet next day's thesis deadline—a situation with which many a science fiction reader can emotionally identify. (By a nice irony, our hero is writing to *disprove* the possibility of time travel.) He is interrupted by his own future self, who has been projected back to his/their boardinghouse room by time machine; then enters another future self, from farther along his, or their, world-line; and the argument the three fall into is interrupted by a phone call from yet another version of the hero's coming self! The lengthened shadow of a man is history, said Emerson, but this four-way metaphysical hassle was not at all what the Sage of Concord had had in mind.

Heinlein managed to tie up all the loose ends before he was done. Some writers left their paradoxes tantalizingly unresolved. There is, for example, P. Schuyler Miller's haunting tale, "As Never Was" (*Astounding*: 32, January 1944). A knife, made of a translucent blue metal unknown to this world, is found somewhere in the future by a time-traveling archeologist (appropriately, his name is Walter Toynbee). Defying all attempts at physical or chemical analysis, the artifact is housed in a glass case in a museum named after the time traveler. Centuries pass. Bombs fall. The building crumbles in ruins. Then at last comes the time traveler, to shovel away the debris and bring the knife back to his own time, where it will be studied and analyzed and housed in a glass case in a museum. . . . But where, or when, did it come from in the first place? "I wish I knew," the narrator cries; "I might find logic and purpose in the future instead of chaos."

Latent in that outcry may be existential revulsion against traveling in time at all. The narrator hints that in trying to solve the paradox of the knife, and utterly failing, the rational intellect of the civilization of his own era has begun to crack. Should a time machine ever actually be invented, people morally committed against venturing outside one's proper place in the continuum might vehemently oppose time travel, much in the spirit of the Apollo space program's detractors.

"Tired men live in the past, ambitious men live in the future,"
says the protagonist of a 1970s story by Gordon Eklund, "The
Stuff of Time" (*Fantastic:* 22, September 1973). "But who lives
in the present? Perhaps healthy men live in the present; it's
hard to say. But somebody must."

There remains moreover that elusive will-o'-the-wisp
known as human freedom, which is not to be captured merely
by spinning endlessly in dizzy circles of paradox. Heinlein's
single/multiple hero in "By His Bootstraps" thinks he has
solved that problem; "freedom" and "determinism" he neatly
separates into "subjective" and "objective" categories. "Free
will . . . could not be laughed off, because it could be·directly
experienced," he muses, "yet his own free will had worked to
create the same scene over and over again. Apparently human
will must be considered as one of the factors which make up
the processes in the continuum—'free' to the ego, mechanistic
from the outside." But that really won't do; it still, basically,
defines freedom as an illusion.

"By His Bootstraps" has most commonly been taken as
comedy. That thrice-repeated conversation between the
hero's first version who wants only to finish his thesis and get
his degree, a second who tells him to enter the future, and a
third who urges him not to, all climaxing in a three-cornered
drunken fistfight that knocks Number One through the time
gate and off on the first of his gyrating travels, still stands up
after repeated readings as a wondrously comic invention. It
might even work on television. But Alexei and Cory Panshin,
in the important article "SF in Dimension: The Search for
Renewal" (*Fantastic:* 22, July 1973), draw a far more bleak
moral to this Heinlein story. "His character is caught in a maze
of time in which he meets himself again and again, acting out
what he has already seen himself act out, helpless to alter his
behavior, vainly repeating himself, trapped in his own futility." Psychologically, the Panshins see this as a classic crisis of
American middle age! Furthermore, it is the character's own
fault: "his older self is responsible for setting the time trap for
his younger self. He is the agent of his own futility." At one

point in his odyssey he has the opportunity to break out of the cycle, but at a psychic cost he cannot bear to pay. "So he must turn from transcendence and run—and remain trapped in his own character, to run round and round and round the maze, without hope."

V

Two roads diverged in a yellow wood, said Robert Frost, and he took the one less traveled by. The twentieth-century scientific universe of Einstein and space-time is also the universe of Heisenberg and statistical indeterminacy. Perhaps, in the chinks and crevices of such a cosmos, there remains some room for acts of free human choice. "We assume that if we travel to futureward there is but one possible destination," a professor lectures in Murray Leinster's "Sidewise in Time," a story that pioneered the philosophic idea of alternate, ontologically real, parallel futures (*Astounding Stories:* 13, June 1934). "There is more than one future we can encounter, and with more or less absence of deliberation we choose among them. But the futures we fail to encounter, upon the roads we do not take, are just as real."

From this perspective, not only did two real roads diverge in the wood, but also there are two real Robert Frosts, each trudging thoughtfully along one of them. Leinster also assumed that the traveler could bushwhack through the forest from one road over to the other. Indeed, in "Sidewise in Time"—published at the height of *Astounding* editor Orlin Tremaine's vogue for "thought-variant" stories, in which marvel must be piled upon metaphysical marvel—entire societies migrate across the continuum into each other's territory. Rice fields, wide-hatted peasants, and Chinese junks suddenly appear along the Potomac, deriving from an alternative past in which the Orient colonized America; San Francisco, displaced by a city from a time-track in which the Spaniards did not get there first, finds itself ruled by the Tsar of All the Russias. This plurality of continua was a stimulating idea, and it has generated an entire inventive subspecies of science fiction.

What if——?

There is a world in which the Saracens beat the Franks, Islam displaced Christianity throughout Western Europe, and a city called Far Damascus stands on the site the natives once named Manhattan ("The Mosaic," by J. B. Ryan, *Astounding:* 25, July 1940). There is another world, described in many science fiction stories, in which the South won the Civil War; it is most logically and imaginatively worked out in "Bring the Jubilee" by Ward Moore (*Fantasy and Science Fiction:* 3, November 1952). There is a world in which the Axis won the Second World War (discussed in chapter 5). There is a world in which the American colonies remained a British possession; a world in which the 1932 assassination attempt against FDR in Miami was successful; a world in which Carthage defeated Rome. And so on, literally *ad infinitum.*

To be sure, this concept of alternate futures and pasts does not *really* resolve the eternal question of determinism versus free will. If each of two possible worlds stemming from a moment of choice actually exists, then not only is the other Robert Frost on his better-traveled road real, but so is the first Frost, tramping along the one less traveled by. Creating a new path through time does not alter the eternal fixedness of the old. "At the end, it's all unchangeable; it merely unrolls before us," wrote David R. Daniels in a story published a year after Leinster's, "Branches of Time" (*Wonder Stories:* 7, August 1935): "Think, for instance, of the martyrs and the things they suffered. I could go back and save them all those wrongs. And yet all the time, somewhere in absoluteness, they would still have known their unhappiness and their agony, because in their world-line, those things have happened."

Suppose, however, that the alternate futures are mutually exclusive? If, for example, the Confederates (in Ward Moore's brilliant story) hesitate in that famous peach orchard and don't get their guns up on Little Round Top, Lee will lose the Battle of Gettysburg next day after all, and the entire future society that would otherwise have arisen from his victory will vanish. In such cases the possibility of human freedom of choice returns in a new form. Indeed, one individual's free decisions may alter the entire pattern of human destiny, as in C. L. Moore's story "Greater Than Gods" (*Astounding*, 23, July 1939), which makes the future of civilization turn upon one person's choice of a mate. The sex stereotyping so typical in 1939, even in a woman writer's work, is somewhat embarrassing today: Shall the scientist-hero marry the giddy blonde who will so distract him from his work that he can never make the great discovery that would have changed history? Or does he go for the hard-driving brunette who will push him into publishing his findings prematurely and in incomplete form, with disastrous results? Both futures, seen via time machine, seem to him unpalatable; our hero therefore plays it safe and marries his calm, sensible secretary, who will presumably see to it that he splits the difference.

The restoration of free will to the time-travel equation makes possible more activist personal vocations than the seminar and library life of the Visiting Time Fellows (as H. P. Lovecraft might have called them) in "The Shadow Out of Time." Moments of choice in the past or present may become so important that soldiers from alternate potential futures are willing to go back to that point in time and fight each other to change the outcome—the stakes being not mere survival, but the possibility of ever *having* existed. Such is the theme of Jack Williamson's three-part serial, "The Legion of Time" (*Astounding:* 21, May, June, July 1938). Fighting men are plucked from the disasters of war—the Western Front, the naval battle of Jutland in 1916, the defense of Paris in 1940 (which, at the moment of writing, had not yet happened)—and recruited into the most foreign of all imagined legions. Traveling by time machine to the point where alternate world-lines diverge from a moment of choice, they must do battle in order that a good (democratic and Utopian) future may prevail over an evil (despotic and reactionary) one.

The wartorn 1930s and 1940s ideologically nurtured this

kind of science fiction, much as they influenced the course of space opera. The hero of Williamson's epic has fought against Franco in the Spanish Civil War, and he is flying for China against the Japanese invader when he is caught up into the Legion of Time. This was to remain a popular form of science fiction adventure in a time-track that remained wartorn, and ideology continued to shape it. The revolutionary and counterrevolutionary currents of the Eisenhower-Dulles years were insensibly allegorized in this time-soldier literature. Thus there were temporal radicals, as in Fritz Leiber's "The Big Time" (*Galaxy:* 15, March, April 1958), who strove to change the past for change's own sake, because in change is creativity and life; and there were temporal conservatives, as in Poul Anderson's "Time Patrol" (*Fantasy and Science Fiction:* 8, May 1955) and its several sequels, who struggled to preserve the known past from time-machined tampering, on the ground that it is better to endure the devil we know than fly to others we know not of.

As our society became ever more police-conscious, it nurtured stories like "Hawksbill Station," by Robert Silverberg (*Galaxy:* 25, August 1967; book version 1968), in which a despotic future government shunts its political dissidents back into a geological era before life had crawled out upon the land, where they cannot possibly affect the future course of history. There, subsisting on brachiopod stew and trilobite hash, they may argue about ideology to their hearts' content—and, in their futility, one by one go mad. Since H. G. Wells first put forth the idea, time travel had thus devolved from high adventure to penal servitude!—a most ominous comment on what was actually happening along our own time-line.

Moreover, despite their philosophic commitment to freedom of the will, in working out the ground rules by which their legionnaires of time were to operate, these writers quite often hedged back in the direction of determinism. There is a Law of Conservation of Reality, one of Fritz Leiber's timefighters explains, in a story warningly titled "Try and Change the Past" (*Astounding:* 61, March 1958). "The four-dimensional space-time universe doesn't *like* to be changed, any more than it likes to lose or gain energy or matter. . . . Change the past and you start a wave of changes moving futurewards, but it damps out mighty fast." Eventually the old pattern tends to reestablish itself. People move as crowds to change destiny, not as individuals; a vast organized array of soldiers may, crudely and brutally, change history, but a man by himself remains in the fell clutch of circumstance. "No, I wouldn't advise anyone to try to change the past, at least not his *personal* past." In contrast, Poul Anderson's Time Patrolmen *do* have the power to change their personal pasts—but they pledge themselves never to use it. "The Patrol exists to guard what is real," one of its leaders explains ("Gibraltar Falls," *Fantasy and Science Fiction:* 49, October 1975). "If ever a mortal takes himself that power, where can the changing end? . . . None less than God can be trusted with time."

Chapter 5

The Phantom Dictator
Science Fiction Discovers Hitler

*The novelists are justified. The war is waged on a Jules Verne basis. It is
the* War of the Worlds *that Wells wrote.* Huxley's Brave New World
*was a satire from which the National Socialists of Germany seem to have
drawn many lessons. Until a thing happens it is fiction.* . . . *No one believed,
once they got over their scare, that the Orson Welles program, where
the United States was attacked by men from Mars, would be duplicated
so terribly, so accurately, or so soon.*

—Stuart Cloete, *Yesterday Is Dead* (1940)

115

"There was a tremendous white flash in the valley, framed by a blue rim of electric radiance; and a black crater yawned where a tank battalion had been."

Deriving its plot and mood from *All Quiet on the Western Front*, this story—by a fo
artillery officer for the Austro-Hungarian Empire—typifies the "next war" sci
fiction of the early 1930s. "The Final War," by Carl W. Spohr. *Wonder Stor*
(April, 1932), p.

IN DECEMBER 1933, at the end of the year in which National Socialism came to power in Germany, *Astounding Stories* published a satire in the form of a time-travel tale entitled "Ancestral Voices" by Nat Schachner. In 452 A.D. a hairy Hunnish barbarian happily engaged in sacking the Roman city of Aquileia is killed in an encounter with a time machine. In the twentieth century, as a result, the descendants of whom he would otherwise have become the remote ancestor—all fifty thousand of them—forthwith disappear. These include two prizefighters—a Jew named Max Bernstein and a German named Hans Schilling—who are squaring off for a championship fight when they vanish.

The author's political point was clear enough: racial mixing has been so extensive over the long history of Europe that everybody has become biologically related to everybody else. Therefore, even if "Nordic" and "non-Aryan" racial differences existed at some time in the remote past, they are meaningless today. All unaware of this fact, a dictator of "Mideurope" (named Herr Hellwig in the story) delivers ranting speeches on the Mideuropeans' alleged racial purity. The artist who illustrated the story made the point still more explicit; he gave Herr Hellwig the black cowlick and toothbrush mustache of Adolf Hitler who, since his rise to power in Germany earlier in that dark year, had already become a dreadfully familiar face and voice to millions (Nat (Nathan) Schachner, "Ancestral Voices," *Astounding Stories:* 12, December 1933).

"Ancestral Voices," declared *Astounding's* editor F. Orlin Tremaine in his advance blurb (November 1933, p. 53), "opens the way for real discussion, discussion deeply connected with social science, the present condition of the world, and its future." The Schachner story would be the first of a new species; each month thereafter, the editor promised his readers, *Astounding* would bring them "one story carrying a new and unexplored 'thought-variant' in the field of scientific fiction." Each such tale would "speak its mind frankly . . . without regard for the restrictions formerly placed upon this

type of fiction," and these controversial "thought-variant" stories would presumably be hassled over by readers in the
"Brass Tacks" letter column.

As with most sales pitches, the promise outran the performance. After that initial example by Schachner, most of the
stories labeled "thought-variant" in the magazine had little if
any connection with social science or with the present conditions of the world. The typical thought-variant as it appeared
in *Astounding Stories* in the 1930s was a dreamily written tale in
which space, time, matter, energy, and thought all were
scrambled together into an unsavory omelet. Mind-boggling
this kind of story undoubtedly was, but despite its seeming
novelty such a theme in the hands of a master hack (such as
John Russell Fearn, who wrote a great many of them) could be
made just as stale and tiresome as the more conventional space
pirate, mad scientist, or bug-eyed monster. A few stories of
this type—such as "Finality Unlimited," by Donald Wandrei
(*Astounding:* 17, September 1936), the unbeatable whopper
along this line—remain more or less readable today, but even
dedicated and omnivorous science fiction readers now find
most of them embarrassing. If any kind of science fiction ever
merited the epithet "escapist," this was it.

Readers in early 1934 responded with enthusiasm to
"Ancestral Voices," the pioneering—and not at all escapist—
"thought-variant" story, just as *Astounding's* editor had predicted they would. However, they focused on the basic theoretical idea in Schachner's story, not its political message, even
though Tremaine in his editorial advance notice had adver-
tised it as a story that "slices deeply through the most precious
myths and legends of mankind" and "attacks boldly a present-
day wave of race-hysteria." Letters in the "Brass Tacks" column (February and March 1934) commented extensively on
the time-travel paradox, and some of them assailed what they
considered the author's faulty logic. But they passed over the
racial and Nazi questions in silence. Perhaps this was evidence
that American pulp fiction readers were not yet ready to take
up the latter kinds of issues and argue about them. Hugo

Gernsback, in vigorous competition with Tremaine, apparently made that assumption; Gernsback's *Wonder Stories* dealt with the question of Fascism in quite a different way.

By that time most of the British and French science fiction classics by Wells and Verne had already been reprinted in the American magazines. *Wonder* therefore turned for fresh reprint material to science fiction in translation from the German, such as "The Shot Into Infinity," by O. W. Gail (see chapter 2). After the rise of Hitler, a few readers assailed this practice on the ground that *Wonder Stories* was thereby contributing—in however small a way—to Nazi Germany's foreign earnings. Replying to one such letter of protest from one of *Wonder's* own budding authors, a politically conscious science fiction fan named Donald A. Wollheim, the editor vigorously defended the reprint policy (*Wonder Stories:* 6, March 1935).

Most of the money paid for these stories, the editor explained, went to the translator; and *Wonder's* two most prominent German writers lived respectively in Switzerland and in Monte Carlo, "and spend most of their money there." (Gernsback, by the way, was notoriously slow in paying his American writers for their work. The magazine at that moment owed Donald Wollheim $10 for his story "The Man from Ariel" [*Wonder:* 5, January 1934], and only by pooling his efforts with other short-changed authors and hiring a lawyer was Wollheim eventually able to collect.) In any case, Gernsback (or his managing editor, Charles D. Hornig) argued, political considerations were none of an American magazine publisher's business. "We have nothing against Germany—we are perfectly neutral—and we are not concerned with the actions of the political parties and leaders outside of the United States," *Wonder's* editor insisted. Then—rather naively, considering what was to happen afterward in the world—he added: "What the leader of Germany does to or for the German people is for the Germans to think about."

Fascism in science fiction was no novelty; Hugo Gernsback's ostrich policy toward Hitler thus seems all the more surprising. Jack London had forecast something very like a Fascist regime in his trenchant political novel *The Iron Heel* (1908): "Out of the ethical incoherency and inconsistency of capitalism, the oligarchs emerged with a new ethics, coherent and definite, sharp and severe as steel, the most absurd and unscientific and at the same time the most potent ever possessed by any tyrant class. The oligarchs believed their ethics, in spite of the fact that biology and evolution gave them the lie."

Jack London's Fascist new order emerged in America; twelve years later another writer moved it to Germany. Milo Hastings, in *City of Endless Night* (1920), predicted a regimented, technological, eugenicist new Reich, centered in a roofed-over Berlin and engaged in war with the rest of the world. Hastings placed this prophecy two hundred years in the future, but the actual triumph of Nazism in Germany prompted far more urgent fictional warnings. In 1935, while Hugo Gernsback was expressing unconcern with the actions of political parties and leaders outside the United States, Sinclair Lewis wrote *It Can't Happen Here;* in that novel Franklin D. Roosevelt is defeated for renomination in 1936 by a demagogue senator resembling Huey Long, and the next American presidential election, therefore, produces a Fascist regime.

Lewis inscribed one copy of his new book to science fiction's own mentor, H. G. Wells, who five years before had uttered a similar fictional warning for England. The usurping "Lord Paramount" in Wells's *The Autocracy of Mr. Parham* (1930) sends the House of Commons packing, holds summit conferences with other European dictators, and in due course plunges the world into war. (To give further satiric bite, Wells described—and the great English political cartoonist David Low drew in pen and ink—the reactions to the new government that might be expected from Wells's and Low's actual contemporaries, notably Mussolini, Ramsay Macdonald, Bernard Shaw, Lady Astor, and Winston Churchill.) Variations on some of H. G. Wells's other themes—Martian invaders,

time travelers, giants, monsters on the moon, and invisible
men—occurred in stories written for Hugo Gernsback's magazines with great regularity, but in them appeared few American versions of Mr. Parham. There *did,* however, appear in
those magazines self-sacrificing technocrats and science corps-
men, some of them functioning in a future world so totally
organized, anti-individual, and also (in some instances) milita-
rist and racist as to make Nazism itself seem relatively loose
and free. A story like Frank K. Kelly's "The Moon Tragedy,"
with its exultant references to storm troopers tramping over
Africa (*Wonder Stories:* 5, October 1933), is enough to make
anyone wonder whether Gernsback's response to Wollheim
mirrored an attitude in science fiction more sinister than
simple isolationism.

        II

Not all the pulp magazines were as circumspect as *Wonder
Stories.* Within months of Nat Schachner's "Ancestral Voices"
in *Astounding,* a cautionary tale by Frank Belknap Long, titled
"The Beast-Helper," appeared (*Weird Tales:* 24, August
1934). In its opening scene, an American correspondent
named Thompson is interviewing the dictator of "Trivania,"
who tells him that "representative government is an absurdity,
an historical anachronism." The regime, called in the story a
"corporate state" (a term also used by Mussolini), intends
"ruthlessly to suppress all dissenting opinion." Scribbling hastily, the correspondent stops and looks up. "May I quote this?"
he asks.

Apparently master of the situation, Dictator Kerriling tells
him: "Yes, Mr. Thompson, you may quote me at length."

The author has previously described Thompson as "a profound skeptic and a scientific humanist." The American considers Trivania's leader "a savage barbarian" and his government a revolt against rational civilization. (This fictional
American correspondent's judgment on Fascism resembles
that of his real-life namesake, Dorothy Thompson, who was

married to Sinclair Lewis at that time, incidentally, and who
had recently secured an interview with Hitler and was beginning to sound the alarm.) In the course of the story, Thompson's argument against Fascism is translated into primordial
myth. Kerriling's unconscious mind has been telepathically
linked to that of a pet gorilla, which the ruler sends out on
missions of assassination. When Thompson in self-defense
kills the gorilla, the resulting psychic backlash causes the
dictator to die also.

Not so easy, however, is the task cut out for the hero of
Wallace West's "The Phantom Dictator" (*Astounding Stories:*
15, August 1935)—a short story that even forty years later
carries a convincing political chill. The teller of this tale comes
back to the United States from six weeks in isolation on a
fishing trip to Canada. He finds a new fad drawing people
into movie theaters across the nation: an animated cartoon
character with an "engaging smile . . . reminiscent of Charlie
Chaplin." Although an element of pathos endears him to a
people "beaten down by the never-ending economic depression," Willie is not as benign as the similar characters in those
Walt Disney color-cartoon "Silly Symphonies" that were so
popular in the actual world of 1935.

On the screens in hundreds of darkened theaters, the car-
tooned Willie Pan holds a magic wand. By its gyrations his
audiences are gradually hypnotized. As they fall into trance,
the animated pictures dissolve from the screen and the real
message softly comes through on audio: "Many of you do not
have jobs. Some of you are hungry. Others have begged a few
pennies with which to pay admission to this theater. Willie is
going to change all that."

For a time this rhetoric sounds merely like a more strident
version of the New Deal. Then comes a disturbing change of
direction, toward militarism. Shortly the papers are blazoned
with banner headlines: "U.S. warships quell uprising in Bra-
zil"; "Western hemisphere must belong to U.S., says President." To thwart the brainwashers, the hero joins forces with
the Hollywood magnate who originally created this cartoon

character; he has refused to see any of the "new," govern-
ment-sponsored Willie Pan films and therefore has not been
influenced by them. Assisted by a stock Girl Friday heroine,
the two men undertake to forge and release an underground
Willie Pan cartoon that will convey another, more pacific
message.

The David and Goliath convention is deep-rooted in American folk culture, and in most of the underdogs-versus-tyrants
epics that were published just before and during World War
II, the reader could have expected the hero and his friends to
succeed. But in "The Phantom Dictator," more realistically,
they fail. The secret police catch up with them. The hero, the
girl, and the film maker are charged with high treason, judged
criminally insane, and clapped into padded cells. "Today they
let me read the newspapers for the first time" since the trial,
the narrator concludes. "The war has started."

However, what the United States actually did in 1935 was
not to start a war, but to pass a Neutrality Act. If well-
intentioned Americans in the 1930s detested dictators, they
also detested war. Hence their tragic dilemma, only temporarily resolved by Pearl Harbor: if the dictators proved so warlike
that their opponents must resort to war to stop them, it
became logically impossible to translate both of these American good intentions into action at the same time. Many people
also shared in the widespread belief that America's entrance
into World War I had been a triumph of Allied propaganda;
that Woodrow Wilson's crusade to make the world "safe for
democracy" had had exactly the opposite result; and that it is
folly to die in the wretchedness of modern war for *any* ideology, be it Hitler's, Stalin's, or even Thomas Jefferson's.

Magazine science fiction caught this disenchanted attitude
fairly early in a story by Miles J. Breuer, "The Gostaks and the
Doshes" (*Amazing Stories:* 4, March 1930). A scientist trans-
ports himself to a nation existing in another universe, almost
exactly paralleling ours: it has drugstores, electric street cars,
movie theaters, beauty shops, and a stock exchange. One day
he hears over the radio and reads in the newspapers an

absolutely meaningless sentence, "The gostak distims the
doshes." Nobody can explain to him what it denotes, but
everybody considers it profoundly important. Enthusiasm
escalates into hysteria, and hysteria spills over into a declara-
tion of war against another nation, which has denied this
incomprehensible but holy belief. Battles are fought, cities are
bombed, rationing is imposed. A mangled veteran returns
from the front, one of thousands. Then someone cries, "The
gostak distims the doshes!" "and the poor wounded fragment
would straighten up and put out his chest with pride, and an
unquenchable fire would blaze in his eyes. He did not regret
having given his all for that."

Antiwar themes, as in Breuer's little parable and in Carl W.
Spohr's "The Final War" (*Wonder Stories:* 3, March and April
1932)—the latter clearly modeled on Erich Maria Remarque's
All Quiet on the Western Front—were a relatively minor element
in the pulp fiction of the 1930s. Certainly they took up much
less space in the magazines than the vast fleets of starships that
swept into battle in space operas such as E. E. Smith's "Skylark" stories, serialized in *Amazing* and *Astounding,* or the
hordes of berserk barbarians who followed Robert E. Howard's muscle-bound, sword-swinging Conan the Conqueror
through many a blood-spattered episode in *Weird Tales.* In
such swashbuckling yarns Might, whether exercised with a
broad-axe or propagated through a force-field, quite
obviously made Right. Throughout the 1930s, however, that
harsh doctrine had to share a few pages in the magazines with
implicit rebuttals.

Nat Schachner, who had warned against Hitler in "Ancestral Voices," warned against global war in a somewhat preachy
story, "World Gone Mad" (*Amazing Stories:* 10, October 1935),
in which a family watches from a twenty-fourth-story pent-
house while civilization is destroyed by gas-laden ICBMs. That
same year, Leigh Keith contributed a grim little fable called
"No Medals" (*Astounding Stories:* 15, March 1935), in which a
scientist during the "next" war, who has learned how to stimulate the motor nerves of a corpse by electrical impulses,

thereby creates the ideal, ultimate soldier. While he is putting his experimental subject through its paces, this military-minded version of Doctor Frankenstein fantasizes as to the difference his invention might make at the front. Unkillable troops could march and fight tirelessly, unless and until physically blown to pieces. Their operators would be safely hidden in blast-proof bunkers, directing these zombies' movements through remote-controlled radio receivers implanted on the corpses' backs. (Medical technicians, meanwhile, would be dragging freshly killed soldiers' bodies into shelter to give them the same treatment.) Once done with the day's work, these animated cadavers would obediently march back, neatly stack arms, and tumble into their preservative vats, conveniently out of the way until needed. "There were no medals, no honors for distinguished services—no heroic sacrifices—but it was most efficient." So the inventor dreams, as he idly plays with his levers. His attention wanders, and quite by accident the naked marionette whose movements he has been directing kills him with its bayonet.

As war approached in the dread spring and summer of 1939, prophecy of the "next" war as the downfall of civilization received some of its sharpest expression. In that year appeared, for example, "Judson's Annihilator," by John Beynon Harris (discussed in chapter 1), and "The Red God Laughed," by Thorp McClusky (*Weird Tales:* 33, April 1939). In McClusky's story, a sentient being from another world lands upon an Earth from which "all races of mankind, all air-breathing creatures save only the deep-sea fishes and the worms that chanced to be far underground—and, perhaps, a few toads and frogs, encapsulated and dormant in dry lake or riverbeds—had perished." Unaware that the Americans and "the yellow men" have killed each other off in a war fought with lethal gas (a substance that served the same doomsday function in prewar science fiction as have nuclear weapons since 1945), Thvall the Seeker touches down in Central Park. He examines a living earthworm, winds up a watch taken from a skeleton, rides in an elevator to a rooftop—and there finds and opens an unused cylinder of war gas. He dies; and therefore his home planet, desperately in need of water, never learns that Earth has that commodity in abundance. Earth's suicidal wars have therefore destroyed not only humankind, but Thvall's people as well. "Mars, the Red God," the sermon ends, "had just claimed his last, and perhaps his most significant, sacrifice."

III

For many in the West, as the springtide of Axis aggression surged across Europe, Africa, and Asia, the horror of war came to seem less than the horror of Fascist rule. This change in priorities had a dramatic impact on American politics, reflected in FDR's "Quarantine the Aggressors" speech (October 1937), and it had echoes in science fiction also. Nat Schachner put aside the pacifism he had preached in "World Gone Mad" and wrote a series of connected stories, leading off with "Past, Present, and Future" (*Astounding Stories:* 20, September 1937), in which three adventurers wander across the world of the ninety-second century trying to warn its complacent, isolated city-states that they are in danger of invasion. Schachner described the aggressors' mountain fortress in language reminiscent of Wagner (Hitler's favorite composer): "the surge of subterranean fires, the thin hiss of steam, the muted rush of falling waters." Like the toiling Nibelungs in the opera *Das Rheingold,* the workers in the depths of that city "looked like huge blond gnomes." The leaders of the city's troops are described as close-cropped and bullet-headed, or else as having "bristling toothbrush mustaches on their lips"; the soldiers themselves are plainly labeled "fascist hordes" ("City of the Rocket Horde," *Astounding Stories:* 20, December 1937).

The prospective victims of those hordes rebuff the three heroes' warnings, on the logical but suicidal ground that to pool their efforts against the legions of Harg would be to succumb to regimentation themselves. Upon the remote

Pacific isle of Asto, in "The Island of the Individualists" (*Astounding:* 21, April 1938), whose spindly, big-domed inhabitants spend their time sitting in the cross-legged yoga posture and thinking, one of the hermits explains their refusal to act collectively even in self-defense: "Even death is better than sinking one's individuality in the common will." Thirty miles high in the stratosphere in Dadelon, the "City of the Cosmic Rays" (*ASF:* 23, July 1939), the biologically individualized citizens—one of them "tall and willowy, with a tiny head that swayed like a fragile flower in a breeze," another covered with a fine fluffy down, another having "great, compound eyes that twirled their many facets round and round," and so on—are as loath to heed the warning that the rocket horde is coming as were the merely mental individualists on the island of Asto. "Dadelon never works as a unit," one of them explains. "That is the method of slaves." In consequence of this attitude, both Asto and Dadelon are attacked and their inhabitants one by one destroyed.

Only when the rocket-powered army encounters Lyv, the "City of the Corporate Mind" (*ASF:* 24, December 1939), whose human components function merely as cells in one great body, does militarism meet its match. The commonwealth of Lyv—which refers to itself as "I"!—calmly wipes out the plunging rocket hosts, and then itself embarks upon a course of conquest. "This is the ultimate totalitarian state, the goal toward which Earth's evolution was obviously working," comments one of the heroes. "A single corporate existence, in which human beings are but mechanical cogs, specialized in function and obedient to the common purpose." If this be a political parable, its moral would seem to be, you're damned if you do and damned if you don't; but the adventurers refuse to abandon their quest for "a city of decent, kindly folk—men who are free and therefore invincible." The helmsman of their refugee craft is told to "point west, always west!" From the Mediterranean, where that story (and the series) ends, to fare westward is both literally and symbolically to head for America.

As war came closer to the United States, the "antidictator" theme in the stories became ever more pointedly and specifically anti-Nazi. On the planet Mongo in Alex Raymond's Sunday comic strip, *Flash Gordon,* whose expertly drawn adventures each week reached a far wider (if probably younger) audience than that of the science fiction magazines, the previously Oriental-looking minions of Emperor Ming the Merciless by 1940 were sporting monocles and *Wehrmacht*-style battle helmets. Ming's political opponents were being herded into what the author called a "concentration camp," guarded by an elite corps—whose dashing uniforms, by an unintended irony, anticipated those worn a generation later by America's own Green Berets.

Even the monsters in outer space began to resemble Nazis. Boskonia, the interstellar "pirate" culture that is fought by the raygun-toting, telepathic Lens-wearing heroes of E. E. ("Doc") Smith's "Galactic Patrol" (serialized in *Astounding:* 20, September 1937 through February 1938), rises to heights of maleficence that make Earth's commonplace Fascism by comparison seem relatively humane. Boskonia's Grand Base, located on "a small but comfortable planet at some little distance from the galaxy," far surpasses all the mystic military dreams of the Nazis' Fortress Europe; its ruthless, efficient personnel practice the Will-to-Power raised to the *n*th degree. Their leader, the "speaker for Boskone," is called Helmuth. That name, although applied in this instance to a being whose eyes, hair, and skin are blue, has nevertheless a supiciously Nordic ring. Such a menace to civilization, author Smith declared, could be overcome in but one way: in "a war of utter, complete, and merciless extinction."

Still more Nazi in outlook are the horrid "Eich" creatures the Galactic Patrol has to fight in the sequel, "Gray Lensman," which appeared in magazine form during the opening months of World War II (*Astounding:* 24, October, November, December 1939; January 1940). Racially prejudiced not merely against differently colored humans, but against *all* "warm-blooded oxygen-breathers," this frightful species nevertheless earns a grudged respect as a foe worthy of Civilization's steel. Evil though they are, "anti-social, blood-mad, obsessed with an insatiable lust for power and conquest," the Eich—like the Waffen SS and other elite Nazi types in the war drama of the 1940s—are described as "brave . . . organizers par excellence . . . in their own fashion creators and doers. They had the courage of their convictions," as "Doc" Smith summed up, "and followed them to the bitter end." Readers of *Astounding* were quick to understand the metaphor, and from time to time in letters to "Brass Tacks," commenting on the contemporary world situation they made reference to "Adolf Schickelgruber and his eighty million Boskonians" (*ASF:* 29, April 1942, p. 115).

A few science fiction writers were slow to get the message. Even as late as the autumn of 1941, after France had fallen and London had taken a year's terrible pounding from the *Luftwaffe,* a story appeared in an American magazine in which Hitler dies a hero. His mighty motorized legions, joining forces with the British and U.S. navies, have fought a gallant losing battle against an invader from outer space (Eando Binder, "Vassals of the Master World," *Planet Stories:* 1, Fall 1941). By that time, however, such judgments were highly atypical. In story after story published in the embattled early 1940s, Hitler got his proper comeuppance. A. E. Van Vogt, turning from menaces in space to a menace closer to home, wrote one story composed of imaginary interoffice memos among the Nazi leaders, "Secret Unattainable" (*Astounding:* 29, July 1942), which ingeniously explained the background for Hitler's suicidal decision to invade Russia. And Ralph Milne Farley, in a story starkly titled "I Killed Hitler" (*Weird Tales:* 35, July 1941), went after the Führer himself.

Farley's protagonist, a distant cousin of the Nazi warlord, decides to go back in time and slay Hitler as a child, thereby preventing him from growing up to launch what Churchill in 1941 would call "this cataract of horrors upon mankind." But the Swami from whom the hero learns the time-travel technique (by crystal ball, not by time machine; Farley was writing for *Weird Tales,* not *Astounding*) warns him that it is impossible successfully to meddle with Karma. Sure enough; when he returns to the present the narrator learns that he has indeed altered the course of history—in such fashion that *he* has now become the ruler of Germany! "My patience is exhausted," he proclaims as the story ends. "At dawn tomorrow we launch our armada against America."

Bustling with millions of other Americans to meet the real armada launched by Hitler's Japanese ally some months later, probably few readers of *Weird Tales* and the other magazines paused to ponder the more profound question implicitly raised by the Swami: is it really possible to do evil, in this case child-murder, in order to do good? And, in a war in which "our side" as well as "theirs" fire-bombed cities and strafed civilians, was there not a bit of Hitler in all of us? "The movement which Hitler was able to kindle in the Twentieth Century has existed potentially in the human soul since the formation of the first society," wrote the Swiss essayist-philosopher Denis de Rougemont (in *The Devil's Share,* 1944); "and it will no doubt exist till the end of the history of our race. Hitler has only given it a face and a name."

Whatever the immediate urgencies of global warfare, the institutionalized violence symbolized in Hitler's regime may not after all have been the ultimate menace to mankind. Aldous Huxley had already suggested in *Brave New World* (1932) that totalitarianism has more powerful mainsprings than simple national aggression, and that it does not need to be triggered by war. Entirely unlike the competing nation-states of Eurasia, Oceania, and Eastasia in *1984,* which need one another as enemies to perpetuate their own domestic regimes, the civilization of *Brave New World* is a planet-wide, cosmopolitan culture from which all the old divisions of race, religion, and nationality have been purged. In achieving the absolute obliteration of freedom, this society has fulfilled also the ancient philanthropic dream of universal peace. It was this theme of totalitarianism as a logical and natural outgrowth of existing tendencies, rather than as a suddenly and forcibly imposed reign of terror, that was to inspire most of the counter-utopian satire in postwar science fiction. "Don't blame the government," says one agent of the new tyranny, in Ray Bradbury's vivid novella *Fahrenheit 451* (first published as "The Fireman," *Galaxy Science Fiction:* 1, February 1951); that future society is the product of ordinary people's ordinary fears. As the cartoonist Walt Kelly put it in the mid-1950s, "we have met the enemy, and he is us."

Much early 1940s science fiction, written during a desperately fought war, had the same purpose as Paul Revere's ride: to "spread the alarm to every Middlesex village and farm." Sometimes the heroes in the stories ventured into the far future and found the Nazis entrenched there; the characters in "Barrier," by Anthony Boucher (*Astounding:* 30, September 1942), travel by time machine to a humorless, regimented world that reckons its years no longer from A.D. but rather N.H.—*nach* (after) *Hitler.* Another wanderer through time, in "The Probable Man" by Alfred Bester (*ASF:* 27, July 1941) finds himself in a future world that has reverted to medievalism, peopled by freebooters dressed up like knights of the Round Table who call themselves "Swasts" (men of the swastika). They do not realize that he is not one of their own until he innocently takes a notebook out of his rucksack, whereupon one of them cries: "The swine's a Reader! He's got a book!" So totally has the Nazis' book-burning ideology prevailed that even Germany's own high technology has been forgotten; this is a future not of television and Volkswagens, but of torchlight and horses.

In all these wartime stories, however, the Good Guys eventually win.

Most of these anti-Nazi epics were potboilers even by pulp magazine standards, no more edifying than any other war propaganda. Alfred Bester's "Probable Man" has an interesting twist on the time-travel theme, but the idea is buried under a fast, jumpy, bang-bang-you're-dead story line—quite different from the effective, sometimes brilliant, writing of which Bester was also capable. (Stories of this type in other magazines, particularly in *Amazing*, were even worse.) Far more interesting, in psychological retrospect, are the stories dealing with Hitlerism written and published *after* the downfall of Nazi Germany. World War II cast some kind of spell on science fiction writers. No longer needing to prophesy a possible German victory to stimulate their readers to pitch in and help win the war, they remained obsessed with the possibility that the war might have gone the other way. In the world of here and now, Hitler's empire lies in ruins; but somewhere on an alternate time-track, like bogeymen in the dark, the Nazis still lurk.

IV

It was the end of March, and the wreck of the Dritten Reich lay in colossal ruin across Europe, where people were only beginning to crawl out of their burrows and face the job of rebuilding a world for better or worse. In Germany itself the Allied Armies . . . were closing in to smash the still-defiant nucleus of the old world that had been for worse.

So begins "Hostage of Tomorrow," by Robert Abernathy (*Planet Stories:* 4, Spring 1949), which appeared in print four years after the Third Reich's cataclysmic end. Driving up a rutted road into the Black Forest, a unit of the U.S. Seventh Army nabs a German physicist who has been building a *Zeitfahrer* (time machine). Transported into the next century, these Americans learn to their dismay that the defeated Germans have secretly built and suddenly used atomic bombs on the occupying powers, thereby turning the tables after all. As a result of that victory, New York has become "Neuebersdorf"; Manhattan's skyline is in ruins, and a neat German colonial town with quiet electric-powered traffic and well-kept green lawns occupies the site of Brooklyn. We are not told what became of New York's Jews.

Atomic energy and automation have made slave labor no longer necessary, and the demographers in Berlin have forecast that in another four hundred years it will be possible to cover the earth with Germans. Therefore, to make room for them, the Greater Reich that rules the world in the year 2051 A.D. has begun to wipe out its conquered peoples with radioactive dust. Russia has already been liquidated, and America is next. The only possible way that a small, fugitive American underground organization can avert this doom is to seize and divert the dust-laden rocket at launch time—and dump its lethal cargo upon Germany!

Admittedly abhorrent as a Final Solution to the German problem, this desperate act brings no utopia to the non-German survivors. In the chaos of a world suddenly released from a century's military rule, they fall to fighting one another, and a new Dark Ages seem about to begin. "What else did you expect?" asks a grim Russian, who has personally escaped the destruction of his own country and joined the American avengers. "You don't imagine that because Germany falls, the rest of the world will become civilized again?"

"I sometimes wonder what would happen if history had taken a different turning," one of the Americans replies—

> if we, instead of the Germans, had been the ones to discover atomic energy. Would we have been any better than they were? Or would we have used the power to make ourselves the masters of Earth and monopolize civilization, just as Germany did?"
>
> "You would have," snorted Vzryvov. "Russia would have. Any nationalism of that time, given such power, would have behaved the same."

Nonetheless, hope springs eternal in the American breast, and at the end of the story the two G.I.'s from 1945 are headed back via *Zeitfahrer* to try and change the past for the better. "We've got our work cut out for us," one of them matter-of-factly remarks as the tale ends.

A story of this kind might be read as an allegorical comment upon the imperial power that America acquired when Germany's was smashed. After Hiroshima, as policies of deterrent terror became standard and the option of total genocide

became thinkable, many in the West had a sinking feeling that
the Nazis had, in a sense, won World War II after all. But that
is not a sufficient explanation for the persistence of such
stories. Postwar Britain, with its old colonial domain falling to
pieces, felt no such burden of empire. Yet British science
fiction also produced a memorable novel about a future in
which the Thousand-Year Reich has become a reality—*The
Sound of His Horn*, by "Sarban" (John W. Wall) (London 1952;
U.S. paperback edition 1960). The horror of Sarban's Reich is
underscored by the unspoiled woodland which is the story's
setting; its villain, Baron von Hackelnberg, is the Reich Master
Forester, who rides out at night in Siegfried costume carrying
a great silver horn as he hunts human beings for sport.

   This society is not the product of barbarian reversion, as in
Bester's "The Probable Man." The Baron's domain has
sophisticated electronic defenses, and his personal physician
competently practices modern medicine. The half-human,
half-feline creatures that add to his guests' excitement at the
hunt are the product of highly advanced bioengineering and
genetic techniques. These Nazis of the far future *choose* to
behave like characters in a Wagner opera, lounging on furs,
eating from greasy trenchers, and quaffing home brew from
drinking horns, rather than luxuriating in gadgets and con-
sumer goods like the urbanized moderns they really are. The
distinguished English novelist and critic Kingsley Amis, in an
introduction to Sarban's book, suggests that *The Sound of His
Horn* is a healthy corrective on "the sentimental consensus—to
be found outside science fiction as well as within it—that it is
only the city and the machine and the ad which kill, that the
country rehumanizes":

The nightmare futures envisioned by writers like Frederik
Pohl or Ray Bradbury are often brilliantly detailed and
imaginative, but . . . they are always urban, metropolitan,
technological, consumptional, managerial. Sarban's rural hell is
just as clearly visualized, furnishing a critique of that huge tribe
of authors who can only see future systems of oppression in

terms of brainwashing and too much television, and acting as a timely reminder that a nonurban hell is not only imaginable, but possible.

And, Amis hinted, a pastoral hell may well be in store for us all (or those of us who survive), should our present metropolitan culture be smashed by city-busting bombs.

The twentieth-century man who wakes up in Sarban's rural future hell is a British naval reservist from World War II; captured off Crete in 1941, he escapes from an ordinary prisoner-of-war camp in eastern Germany before crossing into the alternate future that contains Baron von Hackelnberg's evil domain. Politically and emotionally, this hero is of the same generation as Robert Abernathy's (or Norman Mailer's) G.I.s. But a new generation of young Americans came along, many of whom took their cues not so much from Dwight Eisenhower's bestseller *Crusade in Europe* as from Joseph Heller's bestseller *Catch-22;* they saw World War II less as a heroic struggle against evil, more as an obscene absurdity. In that changing climate of opinion, could not science fiction's fascination with the Nazi menace have been expected to fade away? Quite surprisingly, the answer turns out to be no.

In the middle 1950s, the science fiction fans, polling themselves at their annual World Science Fiction Conventions (or Worldcons) began to award "Hugos"—named after founding father Hugo Gernsback and modeled on the Oscars and Edgars and Grammys and Emmys awarded in other media— to what they considered the best science fiction of the year. The prize in 1958 for best novel went to Fritz Leiber's *The Big Time* (serialized in *Galaxy:* 15, March and April 1958), in which the past has been changed to create "a Nazi empire stretching from the salt mines of Siberia to the plantations of Iowa, from Nizhni Novgorod to Kansas City." In 1963 the Hugo in the book-length category went to Philip K. Dick for *The Man in the High Castle,* a novel in which the United States, defeated in war, has been partitioned between Germany and

Japan. Stroke by careful brushstroke, the author drew his portrait of occupied San Francisco, with its pedicabs, its coin-operated tea dispensers, and its shops where fake American antiques are sold to Japanese tourists. The Japanese in the tale emerge as (more or less) Good Guys; American and Oriental cultures on this time-track are subtly interpenetrating, to the mutual enrichment of both. But the Nazis in the story, working on a Final Solution for Africa and plotting a surprise nuclear attack on Japan, remain as unregenerate as ever.

Still more startling as a measurement of how far science fiction's peculiar "take" on Nazism could go is *The Iron Dream*, by Norman Spinrad (1972). Most of this story consists of a novel-within-a-novel, titled *Lord of the Swastika*—by Adolf Hitler! Introductory notes and an afterword, beautifully burlesquing the pretentious style in which pedants write introductions to other people's books, explain that in 1919 Hitler gave up his dabbling in German "nationalist" politics, emigrated to the United States, and became a science fiction writer. He published a series of well-received novels (*The Master Race, Tomorrow the World,* and such) climaxed by *Lord of the Swastika,* for which he received a posthumous Hugo in 1959. This imaginary story by Hitler that won an imaginary Hugo constitutes the rest of Spinrad's book. The real-world events of the 1930s and 1940s are transferred to a far-distant future in which a glorified Germany (renamed "Heldon") triumphs over the mongrel hordes of a depraved Russia (the "Empire of Zind"). Of course, the supposed commentator on Hitler's opus explains, no political movement could *actually* take command of a civilized modern nation in the manner this pulp writer described; "Obviously, such a mass national psychosis could never occur in the real world."

That comment may be an ironic echo of Sinclair Lewis's *It Can't Happen Here*—or of the radicalism of the 1960s, which bitterly spelled the name of this country *Amerika* on the assumption that Fascism had already happened here. But *The Iron Dream* can also be taken as an exercise in literary self-criticism. Pulp science fiction on our own time-track had known its ego-assertive superman heroes, its military display, its fantasies of unlimited power, its sweeping apocalypses. Therefore, the imaginary *Lord of the Swastika* at times sounds uncomfortably close to what really used to appear in some of the magazines. Algis Budrys has suggested, for example (*Fantasy and Science Fiction:* 49, September 1975), that Spinrad/ "Hitler's" style and treatment owe something to Lovecraft. Thus Spinrad may have been engaged in a subtle purge, helping to write the pulp era's moral and political obituary. The science fiction community, however, received *The Iron Dream* with mixed feelings. Bill Noble 3rd, reviewing the book for *Amazing Science Fiction* (formerly *Amazing Stories*), considered it a joke in rather bad taste: "I don't believe we're quite ready to laugh off Dachau and Auschwitz, *Hogan's Heroes* notwithstanding" ("The Future in Books," *Amazing:* 47, August 1973).

Yet only two years later, *Amazing* published a contribution of its own to this myth of might-have-been, "The Cliometricon," by George Zebrowski (*Amazing:* 49, May 1975). The Cliometricon is a labor-saving device for historians; it visualizes alternate histories on a TV screen. No longer need a scholar pore over brittle newspapers and dusty manuscripts, making notes on 3×5 cards. It is all efficiently computerized; he sits at a console, working permutations on all the possible pasts. Most of the time, however, the narrator watches permutations on one past moment only—the sixth of June 1944. General Dwight Eisenhower walks along the white cliffs of Dover, brooding over a D-Day invasion that has failed. Or General Eisenhower, on those same cliffs, is personally destroyed by the blast from a German nuclear bomb. Or Eisenhower is shot by a passing submarine. Or the D-Day armada makes it ashore, but is then swept back into the sea by a Red army that has changed sides. Or Eisenhower visits the ruins of Moscow with nuclear scientists Oppenheimer and Teller, "while a world away Speer seeks to recruit Einstein and Bohr for work in the victorious Reich." Apart from these vignettes there is no story, no "plot" in the conventional sense.

By way of counterpoint, the author describes a few permutations from the history of classic antiquity that change fortunes of the Greeks and the Persians at Thermopylae.

Why? To broadcast a warning against the Phantom Dictator, in hopes that steps would be taken to prevent his advent in the real world, was surely a legitimate enterprise. So is a search for the enhancement of life and for the relatively more decent course of action, even in a world as ambiguous as that of Mr. Dick's High Castle. But what ghost of our recent past can possibly be exorcised by fantasizing such a series of dire fates for the instinctively well-intentioned Eisenhower? What mileage is to be gained in the future from willing that the *past* be changed for the worse? In stories like "The Cliometricon" the high crusade for civilization of forty years ago has begun to give off a whiff of decay. The alternate-Nazi theme remains popular; 1975 saw also a "mainstream" novel (i.e., one not labeled as "science fiction") by Frederic Mullaly titled *Hitler Has Won,* in which the conquering Führer trumps his own ace by having himself proclaimed Pope. Perhaps that act of consecration is a sign that it is time this particular skeleton in science fiction's closet was laid to rest.

V

"Pulp writers have a job to do," Nat Schachner declared as World War II drew to a close (*The Writer:* 58, August 1945). "Innocently, without meaning to do so," they had for years been creating stock characters in their stories who embodied racial and ethnic sterotypes. "At the first crack of a name—Spinelli, Epstein, O'Hara, Privilovski, Schultz, Hip Sing, Svenson, Pancho, George Washington White—the reader knows exactly what to expect." Not all of this was as innocent and unintended as Schachner charitably assumed; for example, the much-admired Howard Phillips Lovecraft's comments on ethnic minorities—*all* ethnic minorities, save only his own—were at times vicious and colorful enough to have delighted the heart of Dr. Goebbels. Immigrant Americans, Lovecraft confided to an aunt in 1926, "make one feel ill-at-ease, as though one's shoes pinched, or as though one had on prickly woollen underwear" (quoted in L. Sprague de Camp, *Lovecraft: A Biography,* 1975, p. 254).

Racism had been a large part of what the recently concluded war had been all about. Therefore, Schachner argued, if the pulpsters were to commence presenting Jews, Catholics, Italians, Mexicans, blacks, and so on in their stories "not as caricatures or stereotypes, but as individuals, involved in common human situations, with all the wide range of character and personality traits common to all human beings, we will be doing more to eliminate the vicious Nazi myths and propaganda"—and their native American equivalents—"than a thousand pulpit sermons and a thousand ponderous editorials."

Some of this image-breaking had already begun. Lester del Rey has testified (in *Early del Rey,* 1975), that in 1942 he deliberately wrote a sympathetic Japanese-American character into his suspenseful story "Nerves" (*Astounding:* 30, September 1942) in personal dissent from the prevailing hue and cry against that category of citizens. Breaking another stereotype, the Head of Earth's planetary government in a short story, "Q.U.R.," by Anthony Boucher (*Astounding:* 31, March 1943), is a black man. Postwar science fiction continued this trend away from the old caricatures. Racial intermarriage, for example, is the theme of "Dark Interlude," by Mack Reynolds and Fredric Brown (*Galaxy:* 1, January 1951): What does a young white man do in a small Southern town if his sister marries a man from a time so far in the future that all races have blended into one—so that *every* person in that future, by the present-day white South's definition, is "colored"? Editor Horace Gold wryly noted (editorial, May 1951) that some readers misinterpreted this tale as an argument in favor of race prejudice, which demonstrates that even in science fiction circles some fail to understand irony.

Racism, however, had been only one component of the ugly Nazi synthesis. The real lesson to be learned from Nazism was

not how a "small group of villainous men" (as Churchill called
Hitler's henchmen) could terrorize and enslave free peoples,
but rather how a free people could willingly terrorize and
enslave itself. Rejecting the Cold War logic, which says it is
possible to preserve freedom by destroying it, science fiction
in the 1950s again and again warned that "it can happen
here." As a high-ranking security officer explains and ration-
alizes the origins of a computerized American police state in
Poul Anderson's satiric fable "Sam Hall" (*Astounding:* 51,
August 1953): "When we lost World War III, we had to
militarize to win World War IV, and after that, for our own
safety, we had to mount guard on the whole human race. The
people demanded it at the time."

To be sure, after the surrender of Nazi Germany (on our
time-line), Harry Truman and many other Americans simply
substituted Communism for Fascism as the ultimate menace
and Stalin for Hitler as the arch-villain. Some science fiction
shared in the new crusade; for example, Cyril Kornbluth's *Not
This August* (*Maclean's Magazine:* Canada, May and June 1955;
U.S. book publication 1955) begins with a presidential
announcement that U.S. and Canadian forces have just lost
the Battle of El Paso. The United States has therefore surren-
dered to the invading armies commanded by Marshals Novi-
kov and Feng. The rest of the story is a saga of upstate New
York under occupation, first by the Red army and then by the
dreaded MVD; the hero joins the underground American
resistance movement, which eventually strikes for liberation.

However, considering what else was going on in the
1950s—a time of loyalty oaths, atom-spy executions, and rampaging anti-Communist congressmen and senators—there
was surprisingly little Red-fighting in the science fiction magazines. Instead, the 1950s in science fiction were a time of
trenchant social criticism, aimed at what those same congressmen and senators were wont to define as the American Way of
Life. In "that miserable decade we look back on as the era of
McCarthyism," *Galaxy's* editor Frederik Pohl proudly
declared in 1968 (*Extrapolation:* 10, May 1969), "at a time

when presidents and newspaper editors were running for shelter, about the only people speaking up openly to tell it like it was were Edward R. Murrow, one or two Senators, and just about every science fiction writer alive."

No cow was too sacred for science fiction in the postwar era: the fetish of government security, as in "Project Hush," by William Tenn (*Galaxy Science Fiction:* 7, February 1954); police surveillance, as in Ray Bradbury's two-page chiller "The Pedestrian" (*The Reporter:* 5, August 7, 1951, also reprinted in *Fantasy and Science Fiction:* 3, February 1952); the brass-bound Pentagon mentality, as in R. Bretnor's hilarious "The Gnurrs Come From the Voodvork Out" (*F & SF:* 1, Winter-Spring 1950); the American foreign-aid program, as in Poul Anderson's ironic cover story "The Helping Hand" (*Astounding:* 45, May 1950); and capitalism itself, as in "Mars Child" by "Cyril Judd" (Cyril Kornbluth and Judith Merril, *Galaxy:* 2, May, June, July 1951). Long before it became fashionable in other media, science fiction writers vividly denounced the massacre and oppression of native peoples by white Western imperialists, merely transferring the natives to another planet and coloring them green. As a critic shrewdly pointed out in the leading American Marxist quarterly (Oscar Shaftel, "The Social Content of Science Fiction," *Science & Society:* 17, Spring 1953), "The medium's natural camouflage of time (the future) and space (other planets and galaxies) permits some writers to make pungent comments on the here and now."

The future, however, is not the only vantage point from which to judge the here and now. Nat Schachner, the earliest of pulp science fiction's anti-Nazi Paul Reveres, in the end rejected Hugo Gernsback's dogma that the salvation of society must be worked out in futurist terms; instead, he turned for inspiration to the past. "Nat," the penny-a-word pulpster, had coexisted for quite some while with the more respectable "Nathan" Schachner, who wrote for academic quarterlies that paid even less. Books on Aaron Burr and on the medieval universities had appeared under the Nathan byline, while Nat was also churning out the "Past, Present, and Future" series for *Astounding*. Immediately after the war came Schachner's scholarly study of Alexander Hamilton, which won the approval of prominent historian Dumas Malone: "The author is not a professor," Malone wrote (*Saturday Review of Literature:* 29, June 15, 1946), "but he has consulted manuscripts in the approved professional manner." Digging into manuscripts rather than gazing into the future thenceforth engaged Schachner's full attention; his stories stopped appearing in the magazines, and his book on Hamilton was followed by a popular history, *The Founding Fathers,* and a two-volume biography of Thomas Jefferson.

If Schachner had ceased to be a pulp writer, he had not ceased to be a moralist; historians also had a job to do along the line of educating and warning their fellow citizens. That the American republican experiment in its earliest years "survived and did not perish may be considered as something of a miracle," Schachner wrote in 1954 in his Foreword to *The Founding Fathers.* "A world of predatory powers, locked in mortal combat, daily threatened its existence; conflicting ideologies, sectionalisms, social and economic antagonisms, and personal passions nearly tore it asunder." (In such words were there echoes from the ninety-second century of Lyv and Harg, of Asto and Dadelon?) "Today, more than ever, that period merits study and understanding," the author continued. "For once again the United States is groping its way in hitherto uncharted seas."

Schachner's political nightmare—and the nightmare of the 1930s—had been that there might indeed prove to be no middle ground between selfish, anarchic, ego-tripping individualism and soul-destroying, mind-dissolving collectivism. Schachner's dream, and the dream of other Americans in a totalitarian and warring world, was that the wisdom of the revolutionary and constitutional fathers might yet avail to save their sons.

Chapter 6

Alas, All Thinking!
The Future of Human Evolution

For in fact what is man in nature? A Nothing in comparison with the Infinite,
an All in comparison with the Nothing, a mean between nothing and
everything. Since he is infinitely removed from comprehending the extremes, the
end of things and their beginning are hopelessly hidden from him in an
impenetrable secret; he is equally incapable of seeing the Nothing from which he
was made, and the Infinite in which he is swallowed up.
What will he do then, but perceive the appearance of the middle of things, in an
eternal despair of knowing either their beginning or their end.

—Pascal, *Pensées*

143

The ultimate in laissez-faire: wildly mutated *biological* individualism. "It would be an insupportable disgrace for two of us to resemble each other," one of these strange beings explains. "City of the Cosmic Rays," by Nat Schachner, *Astounding Science Fiction*, 23 (July, 1939), p. 47 (See chapter 5)

WHILE THE NAZIS MARCHED ACROSS EUROPE as the advance guard of a coming Master Race, two American science fiction fans and comic-strip continuity writers were dreaming up their own version of Superman. The legendary Clark Kent, that shy, spectacled figure who from time to time steps into a phone booth, shucks his drab business suit, and emerges in muscular splendor to fight crime, has won a secure place in American folklore. For science fiction, however, he represents something of a departure from tradition. Science fiction writers in the Gernsback era, when they considered the future biological evolution of man, quite commonly prophesied the exact opposite of the "Man of Steel" depicted in the comic books. Applying the theory of natural selection to a future environment conceived as mechanized and sedentary, they reasoned that muscle in the long run would have less survival value than mind, and they therefore predicted the atrophy of most of the human body and the hypertrophy of the brain. H. G. Wells, as so often he did in science fiction, set the fashion; both the highly advanced Martians, in *The War of the Worlds,* and the Grand Lunar, in *The First Men in the Moon,* are small-bodied and big-brained. In the pulps, the definitive statement—and then some!—of the same thesis is Edmond Hamilton's "The Man Who Evolved" (*Wonder Stories:* 2, April 1931). A scientist undertakes, by experimenting on his own body, to anticipate the changes in the condition of man that millions of years will bring. His friends' reaction to this proposal, and his reply, dramatize one fundamental ambivalence in science fiction:

> "Why, it's insane!" Dutton exclaimed.
> Pollard smiled. "The old cry," he commented. "Never an attempt has been made yet to tamper with nature's laws, but that cry has been raised."

So, turn on the cosmic rays—whose effects were not very well understood in 1931—and damn the consequences. The first exposure turns Pollard into a physical superman à la

Clark Kent. Not content to let well enough alone, he takes a second dosage. This produces a shrunken body and a ballooning skull that measures eighteen inches from brow to back. A third bout of radiation leaves the scientist with "a huge hairless head fully a yard in diameter, supported on tiny legs—the arms having dwindled to mere hands." At that stage, the superman, to the dismay of his unmutated assistants, decides to master the earth—not ruling it, but owning it, "as you might own a farm and animals." But his erstwhile colleagues persuade him to give himself another ray treatment. He emerges as a brain, supported by two grey muscular tentacles and no longer interested in matters so mundane as world conquest.

Yet another exposure and Pollard is *all* grey brain, four feet across. In this condition he addresses his sometime friends by telepathy: "I am pure intelligence now. . . . The only emotion, if such it is, that remains to me still is intellectual curiosity, and this desire for truth that has burned in man since his apehood will be the last of all desires to leave him." Moved by that desire, the brain asks that the rays be turned on yet once more—and promptly dissolves into a mess of protoplasmal slime. The course of "upward" evolution has after all been a circle; as it was in the beginning, is now and ever shall be, world without end.

"Will that cycle of evolutionary change . . . up from simple protoplasm through myriads of forms and lives of ceaseless pain and struggle, only to end in simple protoplasm again . . . be repeated over and over again upon this and other worlds, ceaselessly, purposelessly, until there is no more universe for it to go on in?" Hamilton's narrator asks. It is a strangely pessimistic conclusion for a brand of fiction that the critics persist in damning for its supposed shallow technocratic optimism. These big-brain stories tended in their outlook to be particularly dismal. Typically, Donald Wandrei in "The Red Brain" (*Weird Tales:* 10, October 1927), depicted a far future in which the great brains that are the apex of evolution wait in their Hall of the Mist on a faraway planet for the last of the stars to go out. One of their number claims to have a remedy even for that ultimate disaster, but he turns out to be insane.

What made the prophets of this particular future recoil in horror was the assertion, as in "The Man Who Evolved," that all human emotions except abstract curiosity are beneath the dignity of Superman, a mere vestige of his animal ancestry. In "Alas, All Thinking!" by Harry Bates (*Astounding:* 15, June 1935), Harlan Frick, a venturesome physicist from an era that still values pride and passion and romance, travels by time machine to a future in which all such disturbing impulses have been damped out. Instead, the highly evolved, big-headed superpeople of that far-off time sit in cubicles absentmindedly munching food concentrates while they think, think, think. A grotesque love affair with a female of that distant future species ends in revulsion, as she too withdraws into her shell of concentration. "Brains will be the ruination of the human race," the hero decides, and he runs through the hall of meditation snapping the superbeings' spindly necks, one by one! Then he returns to the twentieth century, locks the door to his laboratory, and devotes himself systematically to the trivial life of a playboy. "You used to have an I.Q. of 248—" a fellow scientist remonstrates. "I've changed!" Frick insists. "I tell you I'm dumb now—normally, contentedly dumb!"

The problem in writing fiction about Superman, for us normally dumb human beings, is that we can't really imagine him. We can extrapolate a creature who would be in certain measurable ways "higher" than ourselves; faster, stronger, or with sharper senses (X-ray vision, for example) than the present-day *Homo sapiens*. But the *mental* superman, as far beyond us in psychic evolution as we are beyond our primate progenitors, actually presents a formidable philosophical problem. How can we know what by definition is beyond our capacity to know? Could an ape, speculating on the character of its own descendants, have imagined Einstein? No stream can rise higher than its source, and no human at the present stage of evolution can fully describe the coming superhuman being who will transcend us.

Still, to imagine the previously unimaginable is a large part of what science fiction is all about. But this particular barrier has commonly been leaped, in literature, not by logic, but by a trick. The simplest such dodge is never to bring Superman directly onstage at all.

Instead, his transcendent powers are inferred from their impact on ordinary human beings. Such was the method used by Norvell W. Page in a melodramatic but effective novel, "But Without Horns" (*Unknown:* 3, June 1940). As that story's title suggests, the mutated superman is perceived by his less-evolved human contemporaries as supernaturally evil—much as the efficient, methodically genocidal Cro-Magnon warriors in Jack London's classic *Before Adam* were perceived as evil by the shambling Neanderthal men whom they displaced. The human hero of "But Without Horns" seeks to stop a mutant named John Miller from single-handedly taking over the world. This superman's godlike ability to dominate lesser beings by sheer force of will can be inferred from the swath he is reportedly cutting across the midwestern heartland (in the fictitious state of Wichinois). But the reader never sees the Thing named John Miller, and it is just as well. At the climax of the story the human characters do see him, and afterward the hero and his friends walk away from that confrontation transfigured, telling one another they now have "the Master's work to do."

"I am writing for a race of men which does not yet exist," declared Friedrich Nietzsche in *The Will to Power:* "for 'the lords of the earth.'" But it really requires no biological mutation to start men proclaiming themselves lords of the earth; they have been saying so for thousands of years already. "Replenish the earth, and subdue it, and have dominion . . . over every living thing," said God to Adam (Gen. 1:28). Far from being a prophet of *Homo superior,* Nietzsche's Zarathustra may thus himself be "human, all too human," unable to transcend his own limited consciousness and imagine a being for whom the Will to Power could seem just another barbarous survival from the jungle.

Such a gentler variety of superman, quite unlike Nietzsche's, appears in W. Olaf Stapledon's *Odd John,* published in England in 1936 and still widely regarded as the best novel yet written on the superman theme. Born spontaneously by genetic mutation in various parts of the world, John and his friends seek one another out (like many other fictional superbeings, they are telepaths), and they all sail away to establish a commune on a remote Pacific island. Besieged by *Homo sapiens,* who fears and detests the mutants not so much for their greater intellects as for their unconventional lifestyle, the members of *Homo superior* discuss whether they should take time out from their own work to abate this nuisance by conquering the world—and decide against it. "We should be ruined, hopelessly distorted in spirit," John explains. "Violent practical undertakings would have blotted out for ever such insight as we have now gained into the true purpose of life." Rather than allow themselves to be dragged down to the apes' level by playing the apes' own games, these higher beings somewhat snobbishly decide to let the inferior humans win!

The sheer strangeness of this conclusion from the standpoint of *Homo sapiens,* with his long history of domination and slaughter, makes John and his friends seem odd enough that Stapledon could plausibly present them as biological and spiritual aliens. Therefore, he did not need to keep them offstage in the manner of Norvell Page's "But Without Horns." Instead he allowed the reader glimpses of John's personal philosophy, his social criticism, even his sexual activities. But Stapledon's literary trick was to present these details from the narrative viewpoint of an all-too-human Boswell, whom the superman affectionately addresses as "Fido":

> When I told John that I intended to write his biography, he laughed. "My dear *man!*" he said, "But of course it was inevitable." The word "man" on John's lips was often equivalent to "fool."
> "Well," I protested, "a cat may look at a king."

He replied, "Yes, but can it really *see* the king? Can you, puss, really see me?"

Stanley G. Weinbaum, whose scant year and a half in the pulps—from the appearance of "A Martian Odyssey" (*Wonder Stories:* 6, July 1934) until his cruelly untimely death in mid-December 1935—had a powerful impact on all subsequent science fiction, tackled the superman theme much more directly. His novel *The New Adam,* found posthumously in Weinbaum's papers and published in hard cover in 1939 (by Ziff-Davis, the same Chicago firm that then put out *Amazing Stories*), begins on a note of drab realism: "Anna Hall died as stolidly as she had lived, in childbirth." The reader sees her infant son Edmond display an eerie precocity as he employs his extrajointed fingers to drag a pocket watch, not to his mouth—in the fashion of a normal primate baby—but before his eyes for study. Later, when a schoolteacher chides him for apparent inattention, the reader discovers with him that Edmond Hall's mind is uniquely capable of following two distinct and independent trains of thought at the same time. So far so good. Weinbaum played no tricks; the central figure in *The New Adam* is not hidden, as is John Miller in "But Without Horns," nor is he mediated by a human narrator, as in *Odd John*. His story is mainly told from his own point of view. But, as a result, he is not quite plausible as a superman.

Like Odd John, the New Adam briefly considers and rejects the pursuit of power. Unlike Odd John, he decides that the pursuit of knowledge is in the long run equally futile. So he gives himself over to the pursuit of pleasure, which predictably takes the form of sex—not with one of his own kind, but with an unmutated human partner. Her outraged human lover goes after the superman with a gun. The superman allows him to succeed, thereby in effect committing suicide—not, as in *Odd John,* to preserve a transcendent world view from corruption, but simply because by that time he has spiritually run out of gas. Even though he supposedly represents a brand new species, the dominant emotion in Weinbaum's *Homo superior* seems to be sheer world-weariness.

Thirty years later, in an era of literary anti-heroes, Edmond Hall might have been better received than in 1939, when characters in science fiction—whether human or superhuman—were expected to cope and do. But even in more contemporary terms, this protagonist fails as a harbinger of *Homo superior.* Quite apart from the fact that a mental outlook like Edmond Hall's would be a most dysgenic biological mutation indeed, his conversations and soliloquies sound today no more profound than those of any other, merely human, Chicago intellectuals of the 1930s. As for alienness, there is far less of it in this terrestrial superman than can be found in those marvelously bizarre Martian and Venutian intelligences that are Stanley Weinbaum's lasting contribution to science fiction, and that continue to challenge its writers—as *Astounding*'s John Campbell once put it—to "write me a story about an organism that thinks as well as a man, but not *like* a man."

Weinbaum would have been the first to acknowledge that creatures descended from men need not be the final lords of creation. Effective science fiction has been written in which the earth is inherited by dogs or elephants or dolphins. In "Mana," by Eric Frank Russell (*Astounding:* 22, December 1937), Omega, the last man on earth, as weary of life as Weinbaum's New Adam, passes the evolutionary torch to the ants:

> "When the first hairy biped rode the waters on a log, that was *mana*," he proclaimed. "When fire was found, and made, and used, that was *mana*. Whenever men struggled one step higher up the ladder of life, it was *mana*. . . . Even as it was given to us by those whom we could never know, I give it to those who can never know me."

Having provided his ant colony with "a small heap of rotten wood, a midget box mounted upon microscopic wheels," and "a Lilliputian bow with a bundle of tiny arrows," the man commits suicide in a far grander manner than Edmond Hall; by the power of thought he levitates his body upward toward the cold airlessness of space. As Omega ascends, he looks down at "aimless billows surging on a printless shore." His gaze passes "thence to the woodland glade, caught the first flicker of a tiny fire, and he was satisfied." *Requiem aeternam.* . . .

II

Part of the continuing effectiveness of Mary Shelley's *Frankenstein* lies in its being told in substantial part from the monster's point of view. A. E. Van Vogt made his initial mark in science fiction with three stories (all in *Astounding Science-Fiction*) about humans in conflict with extraterrestrial creatures—"Black Destroyer" (vol. 23, July 1939), "Discord in Scarlet" (vol. 24, December 1939), and "Vault of the Beast" (vol. 25, August 1940)—in which the viewpoint of the alien is presented at the beginning of the story, before the reader is introduced to its human opponents. When the time came to undertake his first book-length novel, *Slan* (*ASF:* 26, September, October, November, December 1940; first hard-cover book version 1946), Van Vogt in effect translated the theme of those earlier stories into a conflict between man and superman—but this time he told the story *entirely* from the alien's point of view. As the author remarked to a circle of fans at the Fourth World Science Fiction Convention (the "Pacificon," Los Angeles, 1946), "I imagined one of my alien beings, but put him in a human body. The result was Jommy Cross," the superboy hero of *Slan*.

Actually, Jommy Cross is no more "alien" than Edmond Hall, and he is considerably less so than Odd John. He has two hearts, convenient enough should one of them conk out, and he has tendrils on his head, a feature genetically linked with a faculty of telepathy, but otherwise he is a human—and, at the beginning of the story, badly frightened—little boy. And that, as editor John Campbell was the first to point out, was the way

Van Vogt solved the superman problem, using one of the oldest dodges in the book—simple reader identification.

The opening of *Slan* is a fast-paced chase scene, in which Jommy's mother is shot down by mutant-hunting policemen, and her nine-year-old son makes his escape on the rear bumper of a car in which sits the human police chief who is directing the hunt. The suspense is maintained with very little letup until the final installment, which closes with a double surprise ending. It is a pulp plot, if you will, but in its day it was very good pulp; *Slan* was one of the earliest novel-length magazine stories to be reprinted in hard covers by a major commercial publisher, and a post-pulp generation in science fiction has continued to find it readable.

The basic literary and philosophical problem—how an ape is to tell a man's story, or a man a superman's—remains unsolved. However, as Van Vogt had shown, telepathy offered an easement of this dilemma. J. B. Rhine's ESP (extrasensory perception) experiments at Duke University were quite well known to readers and writers of science fiction, and in the stories ESP could plausibly be described by analogy with sight, touch, and hearing. Thus the coming superman could be described as a conventional specimen of *Homo sapiens*, except for the ability to use ESP to read others' minds. Indeed, telepathy and ESP (or "psi," as it came to be called) need not be a foretaste of human evolution at all; they might be traits that humans unknowingly have always possessed.

Telepaths—human, superhuman, and nonhuman—abounded in pulp science fiction: villains who used the power of thought to further their nefarious ends; heroes who used it to thwart the villains; and bumblers who used it ineptly, as in Donald Bern's ironic short story "The Man Who Knew All the Answers" (*Amazing Stories:* 14, August 1940). Kimball Kinnison, the mighty hero of E. E. Smith's roaring space opera, "Galactic Patrol" (discussed in chapters 3 and 5), used it; in the second installment of that serial Kinnison puts his mind *en rapport* with that of a formidable extraterrestrial being named Worsel who has a "snake-like body, a supple and sentient cable

of living steel, tipped with [a] double-edged, razor-keen, scim-
itar-like sting"—but who, fortunately, broadcasts "wave upon
friendly, surging wave of benevolent power" to his human
companion. In the sequels that followed, Kinnison waxes ever
mightier in mind; by the concluding episode ("Children of the
Lens," *Astounding:* 40, November, December 1947; January,
February 1948), he has fathered four daughters and a son
having even greater mental potency than his own.

"The universe begins to look more like a great thought than
like a great machine." So wrote Sir James Jeans, the eminent
British astronomer, in *The Mysterious Universe* (1930). Logically, a literature that dealt with the power of thought could
have gone in the direction of philosophical idealism, asserting—as seers had been saying from Plotinus's time to Mary
Baker Eddy's—that the world is, in essence, mind. Commonly, in the pulps that statement was not made. An interesting exception was entered in a short story by Clifford D.
Simak and Carl Jacobi, veteran writers for *Astounding* and
Weird Tales respectively; it was entitled "The Street That
Wasn't There" (*Comet:* 1, July 1941). Jonathan Chambers, a
retired professor of metaphysics, leaves his house at his usual
time on the daily walk he has taken for twenty years. But the
street where the cigar store is located that he regularly visits at
this time each evening has disappeared. Closer to home, his
neighbor's solid foursquare Victorian house now looks
strangely lopsided. It rights itself when he looks at it, but when
he looks away, it slumps again. Next morning, an impenetrable fog surrounds his own house; then a familiar old apple
tree emerges from the murk—"but it hadn't been there when
he first looked."

By this time the reader knows that the long wars in Europe
and Asia (the story takes place in 1960) have been followed by
plague, spreading to Africa and South America. The implication is that these millions of deaths have weakened the very
structure of reality:

Man himself, by the power of mass suggestion, holds the
physical fate of this earth . . . yes, even the universe. Billions of

> minds seeing trees as trees, houses as houses, streets as streets
> . . . and not as something else. Minds that see things as they are
> and have kept things as they were. . . . Destroy those minds and
> the entire foundation of matter, robbed of its regenerative
> power, will crumble and slip away like a column of sand. . . .

—leaving room for other, stronger intelligences to come into
our space and take over. The fog thins, disclosing a fantastic
city; behind its parapets gleam thousands of eyes, and behind
them in turn looms "a colossal face, a face of indescribable
power and evil, staring down with malevolent composure."
The vision fades; Jonathan retreats to his accustomed arm-
chair by the fire, a local environment so stamped with his own
personality that it remains "real." But the books he has not
read lately are already gone from the shelves. The clock has
stopped, for the first time in twenty years. The story concludes: "There was a tingling sensation in his feet."

That tale may reflect a particular editor's taste. "The Street
That Wasn't There" appeared in *Comet,* a short-lived (five
issues) pulp edited by F. Orlin Tremaine, who during most of
the 1930s had been the editor of *Astounding Stories,* preceding
Campbell. The turgid "thought-variant" yarns in *Astounding*
under the Tremaine regime quite often had taken this same
tack, that mind is the fundamental reality. So did an occasional fantasy published in the 1940s. A classic example is
"The Ultimate Egoist" by Theodore Sturgeon (*Unknown:* 4,
February 1941), which posits absolute solipsism—the belief
that nothing exists outside one's own consciousness. It ends
with a fragmentary sentence that is surely the ultimate in
shaggy dog last lines: "Is it possible that I myself am a figment
of my own imagi——"

On the whole, however, when they discussed mind and
matter in their stories, pulp science fiction writers remained
resolute materialists. The old supernatural connotations of
mind reading, still present in many stories written for *Weird
Tales,* were sloughed off from most stories on that theme
written for its competitors. "Mental" phenomena were
reduced to physical, and the transmission and reception of

thought waves were treated as in essence no more mysterious than the transmission and reception of radio waves.

Even from the standpoint of the most rigorously mechanistic biology this was a bit oversimple, as John Campbell and his group of young writers for *Astounding* recognized. Radio messages may be drowned in static; to make them intelligible it becomes necessary to improve the signal-to-noise ratio. What would be the telepathic equivalent? Suppose *everything* that was going on in one person's mind could be transmitted to another's? If "the conscious mind is a thin, pale stream, guarded by a censor," as the Freudians say, could a person bear to hear the uncensored version? The hero of Frank Belknap Long's story "Dark Vision" (*Unknown:* 1, March 1939) becomes just such a totally sensitive telepath, and at once every random murderous impulse, every suppressed spitefulness, every masked childish egotism crossing the minds of any of the people surrounding him on the subway comes through to him loud and clear. "The subconscious mind is really frightful," a psychologist later explains to him. "It is utterly direct, utterly without pretense or the indirection called tact." In the end the hero has to have the new talent drugged out of him lest he go mad.

III

Even granting broadcast facilities able to filter out the disorderly unconscious, however, would direct mind-to-mind communication really be possible? Suppose two people who spoke and thought in different languages met and mind-probed each other; would an Englishman "hear" a Frenchman's discourse in English, or would it echo within his brain as a torrent of (to him) unintelligible French? "Interpreters May Still Be Needed," John W. Campbell concluded in one of his typically speculative editorials (*Astounding:* 27, June 1941). The Indo-European languages might be able crudely to get along with each other on a word-for-word basis, making the telepathic translation from *dog* to *perro* to *hund* to *chien;* and of course such things as the names of the chemical elements are uniform in most of Earth's languages. But beyond that point, in situations demanding discernment of the cultural context of words, there might be trouble: "Most of our words have background references that we know so well we tend to overlook them."

One reader who had attempted some ESP experiments of his own, Charles Henry Mackintosh, responded (in "Brass Tacks" for August 1941) by arguing that telepathic communication probably would take place only through images, and rarely if ever in words. "Is it really natural for us to think in words, or is that something we have very painstakingly learned to do in order to facilitate the exchange of ideas?" Mackintosh asked. "Perhaps the true 'thinker' simply reflects—as a mental mirror—and then has to convert what he 'sees' into arbitrary symbols." Casting this conceptual problem into fiction a year later, in a story titled "Impediment" (*Astounding:* 29, August 1942), "Hal Clement" (Harry C. Stubbs) described the painstaking effort by a member of the human species to communicate the thought waves carrying his own language to a telepathic off-planet alien—until he realizes that the biological uniqueness of each human being makes the task quite impossible. Like the whorls on our fingertips, "the tiny currents that pass from nerve to nerve and give rise to the waves that you [the alien] can sense cannot possibly be the same for any two of us [humans]; and so no two sets of 'thought waves' could be identical." Therefore, if the alien wanted to learn to "talk" telepathically with any other human being besides the hero, that alien would have to begin all over again.

Simply and baldly put, perhaps, but philosophically this is pretty heady stuff. Benjamin Lee Whorf's profound studies of the grammar of Hopi, which concluded that the way a language is put together largely determines a culture's entire world view, were at that time very little known even among specialist scholars. Other, still more arcane, researches into structural linguistics had not yet been done. Investigation of the neurological origin of symbol formation, and the identification of particular brain waves with specific areas and functions of the brain, were still in their infancy. In short, the science fictionists were getting into something not so generally accessible to writers and readers as basic rocket technology or the geography of the Solar System. It is not surprising that most of them ducked out of the question.

Not until after the space rocket and the nuclear power plant had passed from extravagant fiction into cold fact did the science fiction magazines do much with what is now sometimes called "inner space." Even then, most writers of "psi" stories for *Astounding/Analog* dealt with their theme in an engineer's manipulative way. Strangely, the most exciting of all the new frontiers of knowledge was handled so unimaginatively that most of the fictional treatments of ESP in the 1950s and 1960s were downright boring—or else they went to the other extreme and slid into occultism.

The May 1950 *Astounding* featured a forty-page article by one of its regular (and most popular) writers, L. Ron Hubbard, "Dianetics: A New Science of the Mind." Simultaneously, Hubbard's hard-cover book, *Dianetics: the Modern Science of Mental Health,* came off the press, and by August it had sold 55,000 copies. Never had a writer more spectacularly broken out of science fiction's magazine ghetto, and seldom had science fiction so confidently put its worst foot forward. Hubbard's book and article dealt not in psi power but in psychotherapy; dianetics promised a radical, quick new way of curing all the ills that mind is heir to (and some of the body's as well), where all previous therapeutic techniques from acupuncture to Freud had failed. Dianetic "auditing" groups sprang up everywhere, especially on the West Coast where Hubbard's colleague A. E. Van Vogt became a dianetics therapist; references to "clears"—dianetically cured individuals—began to turn up in some of the stories. Van Vogt, Blish, and other writers who flirted with the movement eventually returned to science fiction (Blish revising the "clears" out of later published editions of the stories), but for L. Ron Hubbard dianetics was only the beginning. The movement he launched in 1950 evolved into the Church of Scientology.

One *Astounding* reader at the outset expressed great skepticism: "It sounds very much like the kind of talk I hear from some of the patients in the mental hospital where I am taking psychiatric training," intern J. S. Horan wrote ("Brass Tacks," *Astounding:* 46, December 1950). But the editor chided him for this reactionary attitude. In an editorial accompanying the Hubbard article ("Concerning Dianetics," *ASF:* 45, May 1950), Campbell proclaimed: "I want to assure every reader, most positively and unequivocally, that this article is *not* a hoax, joke, or anything but a direct, clear statement of a totally new scientific thesis." It is ironic indeed that what John Campbell proposed to treat as a hypothesis should so speedily have evolved into a religion, and after about a year's flirtation with Hubbard's new faith, Campbell backed off. Haywiring electronic circuitry, he admitted, was a good deal simpler than tinkering with the mind. "Render unto introspection the things that are introspective," the editor declared (*ASF:* 48, October 1951), "and unto spectroscopes the things that belong therein."

Fiction about the future of psychotherapy fared considerably better in the magazines than this abortive experiment with dianetics would have led one to expect. Telepathy in particular offers all kinds of diagnostic and therapeutic possibilities, as the therapist becomes able to enter the patient's own state of consciousness. As John Campbell gleefully put it, introducing a story by a new British writer in 1948 (headnote for "Dreams Are Sacred," by Peter Phillips, *Astounding:* 42, September 1948), one method of "curing the schizo who retires from reality into his own world of dreams" might be simply to "louse up his dreams!" This idea has generated a substantial body of writing, some of it quite well done. Roger Zelazny's Nebula award-winning "He Who Shapes" (*Amazing Stories:* 39, January, February 1965), in which the dreamshaper is trapped in the mental universe of a patient whose will is stronger than his own, is probably the best known of such stories; rich in symbolism and in subtle personal interplay, it is a measure of how far science fiction has come from its flat-footed, wooden-charactered early days.

The sociology of telepathy, as distinguished from its clinical possibilities, has not fared nearly so well. It got off to a very bad start; space opera of the kind "Doc" Smith wrote, steeped in the Gernsback technological tradition, tended to treat "psi" power as just another gadget, like the ray gun. There was some rudimentary discussion of the ethical implications of mind reading: does it invade privacy, ought one to use it to cheat on exams, and so on. But E. E. Smith's conclusion on this matter was not very different from what J. Edgar Hoover's might have been: in a cops-and-robbers situation the police may use any unorthodox method in line of duty so long as it gets results. The whole process was conceived in terms of offensive and defensive armament; if the Galactic Patrolmen employed Lenses to amplify their thoughts, their space-pirate opponents developed thought-screens.

After World War II, however, matters were considerably improved. The nuclear bombs of 1945 inspired swarms of stories about radiation-induced human mutation, taking place no longer in rare isolation (as in "But Without Horns," *The New Adam,* and *Odd John*), but in populations large enough to constitute substantial colonies. Authors thus could address themselves to the question of how such societies might function internally. (What changes in social behavior may be expected, for example, when all minds are open to all other minds, and it is therefore impossible to lie?)

One such subculture of telepaths is the subject of a memorable story that was published shortly *before* the atom bomb fell, flooding two cities in Japan with radiation; this was "The Piper's Son," by Henry Kuttner (writing as Lewis Padgett in *Astounding:* 34, February 1945). Normal, non-mind-reading humans in the post-Blowup world of this story know the mutated members of their species as "Baldies," a reference to a secondary trait of hairlessness that is genetically linked with the telepathic ability. The Baldy community is divided against itself. Ought its members discreetly to hide their identity under wigs, to get along as tactfully as possible with the nontelepathic majority that may otherwise turn against them—as it has turned against other unusual-looking "ethnics" throughout the centuries? Or should they flaunt their baldness openly, proclaiming to the less-talented humans around them that they are biologically a superior race? "Superman" during World War II had acquired, for the best of reasons, a bad name; author Kuttner's sympathies in early 1945 were therefore understandably with the moderates. The villainous character in the story, who proclaims the opposite view, appears at the climax as a caricature Nazi: "We are the Future! The Baldies! God made us to rule lesser men!"

In "The Demolished Man," by Alfred Bester (*Galaxy:* 3, January, February, March 1952), set two centuries beyond the post-nuclear-war world of "The Piper's Son," moderation has prevailed. The telepaths, colloquially named "peepers," play licensed, legitimate roles within a predominantly nontelepath civilization. That society has, however, not solved all its problems. The story describes an individual's attempt to commit a premeditated murder, knowing all the while that his mind can be read by the police—and such is the ingenuity of science fiction that he almost gets away with it. That plot is transcended by the author's virtuoso writing; Bester, for example, was able plausibly to convey the ebb and flow of "conversation" at a telepaths' cocktail party, using tricks of typography on the printed page. At the end of the novel, the telepaths' message to the mentally silent majority is definitely not Nietzsche's. "We see the truth you cannot see," the telepath hero tells the "normals" around him, "that there is nothing in man but love and faith, courage and kindness, generosity and sacrifice." If the normals also strive to apprehend that truth, "one day we'll all be mind to mind and heart to heart."

IV

Those spindly, big-domed men of the future who used to appear so regularly in Frank R. Paul's cover paintings on early 1930s issues of *Wonder Stories* have by now all but disappeared from science fiction. One sentence from a 1970 serial succinctly explains why: "Man's brain had not evolved appreciably since he achieved competent verbal communication because there had no longer been a competitive advantage in higher intelligence" (Piers Anthony, "Orn," *Amazing Stories,* 43, July; 44, September 1970). Man the chattering primate, who can store his chatter on papyrus scrolls or magnetic tape if he needs to remember it, does not really require a larger or more convoluted brain. (By the same logic, the successful evolution of speech may have inhibited him from developing telepathy.)

Still, there are other things that might be done to a brain. The speed with which its neurons fire might be increased, as in *Brain Wave,* by Poul Anderson; or, its capacity to absorb knowledge might be enlarged by a surgical procedure, as in "Flowers for Algernon," by Daniel Keyes (*Fantasy and Science Fiction:* 16, April 1959), the story upon which one of the very few good science fiction movies—*Charley*—was based. Or—as has been done in countless horror films—it might be removed from the body altogether, or transferred into that of someone else. Nourished by continuing research in this area (animal brains have, in fact, been separated from the rest of their bodies and temporarily survived), this remains a viable if scary option for science fiction today. Over the years, a host of brain-transplant stories—an early, melodramatic example was "The Brain in the Jar," by Norman E. Hammerstrom and R. F. Searight (*Weird Tales:* 4, November 1924)—have assumed that the human ego can be scooped up intact out of a skull and deposited in a bottle, from which it may go on functioning as if not very much had happened.

Properly supplied with nutrients, it may even be biologically immortal, as in "The Jameson Satellite," by Neil R. Jones (*Amazing Stories:* 6, July 1931). That story tells of a scientist who dies and leaves a will directing that his body be sent into earth orbit by rocket, so that it may be perfectly preserved for all eternity. Forty million years later, visitors from another world find Professor Jameson in space, remove his brain, place it in a mechanical body, revive it, and rename him 21MM392. He then joins his rescuers in a succession of bizarre adventures on other planets. These tales ran in the Sloane-edited *Amazing* of the 1930s and, evidently popular with readers, they resumed in one of the new pulps of the 1940s, *Astonishing Stories,* under the editorship of Frederik Pohl. "The Jameson Satellite" in particular fired the imagination of then-eighth-grader Isaac Asimov, as he has since confessed (in *Before the Golden Age,* 1974). However, to anyone encountering them today for the first time, these Professor Jameson stories are unreadable. Their basic plot, which author Neil Jones used over and over again, appears in capsule form in a conversational two-liner toward the end of the first of these tales: "I'm wrecked." "We shall repair you." It is a curiously shriveled conception of the nature of man.

Even more relentlessly than the "psionics" stories published in Campbell's *Astounding,* the typical brain-transplant story assumed the narrowest kind of biological materialism. "The brain secretes thought as the liver secretes bile," quipped the eighteenth-century French *philosophe* LaMettrie, and many a twentieth-century American pulpster would have agreed with him. Ignoring not only the Platonists, but also the Freudians, science fiction writers came close at times to saying that the brain *is* the mind. But if sex is so central to the human psyche as Freud said it is, could a totally sexless brain, lacking any chemical input from normally stimulated endocrine glands, claim full stature as a human being? Again, would an athlete, who had experienced all his or her highest moments through intense physical exertion, be *exactly* the same person if his or her brain were transplanted into a body whose previous ten-

ant had been a lazy slob? Or, if criminal behavior is traceable
in part to chemical deficiency—as some current research suggests—might not a law-abiding brain transferred into a criminal's body succumb also to that body's criminal tendencies?

Don Wilcox, a frequent contributor to *Amazing* in its Chicago era under Ziff-Davis, crudely but effectively challenged
the brain transplanters' purely cerebral view of personality in
a thriller called "The Whispering Gorilla" (*Fantastic Adventures:* 2, May 1940). The hero, a newspaper reporter, is slain in
Africa while uncovering evidence on an international ring of
munitions makers who are plotting a profitable world war—a
story idea, by the way, which seems not so naive in the 1970s as
it may have sounded only a few years before. His body is
buried, but his brain is saved, transplanted into the skull of a
great ape. In that form—posing as a member of a theatrical
troupe!—he returns to America where he resumes his exposé
of the munitions kings, goes on the air in his show business
disguise ("This is the Whispering Gorilla speaking"), and
eventually starts an antiwar campaign for a seat in Congress.
At that point the merchants of death play their trump card:
they confront the transplanted hero with the killer who had
gunned him down beside the Congo. He goes berserk. A
policeman's billy bashes his unstable psyche back to apedom,
and the scientist who performed the original surgery takes
him back to a presumably happier life in the jungle. In this
instance, pulp magazine conventions—placing a high pre-
mium on two-fisted action, in which the body was all-impor-
tant—may have corrected science fiction in the direction of
greater realism.

As for the brain-in-a-box stories, some writers began to
perceive that the absence of a body, or the presence of a new
and artificial one, would indeed make a personality difference, much as amputation does: can one imagine Captain
Ahab without his ivory leg? In a story written with Lester del
Rey's usual human sensitivity, "Reincarnate" (*Astounding:* 25,
April 1940), a man injured in an accident and transplanted

into a robot body struggles to learn the use of magnets for muscles (with piezoelectric crystals to simulate muscle sense), gyroscopes for balance, and television lenses of the right focal length for eyes. "A man's senses are liars—but consistent liars," commented editor John Campbell. "If a man lost his body, could he learn the lies of another set of senses?"

Del Rey's story was only moderately successful in developing this theme, but it paved the way for C. L. Moore's magnificent "No Woman Born" (*Astounding:* 34, December 1944). The brain of an actress and dancer who has "died" in a theater fire is endowed with a graceful robot body in which she is able not merely to live, but to return triumphantly to the stage. The scientist who has wrought this miracle worries over whether he has been a Frankenstein creating a freak; but at the story's climax the heroine assures him she is not sub- but superhuman. In a sense never intended by St. Paul, this corruptible flesh has put on incorruption. Indeed, adds Damon Knight in a bleak, deliberately ugly story he says he wrote more or less in rebuttal to Moore's, titled "Masks," a psyche housed in cleanly functioning metal might come to regard all other kinds of organisms with revulsion. "When he looks at the sweaty, oozing meat that other people are made of," Knight states (in Robin Scott Wilson's anthology *Those Who Can,* 1973) "his one possible emotion is disgust, brought to an intensity we cannot imagine."

Superman, or in Moore's case Superwoman, has arrived in such instances not by the insensate trial and error of biological evolution, but by a creative—or demonic—fusion of engineering with medicine. Updated to take account of actual experimentation, and employing newer words such as "cyborg" and "bionics" (as in the popular, if critically overlooked, TV series *The Six Million Dollar Man* and *The Bionic Woman*), this kind of science fiction more recently has become a major emphasis within the field. For his first book-length work in a decade, "Man Plus" (*Fantasy and Science Fiction:* 50, April, May, June 1976), Frederik Pohl chose to write about the

bionic adaptation of a human being for survival on Mars—the
real Mars, not that of Burroughs, Brackett, and Bradbury. In
"Man Plus," and in such tales as Alan Brennert's "All the
Charms of Sycorax" (*Analog:* 95, July 1975), in which a bioni-
cally rebuilt U.S. senator frets that the voters are responding
not to his human charisma, but to his machine image, or Anne
McCaffrey's "The Ship Who Sang" (*F&SF:* 20, April 1961), in
which the "body" the female protagonist's brain operates is an
entire spaceship, we are light years beyond the metaphysical
crudity of "The Jameson Satellite." These newer cyborg stories spell out the point made thirty years ago by the author of
"No Woman Born"; namely, that the boundary between
"man" and "machine" may have become as abstract and arbitrary as the line traditionally drawn between "body" and
"mind." The old, simple materialism that reduced mind to
brain, or thought to electromagnetic radiation, has been subtly outflanked and transcended. "I've begun to realize,"
declares Moore's heroine, "what a tremendous force the
human ego really is."

V

What then of the robot, that "spare, simple paradigm of
man" as Eric Hopkins calls him, whose brain as well as his
body is an artificial creation? "Science-fictional man," Hopkins
argues in an essay on SF titled "New Maps of Heaven" (*Theo-
ria to Theory:* 1, 1966), "is seen essentially as a rule-following
animal"; and following rules is something a machine can do at
least as faithfully as a man. Can it do so consciously? And can
it reprogram itself if the rules prove unsatisfactory? Debate
still rages among computer designers on that point, although
Doctor Asimov's robot and human engineers were already
wrestling with his Three Laws of Robotics three decades ago.
Still earlier Samuel Butler, in his splendid counter-Utopian
satire *Erewhon* (1872), had suggested that man's machines
rather than his mind (or brain) might be the next frontier for
Darwinian evolution: "Who can say that the vapor engine has

not a kind of consciousness? Where does consciousness begin, and where end? Who can draw the line?"

Living, conscious machines need not look like people. The bellowing dinosaurian vitality of earth-moving machinery, to which anyone can testify who has ever driven through a bad stretch of road construction or watched a foundation being dug, was skillfully exploited in a story by Theodore Sturgeon titled "Killdozer!" (*Astounding: 34*, November 1944), about a rampaging intelligent machine that stalks and kills the members of a work crew who are building an island airstrip during World War II. Sturgeon, with an experienced operator's first-hand knowledge of such equipment, made that clash solidly convincing, particularly the climactic boxing match between the self-operating bulldozer and a human-operated power shovel. (It is regrettable that the 1974 attempt to translate this exciting tale for television failed; this should have been a natural for one of the visual media. Science fiction's relationship with TV and the movies has been, on the whole, an unhappy trail of lost or botched opportunities.)

If living machines need not look like people, they likewise—as Samuel Butler had also pointed out in his *Erewhon*—need not require sex to reproduce. "The Mechanical Mice" by Maurice A. Hugi (*Astounding: 26*, January 1941), tells of a buzzing, whirring, ticking Robot Mother that snatches alarm clocks, small car parts, radio components, and other mechanical odds and ends, and fashions them into active (and murderous) offspring. At the end of the story, having destroyed both this ingenious device and an equally proficient replica it has created, the hero and his friends are alarmed when they again hear the sound of ticking. They are only momentarily relieved when they learn its actual source: an ordinary, cheap, noisy wristwatch. "'*Tick! tick!*' said the watch, with mechanical aplomb," and the story ends—implying that although this round has been won by the humans, the future belongs not to them—nor to a Superman descended from them—but to the Robot Mother.

By creating a robot with a trait so biomorphic as motherhood, the author has already implied that to be a person means something more than the mere ability to follow rules. If a machine that has consciousness breaks one of those rules, can it be held legally or morally responsible? If, for example, a robot kills its maker, is that act murder, or is it only an industrial accident? That thorny issue was raised in "The Trial of Adam Link, Robot" by Eando Binder (*Amazing Stories:* 13, July 1939). In the course of this unprecedented court proceeding, it is brought out that the sheriff, had he thought of it, could have obtained an order from Washington to have Adam Link scrapped as a dangerous weapon rather than executed as a criminal, which would have enabled the court to evade the philosophic (and ultimately religious) question of sentience and responsibility. The prosecutor, as he argues that Adam is "a *thing* without a soul" who therefore "can know nothing of the emotions of kindliness, sympathy, mercy," up to a point accepts that line of reasoning. Then, inconsistently, he asks for the death penalty: "No thing that mocks the human body and its divine intellect," he sums up, "can have a place in our civilization."

Counsel for the defense—and the author—missed an opportunity at this point to plead the classic legal defense of homicide, namely insanity: if Adam Link be a thing without a soul, then by definition he does not know right from wrong. Instead, however, the defense elects to plead simple innocence. The reader already knows, from the story "I, Robot" to which this was a sequel (*Amazing:* 13, January 1939), that Adam in fact did not kill his creator; a loose angle iron had fallen on the scientist's head, and the case rests on circumstantial evidence. Nevertheless, mob hysteria over "Frankenstein," whipped up by the prosecution and the press—at bottom, simple fear of the unknown—makes a "guilty" verdict inevitable.

At the end, the robot reflects that he could, if he chose, tell them how to open the power pack on his chest and simply turn him off. Instead, he decides to let them put him in the electric chair, which can disrupt the delicate circuitry in his artificial brain as effectively as if it were a human's natural one. In effect, by thus willing his own death, Adam has achieved at least a minimal stature as a being. From that desperate affirmation—I can die, therefore I am alive—it is not a very long step to the situation described in Charles Beaumont's quiet, touching story "Last Rites" (*If: Worlds of Science Fiction:* 5, October 1955), in which a dying robot persuades a troubled priest to administer extreme unction, on the chance that an intelligent and compassionate machine may somehow, in the face of all man's (and the Church's) logic, have acquired a soul; or to the ethical trauma of the robot menace-hero in Roger Zelazny's "Home is the Hangman" (*Analog:* 95, November 1975), for whom acquiring a sense of guilt for murder is what makes him cross the gulf from mechanism to personhood.

But Adam Link, anticlimactically, is reprieved, so that author Binder could go on writing new stories about him. In the next sequel, "Adam Link in Business" (*Amazing Stories:* 14, January 1940), the robot hero's effort to establish himself peaceably in the American economy goes astray when he falls in love with a human young woman ("The capacity for emotion, rooted in me by my creator, has again betrayed me," Adam muses); and in the tale following, "Adam Link's Vengeance" (February 1940), he fashions a robot mate—named, inevitably, Eve—to share his loneliness. Readers had and have accepted the reverse situation, of a human male who loves a feminine robot, in Lester del Rey's Hall of Fame story "Helen O'Loy" (*Astounding:* 22, December 1938). They were quite merciless, however, toward these two Binder stories, invoking the eternal male sophomore's worldly wisdom, which says that love is (in Harlan Ellison's apt phrase) nothing but sex misspelled. As Clayton Stoddart put it in a letter to the editor (*Amazing Stories:* 14, April 1940): "For Adam Link, love is impossible. His iridium sponge-controlled mind wouldn't be sufficient to make him fall in love with any woman, much less a robot. You see, love is an emotion governed entirely by sex and the sexual instinct. Link (Adam, I mean) has no sex, and therefore, I think you will agree, could not be sexually attracted to Eve, nay—even to Hedy Lamarr."

"Personally, your editor won't admit . . . that love is just a sexual emotion," *Amazing*'s editor Raymond A. Palmer responded. "We're not that scientific." Reader Stoddart was certainly wrong when he said that "the mind Binder gave Adam Link, which was on a par [with] the best human minds, was not capable of developing regard for another." But that did not end the argument. Adam Link went on in another story to take up competitive sports, becoming a champion bowler; and reader Konrad Maxwell wrote in to complain (in "Discussions," October 1940) that Superman really ought not to descend to such trivia: "Don't you think that Adam, who has such a brilliant brain, is wasting his time fooling around with bowling and metal gals instead of working on science? There is space travel yet to be conquered and so sic A. Link after this problem and break up some of his moonlight walks! Metal gals, bah! Real ones are bad enough when it comes to science."

This outburst has unmistakable emotional echoes from that time in a male American's boyhood when any friendly overture from the opposite sex prompts the disdainful response "Aw—*girls!*" Go away, and leave me and my chemistry set alone. One begins to understand why pulp science fiction for so many years was virtually an all-male ghetto.

Chapter 7

The Bright Illusion
The Feminine Mystique
in Science Fiction

Men are allowed diversity. Some are libertines, others are husbands; a few are lawyers, many are clerks. They wear no insignia of masculinity or badge of paternity and they are never expected to live up to being Man or Mankind. But every woman has the whole weight of formulated Womanhood upon her shoulders. Even in new times she must carry forward the design of the ages. . . . There may be men who are able to think of woman apart from the pattern of female, but they are inarticulate. Most of them spend their lives associating with a symbol. . . . As long as women are pictured chiefly as wife, mother, courtesan, or whatnot—defining merely a relationship to men—nothing new or strange or interesting is likely to happen. The old order is safe.

—Florence Guy Seabury, "Men Who Understand
Women," *The Nation,* 119 (November 12, 1924)

171

Artist: Frank R. Paul.

"They laughed and passed comments on the Last Woman. Her face flushed under their cold merciless humor. She was to them another animal of earth."

This may be the most male-chauvinist science fiction story ever written. It is a rebuttal, of sorts, to "The Last Man," by Wallace West, in *Amazing Stories*, 3 (February, 1929). 1030–1040. "The Last Woman," by Thomas S. Gardner, *Wonder Stories*, 3 (April, 1933), p. 1238.

M OST OF THE READERS OF SCIENCE FICTION are male and most of them are young," says science fiction writer, critic, and teacher Joanna Russ. The science fiction readers she has met, Russ declared in an essay "The Image of Women in Science Fiction" (*Red Clay Reader:* 7, 1970, reprinted in *Vertex:* 1, February 1974), "are overwhelmingly likely to be nervous, shy, pleasant boys, sensitive, intelligent, and very awkward with people. They also talk too much." Such boys have been turning the cranks of mimeograph machines, attending fan conventions, and talking away the night almost since magazine science fiction began, and magazine editors have had to take account of them as an ever-present commercial reality. Jerry Westerfield, who was assistant editor of *Amazing Stories* and *Fantastic Adventures* a quarter-century ago, stated (in his essay "The Sky's No Limit," *Writer's Digest:* 20, January 1940) that "the science fiction reader is usually a boy in his late teens," and a fellow editor of that era agreed that "90% of our readers are masculine youngsters who are learning and who don't know just what to believe and what not to believe." Especially, one might add, about the opposite sex.

Youngsters do eventually grow up, however, and not all of them "quit reading the stuff in their middle twenties," as Joanna Russ contends. In 1949 John Campbell tabulated three thousand reader questionnaires and reported that the typical *Astounding* reader by that time was "just under thirty" ("The Analytical Laboratory," *Astounding:* 43, July 1949); he remained, however, overwhelmingly—93.3 percent—male. Still later, after the magazine had changed its name from *Astounding* to the more respectable *Analog,* Campbell warned prospective writers: "Do not make the egregious error of thinking science fiction is for kids." Considerable statistical evidence existed to back up the editor's claim that "corporation executives—research laboratory directors—patent attorneys—all types of astute and highly competent men interested in the future" enjoyed science fiction (John W. Campbell, "Science Fiction We Can Buy," *The Writer:* 81, September 1968). However, judging from that editor's guidelines for his writers, some of these more grown-up readers seemed as little inclined to explore the intricate relationships between the sexes as any of those talkative kids.

"Sex in suburbia—or elsewhere—is *not* the only motivating force in a real yarn," *Analog*'s editor insisted. "A *man* has a lot of other motivations; ask Joseph Conrad, Shakespeare, or Homer—who managed to write yarns without much sex that outlasted their decade." In one sense, Campbell's point was well taken; carnality in the suburbs, or elsewhere, can make dull fiction indeed, as even the pornography-mongers have lately discovered. Nevertheless, that chauvinistically italicized word *man* betrays a crippling incompleteness in science fiction. Philip K. Dick, interviewed in 1969 for a fan magazine (as quoted by Dick Geis in his column "The Alien Viewpoint," *Worlds of If:* 22, June 1974), declared that "the greatest weakness of science fiction today" was its failure to deal adequately with "the man-woman aspect of life." "S-f simply must learn to do this," that writer warned, "or it will always be retarded—as it is now."

John Campbell, offering his restrictive advice to would-be writers in 1968, was only echoing in more sophisticated fashion what Hugo Gernsback, when he founded the first science fiction magazine in 1926, had said more priggishly. As the earliest letters to the editor poured in, said Gernsback, he noted "with a feeling of gratification" his readers' "almost unanimous condemnation of the so-called 'sex-appeal' type of story that seems so much in vogue in this country now"—at the height of the Roaring Twenties. "Most of our correspondents seemed to heave a great sigh of relief in at last finding a literature that appeals to the imagination, rather than carrying a sensational appeal to the emotions" (editorial, *Amazing Stories:* 1, May 1926). From the fact that Gernsback later founded a highly successful digest-format magazine titled *Sexology,* we may infer that in this early editorial he expressed no personal taboo or prejudice of his own; rather, he articulated what he thought readers of the first science fiction magazine in the field really preferred. (Incidentally—a point worth pondering—where except in science fiction would imagination have been *contrasted* with the emotions?)

The old science fiction pulps have a reputation for gaudy cover paintings that featured attractive young women struggling in the clutches of bug-eyed monsters. Actually, for the first four or five years, the magazines' covers all but ignored women as a possible subject. Frank R. Paul's first cover painting for *Amazing Stories* in April 1926, illustrating *Off on a Comet* by Jules Verne—the planet Saturn behind a wrecked sailing ship, with parka-clad ice skaters in the foreground—set the tone. Typically, the July 1926 cover depicted Navy bluejackets fighting a giant fly; November's showed a crowd scene from Garrett P. Serviss's modern flood story, "The Second Deluge"; the one for February 1927 exhibited lizards attacking a submarine. The first woman did not appear until the first anniversary number (April 1927), in a decorous scene with elderly male scientists; a second appeared the following month. But then the women vanished, in favor of such subjects as the Martian stalking-machines in H. G. Wells's *War of the Worlds* (August 1927); an enormous pitcher plant snagging an explorer (September); a resplendent planet Jupiter (November 1928); or a roaring tyrannosaurus. T. O'Conor Sloane, as editor of *Amazing,* continued this antiseptic tradition; except for one group nude scene, "arty" rather than erotic in theme (August 1934), the human body, female or male, was generally absent. Instead, the magazine caught the customer's eye on the newsstands with such dangerous visions as the one that Leo Morey painted for April 1931, of a warship being smothered by a mass of sentient green protoplasmic glop.

Hugo Gernsback's *Science Wonder Stories,* founded in 1929, with rare exceptions was equally devoid of women. For one thing, artist Paul could not draw them very well. Fantastic cities, towering machines, and extraterrestrial creatures were more his forte; indeed, as pictorial art they hold up surprisingly well today. It was the early *Astounding,* closely aligned with other, non-science-fiction pulps, that really broke with the Gernsback art tradition. A woman appeared on its first cover (January 1930) in a fur miniskirt, although in pictorial interest she was subordinate to a battle between a man and a giant beetle. In December of that year, cover artist H.W. Wesso introduced what was to become science fiction's version of the Eternal Triangle: the man, the woman, and the monster all sharing space on the cover more or less equally. But after *Astounding* changed hands in 1933, the covers reverted to bizarre landscapes and machines. John Campbell, when he took charge in 1937, perpetuated that tradition and added carefully drawn, astronomically accurate views of the solar system: the sun as seen from Mercury (February 1938), Mars as seen from its satellite Deimos (June), Jupiter from Ganymede (November), and a serene image of Saturn with its rings (April 1939). The message for the boys seemed to be: look not to the other sex for inspiration, but to the stars.

Weird Tales was something else again. While the other magazines focused the newsstand browser's attention upon rocket ships, giant insects, or disembodied brains, the oldest of the fantasy pulps for a span of about six years during the 1930s caught his (or her?) eye with covers depicting flamboyant female nudes. Interestingly, most of them were drawn *by* a woman, Margaret Brundage, who was identified by the editor at first only as "M. Brundage" or "the artist," and who—even after the magazine had publicly acknowledged her gender— was still occasionally referred to by an unaware reader as "Mr. Brundage." Typically, she illustrated Robert E. Howard's swaggering, male-sexist stories of Conan the Conqueror. She used her own daughters as models, and worked not in oils, like most pulp magazine color artists, but with pastel crayons. "The originals are so delicate," wrote editor Farnsworth Wright ("The Eyrie," *Weird Tales:* 22, August 1933), "that we are afraid to sneeze when we have a cover design in our possession, for fear the picture will disappear in a cloud of dust." In production, however, the pictures came out bold and strong.

Reader reaction to such covers ranged from enthusiastic

approval to vociferous protest. "Personally I prefer any kind of monster that it is possible to think of rather than the sexy covers you have been having," wrote Lionel Dilbeck ("The Eyrie," *Weird Tales:* 22, October 1933). "And I really hate to tear the covers off the magazine, as that also spoils the looks of them." But Brundage had her champions. "By all means," wrote E. L. Mengshoel (vol. 27, June 1936), "let her continue with her nudes offending the prudes." Opinion on this point does not seem to have divided entirely along sex lines. "Please, please dispose of the unclad ladies on your covers for good," wrote one woman reader, Margaret Sylvester (vol. 22, December 1933). "They cheapen and degrade your otherwise splendid magazine." In contrast, however, Gertrude M. Brezeale responded to one Brundage cover—whose subject was naked except for high heels—by exclaiming: "What could be more breath-takingly *lovely?* . . . Without a trace of vulgarity, too" (vol. 29, February 1937). Bear in mind that the letter columns in *Astounding Stories* during these same years ran heavily to mathematical equations, and ponder this question: is sexuality perhaps more compatible with the supernaturalism of antiquity than with the naturalism of the modern world?

II

The stories in *Amazing, Astounding,* and *Wonder Stories* in the 1930s for the most part were as strait-laced as their covers (*Weird Tales,* with its witches, high priestesses, female vampires, victims of exorcism, and so on, was again the exception). Science in America was, and is, a heavily male-dominated activity. Ordinarily, therefore, the Gernsback-Campbell engineering gadget kind of story—regrettably but realistically—required no female characters at all. When a writer, as in "Star Light" by Hal Clement (*Analog:* 85, June 1970) states that two of his male characters "turned to their equipment, and for several minutes their activities meant little to the woman," he may simply be reporting a social fact. But it is terribly easy to attach masculist value judgments to such facts. If that is done, then the highest status to which a woman could ever aspire in such a story would be that of Hero's Girlfriend, sometimes combined with the role of Scientist's Beautiful Daughter—who, as Joanna Russ sarcastically observes, "knows just enough to be brought along by Daddy as his research assistant, but not enough to be of any help to anyone." This is the kind of science fiction that persists in the movies, where, as science fiction writer Ursula LeGuin puts it (interview in *Vertex:* 2, December 1974), "If there are any women at all, all they do is stand aside and say, '*Eeeee* . . .' and get carried off by a monster."

When E. E. Smith wrote his immensely popular first novel, *The Skylark of Space,* serialized in *Amazing* in 1928, he hired another writer to do the "love interest"; in other words, so incidental was the heroine to the plot that the author himself need pay no attention to her! Villains, as in Nat Schachner's wretchedly written "Pirates of the Gorm" (*Astounding:* 10, May 1932), were permitted at least to ogle the heroines (" 'By Jupiter, she is a tempting morsel,' and his red eyes took in the flushed beauty of the panting girl speculatively"), but the heroes' minds seem to have been on higher things. Jack Williamson, in "The Plutonian Terror" (*Weird Tales:* 22, October 1933), has the first explorers of space come back to earth after a perilous year on the moon; only at the end of the story does the hero realize that his sole companion *for a year*—all bandaged and husky from X-ray burns, to be sure—has been the girlfriend he thought he had left behind on earth! "The not-very-believable twist at the end of the story seems to suggest," its author now cheerfully admits (in *The Early Williamson,* 1975), "that I wasn't yet fully aware of women."

Yet the science fictionists of that early era were already interested in such questions as population pressure and eugenic control. Surely that concern required some specific attention to the future of the sexes; H. G. Wells, the mentor, had certainly expressed some emphatic views on the subject. But only very occasionally, as in "The Last Man," by Wallace West (*Amazing Stories:* 3, February 1929), whose hero sits in a glass demonstration cage while an all-female civilization bustles around him, or in "The Last Woman," by Thomas S. Gardner (*Wonder Stories:* 3, April 1932), which exactly reverses that situation, was any attempt made to deal with this question in personal and human terms.

Both of these stories, significantly, assumed that in the battle of the sexes there can be no truce; one or the other must prevail. "Having lost the mastery of the world," wrote Wallace West, "the men found themselves helpless and in the way." Conversely, Thomas Gardner attributed the rise of his all-male society to biochemical research by a twentieth-century student "who was considered peculiar by the young men of his time because of his dislike of girls." In West's story, an atavistic, "womanly" female rescues the museum-caged hero, and they run off together as Adam and Eve, presumably to beget children and start the cycle all over again. In Gardner's story, the heroine's attempt similarly to escape from Earth with a male astronaut is foiled, and the star-crossed couple are executed, having first been told that they "represent that influence that for ages dragged mankind back to the primeval slime out of which he had struggled." No reader of *Wonder Stories* seems to have quibbled at that harsh and prudish verdict; "a truly wonderful story with a clever plot, ingeniously worked out," one correspondent termed "The Last Woman" (Fred J. Walsen, letter to the editor, *Wonder Stories:* 4, June 1932).

Nobody writing a letter—or submitting a story—to a science fiction magazine would take so extreme a misogynist stand today. However, Wallace West's complementary version, "The Last Man," has spawned innumerable imitations. Stale though it has become since West's use of it forty-five years ago, his theme of the lone male who finds his mate (or, more often nowadays, his mates), thereby foiling the oppressive matriarchy—or who heroically fails in his effort to do so—nevertheless continues to find its chroniclers, such as Edmund Cooper (*Five to Twelve,* 1968) and Charles Eric Maine (*Alph,* 1972). Another variant is *Amazon Planet* (1975, serialized in *Analog:* 78, January, February 1967) by the highly popular writer Mack Reynolds, who teases his male readers by describing a "matriarchal" civilization, and then reassures them by revealing in the course of the story that the matriarchy is only a facade; that the planet is not really gynocratic at all! Until very recently there have been few modern imitators of that most exceptional story on the matriarchal theme, "The Conquest of Gola," by Leslie F. Stone (*Wonder Stories:* 2, April 1931), in which "the ignoble male creatures" from Earth who invade a female-controlled Venus are justly defeated; and that story, a male chauvinist might complacently observe, was after all written by a woman.

"Science fiction is far less a man's world than it used to be as far as the readers are concerned," noted Isaac Asimov in his editorial introduction to Anne McCaffrey's award-winning story "Weyr Search" (*The Hugo Winners:* 2, 1971). "The *writers,* however, are still masculine by a heavy majority. What's more, they are a particularly sticky type of male, used to dealing with males, and a little perturbed at having to accept a woman on an equal basis." Not all women who now write science fiction would agree with that statement. Leigh Brackett, successful both in science fiction and in the likewise predominantly male field of Hollywood script writing, feels that she has not been discriminated against on account of her sex. But when Brackett sold her first stories to the pulps in the early 1940s, she and Catherine Moore—who bylined herself as "C. L. Moore" and received fan letters (including one from her future husband, Henry Kuttner) addressed to "Mr. Moore"—were the only women regularly writing science fiction. Prior to that first Brackett sale—to Campbell's *Astounding* in 1940—Moore stood virtually by herself.

If only two women are writing for an overwhelmingly masculine audience, what kind of fiction will they write? Much of what C. L. Moore and Leigh Brackett turned out was swashbuckling, male-oriented space opera. Catherine Moore's first story, "Shambleau" (*Weird Tales:* 22, November 1933), introduced a steely-eyed, heatgun-toting, masculine-stereotyped character named Northwest Smith, together with a Venutian male sidekick who plays Chingachgook to Smith's Natty Bumppo. In the next decade Leigh Brackett created a similar interplanetary wanderer and womanizer, Eric John Stark, of whose adventures we have already taken note (chapter 3). "Most of my own heroes are fairly hard boys, not above using their boot-heels in a scrap and giving a handsome wench one of those 40-second Bogart-type kisses," Brackett once acknowledged ("The Science-Fiction Field," *Writer's Digest:* 24, July 1944). C. L. Moore has retired from writing science fiction, but Leigh Brackett and Eric John Stark are still going strong.

This development is not quite so surprising as literary critics—sleuthing for "feminine sensibility" in fiction à la Jane Austen, or for heightened female consciousness à la Erica Jong—might think. Especially it is not surprising in the pulp field. "The hard-boiled detective story by J. R. Doe may seem absolutely masculine—until one day Jean Rose Doe admits she wrote it," Lester del Rey has noted in his book review column (*Analog:* 95, June 1975). "And the gushy love-pulp or over-female confession was written by a man in more than half of the cases. . . . No editor can ever be sure (without knowing the writer) whether a story has been submitted by a man or a woman." In the case of C. L. Moore, del Rey argued, "What difference can it really make that the Northwest Smith stories were written by a very feminine woman? Their vigorous masculinity grew out of the stories they were, just as the female-centered nature of 'No Woman Born' [discussed in chapter 6] developed from the story it was."

Other early work by Moore, however, might be read as a challenge to this thesis of del Rey. *Weird Tales* in the 1930s, as already noted, had a wider latitude in matters of sex than its all-science-fiction competitors. In addition to the Northwest Smith stories, C. L. Moore also wrote for that magazine several stories, classifiable as "sword and sorcery" rather than as science fiction, about a lithe, red-haired, chainmail-clad young warrior woman, "tall as most men, and savage as the wildest of them," named Jirel of Joiry. Jirel lives not in a future world of spaceships and robots but in a medieval French troubadour's world of castles and magicians. At the opening of the first of these tales, "The Black God's Kiss" (*Weird Tales:* 24, October 1934), Jirel's fortress has been taken by storm and she has suffered the humiliation of capture by a swaggering male knight. Moore continued to play variations on this theme, of a woman in the power of a domineering man who must fight her way to freedom, in other Jirel stories.

In one of the best-told among them, "The Dark Land" (*Weird Tales:* 27, January 1936), Moore's medieval heroine is trapped in a vivid, seemingly real world, which is actually the mental creation of the man-god Pav, who seeks not merely to possess her as a male but also to absorb and destroy her identity. As in an ancient myth or fairy tale, Jirel is tempted: to accept Pav's material gifts, to let his sheer strength overpower her, to resign herself to her situation and submit. Only when she meets, out at the far fringe of Pav's domain, a sorceress whom he has loved and cast aside—which is to say a woman who has at great cost learned how to survive in, yet not be a part of, this man-created world—can Jirel acquire the power to destroy Pav and set herself free. Taken allegorically, "The Dark Land" is a testament of women's liberation.

Equally striking as allegory is Moore's science fiction story "The Bright Illusion" (*Astounding:* 14, October 1934). A man of Earth, wandering through the Sahara, is plucked from the shimmering hot sands by an alien intelligence and thrust into a far universe, a place of "incredible angles and impossible colors, the tints and the tilts of madness," with appropriately hideous inhabitants. To shield his sanity, a telepathic veil deludes his senses, so that he seems to see a splendid and beautiful city tenanted by humans. In that illusory situation, Boy meets Girl, and in the classic tradition they instantly fall in love. Knowing that she is not what she seems—and that she in turn perceives him as one of her own kind, rather than as an utterly alien being—the hero wonders: "Could love rise from no more than a scrap of beautifully shaped flesh?" Love, he concludes, transcends the accidents of physical form. "Somewhere at the very core of our beings is the one vital spark of life, which in the last analysis is *self,* and with that one spark we love each other." It would be many years—three and a half decades, in fact, until Ursula LeGuin won the Hugo and Nebula awards for her novel *The Left Hand of Darkness*— before science fiction again would so far transcend sexual chauvinism.

III

When *Amazing Stories* moved to Chicago, changing ownership for the second time in its fifty-year history, the magazine's first cover under the new regime (June 1938)—a photograph, not the usual painting—depicted a helmeted villain on a ladder cradling an unconscious woman in a red evening gown. It was the herald of a new order. Male and neuter (robot or monster) themes predominated for another year or so; it is a fully dressed man, not a woman, that the Whispering Gorilla (wearing a tux with white tie!) holds overhead before the terrified crowd on the cover of *Amazing*'s companion magazine *Fantastic Adventures* for May 1940. But by mid-1941—and surely the war had something to do with this—cover artist H. W. McCauley was regularly painting for both of these magazines a glamorous Hollywood type of woman whom readers and editors soon dubbed "the MacGirl." *Thrilling Wonder* and its new companions, *Startling Stories* and *Captain Future,* picked up the same cue; month after month on their covers the monster charged, the hero's ray guns blazed, and the heroine screamed.

The new magazines that were launched in the general pulp proliferation of 1939 followed the same pattern. The cover painting for the first issue of *Planet Stories,* for example (Winter 1939–40), illustrating a lead story entitled "Golden Amazons of Venus," was a Busby Berkeley MGM song-and-dance spectacular, showing a host of blondes in golden helmets and breastplates firing crossbows at a horde of scaly Venutians.

Another new magazine, *Astonishing Stories,* on its cover for March 1942 carried the triangle of Boy, Girl, and Creature to its logical, laughable conclusion. Near the open hatch of a spaceship, the hero, clad in one of the realistically bulky space suits that artist Wesso always put on his astronauts when they had to go for a walk in high-vacuum conditions, is rescuing a young woman from a monster, in this case a green dragon equipped with several sets of wings. Nearby hangs a swollen sun, larger than it would look to the eye even from the orbit of Mercury, and presumably hotter. But the lady over whom the other two characters are fighting is wearing, not a refrigerated space suit, but a red dress and tennis shoes; and—wondrously absurd touch—her hair is blowing! (In what? The solar wind?)

John Campbell's *Astounding* never really adjusted to this pictorial revolution; the blue-skinned, modestly swimsuited young woman who appeared on its cover for July 1940 was an exception to the magazine's continuing emphasis on men, space, and machines. (Besides, she was scientifically plausible; the story for which that cover was painted, "Crisis in Utopia" by Norman L. Knight, described a mutated race of undersea-dwelling, water-breathing humans.) She made far less of an impact than the burly hero of E. E. "Doc" Smith's space opera *Gray Lensman,* whom cover artist Hubert Rogers painted for October 1939. Ray Bradbury, not yet a practicing professional writer, was moved to compose a fan letter: "If you could have been at the Thursday meeting of the Los Angeles Science-Fiction League, you would have heard a chorus of excited oh's and ah's echo far into the night as Forrest J. Ackerman produced the October issue of *Astounding,*" Bradbury wrote (in "Brass Tacks," *Astounding Science-Fiction:* 24, December 1939). "Kimball Kinnison, as coverized, is enough to make [Charles] Atlas melt away into his original ninety-seven pounds."

Meanwhile, paradoxically, flamboyant old *Weird Tales* under a new editor, Dorothy McIlwraith, had considerably toned down. Cover artist Margaret Brundage began to put clothes on her women in the summer of 1937, and by March of 1941 they were as properly dressed as any other young female American clad in what would have been called in those days a "formal." However, another *Weird Tales* artist, Virgil Finlay, found a new market for his nudes in the reprint magazine *Famous Fantastic Mysteries,* and he continued exploring this theme also in many of his interior illustrations (not so visible on the newsstands). The science fiction pulps as a group seem thus to have evolved from the primary grade level of "Don't look now, boys," at least to the Hollywood or Miss America level of "Look, don't touch!" Nearing draft age with the world on fire, science fiction's little boys now faced some quick growing up.

The stories inside those garish covers on the whole remained quite innocuous, however. As Sam Moskowitz puts it (in *Seekers of Tomorrow,* 1967), most probably the bug-eyed monsters in pursuit of all those girls were merely hungry. Sexual behavior had become discussable, although not describable, in the stories; there is a note of mild bawdy humor in L. Sprague de Camp's science fiction and fantasy, for example. Occasional off-trail yarns like "The Facts of Life," by P. Schuyler Miller (*Comet:* 1, May 1941), in which a scientist trains hothouse flowers to a more active kind of lovemaking than plants are accustomed to (only to be thwarted by a disapproving spinster who works in the florist's shop next door), could now be tolerated. However, if an opportunistic editor sought to boost his sales by pushing his story policy toward what we would nowadays term "soft porn," perhaps with a dollop of sadism as in John Wallace's short story "Perfectionist Perdition" (*Marvel Tales:* 1, December 1939), a clamor of protest would drive him back in the direction of innocence—as later, less lurid issues of that same magazine attest.

As for character, as distinguished from physical attractiveness—a distinction American males have always had difficulty in making—the predominant female type in science fiction remained, as before, the heroine who exists only as a reward at the tale's end, like candy, for the hero's good behavior; or who functions earlier in the story as a sounding board for his scientific soliloquies. Stronger, more complicated women, however, were beginning to appear. Leigh Brackett, as she began to publish in the early 1940s, had no patience with the previously typical science fiction heroine, that "vision of feminine loveliness" who "does nothing but have tantrums, shriek, and generally gum up the action." The tales Brackett turned out for *Planet Stories* during the wartime years presented quite another model: "My women are usually on the bitchy side—warm-blooded, hot-tempered, but gutty and intelligent" (the first adjective, the present-day reader should understand, was intended as a compliment). Similarly, C. L. Moore's heroines of the early 1940s—Deirdre in "No Woman Born," previously discussed, or Quanna in "There Shall Be Darkness" (in chapter 9)—were developed with far greater subtlety than her warrior-woman Jirel.

Women in science fiction were still, ordinarily, "won" or "lost" by a male protagonist before the story was over. But that convention was changing also. Rarely, but increasingly, hero and heroine would be found living together as husband and wife *before* the action of the story began, a circumstance forcing the writer toward more mature characterization; they couldn't be shown just as "living happily ever after." An early and refreshing example of this greater maturity is "Sculptors of Life," by Wallace West (*Astounding:* 24, December 1939), in which a husband and wife commute to their laboratory job together and talk over its problems, more or less as equals, back home at the end of the day—a substantial advance over the situation described in West's "The Last Man"!

Once in a long while, in fact, it had become possible for a writer to portray a woman with an active, autonomous role independent of her relationship to a particular man or men. Isaac Asimov began his well-received series of robot stories with a couple of tinkering Gernsbackian male engineer-heroes having the interchangeable names of Powell and Donovan. But the third story in the series, "Liar!" (*Astounding:* 27, May 1941), introduced the formidable Dr. Susan Calvin, a special-

Artist: Elliot Dold

"Before his eyes a splendid and stately city was taking shape. Out of the ruin of eye-wrenching color rose tier beyond tier of white pillars and translucent domes. . . . Over the crowded streets with their swarms of multicolored horrors a stranger change was falling. Out of the mingling indistinctnesses of those colors without name, the semblance of humanity grew."

"The Bright Illusion," by C. L. Moore.
Astounding Stories, 14 (October, 1934), p. 120.

ist in the psychology of robots. By the time Asimov gathered
these short stories into book form under the title *I, Robot*
(1956), Dr. Calvin had clearly become the central—and
strongest—character.

Even such old-timers in science fiction as E. E. Smith got
some of the new message. Gone were the days when Smith
had had to engage someone else to write the "love interest";
his heroines, one reader noted in 1942, were no longer "useless props acting as resonators for his heroes" (W. B. Hoskins,
letter to the editor, *Astounding:* 29, April 1942). "Smith has, in
the Lensman series, discovered that a female can, in fact, once
in a while, get in there and *do* something." Moreover, the
ideology of the Lensmen series—unlike that of the earlier
Skylark stories—was, pro forma, equalitarian. The galaxy-
spanning Civilization and the equally vast Boskonian culture,
which struggle against each other in these space sagas, each
contain a great diversity of bizarre life-forms and societies;
there are conventional human beings who work for evil Boskonia, and there are "frigid-blooded poison-breathers," as
Smith called them, who are Good Guys and enlist in the
crusade for Civilization. About the only biosocial trait the
many peoples of Civilization have in common, Lensman Kimball Kinnison surprisingly discovers, is the equality of the
sexes. In contrast, Boskonia prefers to employ as its top
human agents either absolute male supremacists or, more
rarely, matriarchs. Its ultimate Bad Guys, the mysterious
Eddorians, are not "guys" at all; they are sexless beings that
reproduce like amoebae, by fission.

But if "Doc" Smith's heart was theoretically in the right
place regarding the status of women, in practice he couldn't
quite bring it off. The Galactic Patrol to the end of that series
remains an overwhelmingly masculine enterprise, and its civilian context remains a Civilization some of whose strangest
nonhuman adherents practice Earth-style, implicitly male-
dominant capitalism. If Nurse Clarissa MacDougall is built
up into a heroine fit to be Lensman Kinnison's mate, Kinnison
himself is built up still more, to the point that even by pulp

standards—as reader Hoskins also noted—he becomes too superhuman to be credible. Thus, if the woman gains, the man raises the ante, leaving their relative situation just where it was before.

As already noted in chapter 5, the intergalactic conflicts chronicled in E. E. Smith's Lensman stories had allegorical overtones from the wars then raging on small, green Earth, with the West cast as Civilization and the Nazi New Order functioning as Boskonia. Perhaps we may carry the allegory one step further and say that women in the science fiction of the early 1940s were winning as much as—but no more than—their real-life sisters were winning in World War II. They could work for a living, in the patriotic context of total mobilization; they could serve in clerical positions in the armed forces, if that would free some of their men for combat (*Planet Stories* at times went one step further, and let the women do some of the fighting). Beyond that point, in reality as in fantasy, they could expect token representation only: in actual, present-day nuclear physics, the occasional Lise Meitner; in the fictional future science of "robotics," the occasional Susan Calvin. Summing up in a "how-to" article for aspiring authors ("It's a Science," *Writer's Digest:* 25, May 1945), seasoned pulpster Arthur K. Barnes advised a person trying to write for the science fiction magazines to create, as the leading female character in a story, "the 'golden girl' type who can do anything except lick the hero." That word *except* exactly measured, as of the mid-1940s, the iron limits to women's liberation.

Still, for pulp science fiction—with its Gernsback-nurtured "for men (and boys) only" tradition—this was respectable progress. For the first time it had become possible on occasion to challenge the male-dominant values that existed outside the science fiction ghetto by means of insights gained from within. "I once had an English teacher who continually drilled into me the fact that men wrote stories, and women read them," reported Victor King after having read and enjoyed one of Leigh Brackett's yarns (letter to the editor, *Astonishing Stories:*

4, October 1942). "Adding that that was as it should be, said teacher made some rather caustic remarks about the puerile sort of tripe ground out by the *femmes*. Incidentally, that teacher was a woman." The Brackett story the young reader was defending, a pulp thriller titled "Out of the Sea" (same magazine, June 1942), was no doubt less edifying than the kinds of works almost any English teacher in those days, male or female, would have preferred to have students read. But this example of a free-lance professional writer, who happened to be a woman, may have taught one male student in a sexist American classroom a far more important lesson than he could (at that time in his life) have learned from more polite literature.

IV

The real problem with women in the older science fiction, Ursula LeGuin points out, was a problem with *people* in science fiction; the males in most of the stories had been as stereotyped as the females. "When they began using characters in science fiction," LeGuin concludes, "they began using women." Science fiction has its trends, C. L. Moore's husband, Henry Kuttner, observed in another of these authors' "how-to" articles ("Selling Science Fiction," *Writer's Digest:* 19, October 1939), and "the trend in science-fiction today is away from super-colossal characters and ideas." Despite the glowering persistence of Kimball Kinnison—and his even more juvenile equivalent, *Captain Future,* hero of the most comic bookish of all science fiction magazines—Kuttner nevertheless believed that "the jimber-jawed, steely-eyed interplanetary cop, with a blazing ray-gun in each hand, has gone out of style." Encouraged by John W. Campbell, male writers such as Theodore Sturgeon and L. Sprague de Camp and Lester del Rey in 1939 and 1940 produced some low-keyed, well-characterized stories for *Astounding* and *Unknown* whose male characters were unpretentious introverts rather than high-spirited knights. Pathos and gentle comedy were as likely to befall this new breed of hero as epic adventure. If LeGuin is right, then by fostering this type of story that unabashed male chauvinist John Campbell quite unwittingly may have furthered the eventual enlightenment of his male readers; to deal adequately with "the man-woman aspect of life," as Philip K. Dick has said science fiction must learn to do, a necessary first step for the young (or not so young) male science fictionist is to attempt to understand at least the male half of that equation— rather than fantasize about Kinnison or Conan.

But the old attitudes die hard, and a less assertive male in his own quiet way can be as chauvinistic as the more bumptious type. In "The Job Is Ended" by Wilson Tucker (*Other Worlds:* 2, November 1950), a meek man "wearing his troubles on his face" walks into a counselor's office to tell him those troubles, the chiefest of which is that he has married a woman far more intelligent than himself. "A man wants a woman who needs his advice, who needs to lean on him, who needs his greater reasoning powers," the client explains. "That is the kind of woman every healthy man desires." There is no indication that the counselor, who narrates the story, disagrees; and the author thought so well of the ploy that four years later he wrote it word-for-word into a book-length version of the same tale, adding to man's "greater reasoning powers" his "mechanical knowledge" as well. (The superior woman turns out to be a ten-thousand-year-old castaway from outer space, and the counselor to be another of her own sort; he at least, a member of her own species, is able to outsmart her, even if her dumb Earthbound husband is not—so that the supremacy of the male ego is after all preserved.) Published in 1953 as *The Time Masters,* Tucker's sexist parable continues in print in paperback; evidently its message is one that a new generation of talkative young science fiction fans, ignoring the more emancipated views that emerged after the war, still want to hear.

They are far less likely, however, to show the downright ascetic bias that their predecessors expressed in the era of Hugo Gernsback. Quite the contrary, they expect the story's heroine to hop into bed with the hero at the earliest opportunity. After World War II, the famous (or notorious) Kinsey Report signaled—or reflected—a demand in various quarters for the relaxing of conventional sexual standards, and in due course that argument reached the pulp magazines. "Discussions of sex have just as legitimate a place in science-fiction as nuclear physics and military technology and synthetic foods and the eternal struggle of dictatorship vs. freedom," John Higgins asserted in a letter to *Planet Stories* (vol. 4, Summer 1949). "So let's start jettisoning the taboos!"

Actually, the magazines—and *Planet* in particular—had cautiously started to jettison the taboos well before the advent of Dr. Kinsey. Leigh Brackett, in her *Writer's Digest* article of 1944, maintained that "You can get away with practically anything as long as it's well and subtly done." Over the next twenty years the subtlety disappeared as science fiction enlisted in the so-called sexual revolution of the 1960s. But if the sexual behavior in the stories became more explicit, the conventions surrounding it remained archaic. We should not single out the science fiction and fantasy writers alone for this failing; many a supposedly avant-garde writer out in the literary "mainstream" also commonly confuses freely available sex with genuine human liberation. Often, however, it only gives male supremacy a new form; the woman, instead of being the property of one man, becomes the property of any and all.

Robert Heinlein's more recent novels, with their recurrent theme of the benevolent old satyr and his obliging playbunnies, painfully exhibit this confusion. So does the lengthy, much-debated novel by science fiction writer Samuel Delaney titled *Dhalgren* (1975). Delaney uses a great many words one would not have found in the lowly pulps or even in general hard-cover fiction not so many years ago; whole pages in it read as if transcribed directly from lavatory walls. But the message conveyed by this four-letter language is ultimately more male chauvinist than anything in the politely censored pages of Jack London or Zane Grey.

A debate within the pages of *The Magazine of Fantasy and Science Fiction* in the mid-1950s illustrates the point. It began when R. S. Richardson, of the Mount Wilson Observatory, who had published articles on astronomy (and fiction, under the pseudonym Philip Latham) for John Campbell's *Astounding*, wrote on the topic "The Day After We Land on Mars" (*F&SF:* 9, December 1955). Mars voyaging was going to be monotonous and prolonged; and if male explorers were going to be required to live apart from women for spans of up to five years, they would be subjected to unhealthy and abnormal stress. "One hardly needs to be an expert," Richardson pontificated, "to know that men and women were meant to live together, and that when compelled to live alone they undergo personality changes of an undesirable nature." Family life would be impossible under the conditions prevailing on the real, non-Burroughs Mars; therefore, Richardson recommended, "the men stationed on a planet should be openly accompanied by women"—not wives—"to relieve the sexual tensions that develop among healthy normal males."

The response was vigorous. "It is pretty disheartening, after all these years, to discover how many otherwise enlightened and progressive-minded men still retain in their subconscious this throwback attitude toward half of humanity, which relegates women to the position of possessions, of ancillary adjuncts to men," wrote Miriam Allen DeFord ("News for Dr. Richardson," *F&SF:* 10, May 1956). The only real solution to the problem—if it was a problem—would be equal access for women to the kinds of jobs men had to have to qualify to go to Mars in the first place. If women physicists, chemists, astronomers, geologists, meteorologists, and engineers qualified for enrollment on the roster of the first Mars expedition, there would arise no need for Richardson's "extraterrestrial bordello." And if, in the interim before such equality was achieved, a celibate all-male crew landed on Mars, male science fiction writer Poul Anderson added, there was abundant historical precedent for the success of such a mission: "Even on Mars, a camp of Jesuits ought to manage quite well."

On this issue the science fiction emanating from the socialist countries is not of much help; Kate Millett has devastatingly shown (in *Sexual Politics,* 1971) that socialism does not automatically and necessarily lead to women's liberation. A novel by the highly prestigious Polish science fiction writer Stanislaw Lem titled *The Invincible* (1975; translated from the East German edition, *Der Unbesiegbare,* 1967) presents the adventures and mishaps of an all-male interstellar expedition on a typically rugged-landscaped planet of the Lyre constellation; women are not present in the story, and the besieging native life-forms—machines left over from a previous expedition that have undergone Darwinian evolution—leave the crew no time to brood over what Dr. Richardson assumes must be man's constant and all-absorbing preoccupation.

V

Far more interesting as indicating some real substantive change in science fictionists' attitudes about the proper role of women are a pioneering handful of stories published as the 1940s became the 1950s, especially in the new and more literary magazines that were founded just as the pulp era came to an end. The surviving older pulps also made room for an occasional tale that broke loose from their own stereotypes. A small but pointed example, which begins as if following the typical *Planet Stories* formula for romantic adventure, is "Garden of Evil" by Margaret St. Clair (4, Summer 1949).

In St. Clair's ironic tale, an interplanetary ethnographer is rescued from death by a green-skinned native girl named Mnathl, who feeds him, bathes him, medicates him, dresses his wounds, and cures him of drug addiction—the domestic services that patriarchal males traditionally have expected their women to perform. The catch is that all this nurturing activity is, literally, mere fattening for the slaughter; Our Hero is duly beheaded and consumed at a cannibal feast by Mnathl and all her friends and relations (of both sexes). "Mnathl's devotion, her self-sacrificing tenacity, her long kindness to him, everything—had all been nothing but the prelude to a ritual meal in which his rare blonde body was to be the chief support." C. L. Moore's Northwest Smith had regularly gotten himself into equally dire predicaments, and so did (and does) Leigh Brackett's Eric John Stark; but Smith and Stark always got out alive!

Planet Stories, most of the time, remained locked into its own pulp formulas until its demise in 1955; Mnathl is rather a rudimentary figure in the literature of women's liberation. In contrast, stories in Horace Gold's *Galaxy Science Fiction,* founded in 1950, represented a real break with most of science fiction's past. It published, for example, Fritz Leiber's short story "Nice Girl With Five Husbands" (*Galaxy:* 2, April 1951), whose heroine has not only five husbands, but four "kwives" (= "co-wives"); they all live together in a future commune. However, as she confides to a man from the present (her past), she has her own special emotional problem: secretly she yearns for lifelong monogamy, which in this world of the future is morally tabooed. *Galaxy* also published "Double Standard," by Alfred Coppel (3, February 1952), whose male hero resents the fact that *men* are not permitted to go into space; they have too little stamina and too much mass. He tries to sneak aboard a spaceship disguised as a woman, and fails. In these and other such stories, the shoe was beginning at last to be placed on the other foot.

Simultaneously, a new generation of women writers of science fiction was emerging. Even John Campbell, whose "long chatty editorials in *Astounding* had the style of an after-dinner speaker at the Elks Club"—he typically addressed his readers as "Gentlemen . . ."; so notes Terry Carr in a guest editorial for *Amazing Science Fiction* (49, November 1975), introduced two able writing women to *Astounding*'s predominantly male readers—Judith Merril ("That Only a Mother," *ASF:* 41, June 1948), and Wilmar H. Shiras ("In Hiding," 42, November 1948). Quite different in background and personal tastes from the engineering-trained Campbell, the liberal Catholic humanist Anthony Boucher in *The Magazine of Fantasy and*

Science Fiction printed in the 1950s the work of Miriam Allen DeFord, Idris Seabright (a pseudonym of Margaret St. Clair), Zenna Henderson, Mildred Clingerman, Andre Norton, and Evelyn E. Smith. They remained a minority among the writers, but the tokenism of the Moore and Brackett era was obviously over. Pamela Sargent, in her anthology *Women of Wonder: Science Fiction Stories By Women About Women,* a collection put together from a markedly feminist point of view, estimated that at the time of publication (1974) women who wrote science fiction made up between 10 and 15 percent of the total.

Some &f the work of the women writing in the 1950s has been faulted as "ladies' magazine fiction," in which (to quote Joanna Russ again) "the sweet, gentle, intuitive little heroine solves an interstellar crisis by mending her slip or doing something equally domestic after her big, heroic husband has failed." Still, it was something to have persuaded male readers brought up on boom-boom pulp action and an engineering mystique to read and enjoy stories which told them that gentleness, intuition, and domesticity are as legitimately part of the scheme of things as aggressiveness, logic, and high adventure.

By the end of the 1960s, despite Philip Dick's caveat, it was evident that a greater maturity in dealing with "the man-woman aspect of life" had arrived in science fiction. It had become possible even for a male science fiction writer, for example, to tell a story convincingly while shifting the narrative viewpoint back and forth between male and female protagonists, as in *Orn,* by Piers Anthony (1970; serial version in *Amazing Stories:* 43, July, and 44, September). In *Orn* and in the story to which it was a sequel, *Omnivore* (1968), the leading characters constitute a triangle of two men and a woman. It would have been very easy to do them badly, in the stock Hollywood tradition of Hero, Heroine, and Hero's Best Friend, or, in the alternative and more modern manner, to merge them into a convenient *ménage à trois.* The author, however, declined to have it the easy way. In these stories, unprecedentedly for science fiction (and unusual in any twentieth-century fiction), a man and a woman who are attracted to each other become aware that for them to pair off sexually would injure the relationship each has with the third partner, and destroy the mutually supportive community the three constitute as a whole. Sadly, having taken this high ethical ground, the author then reneged; in another sequel, _OX_ (1976), he introduced a second woman character, converting the triangle into a quadrangle and thereby neatly pairing everybody off.

Women writers were meanwhile blazing new trails in science fiction, in stories like Vonda McIntyre's deservedly award winning "Of Mist, and Grass, and Sand" (_Analog Science Fiction/Science Fact:_ 92, October 1973), published under John Campbell's young successor as editor, Ben Bova, who during his tenure at _Analog_ has quietly erased a number of traditional Campbell biases. They have also shown that feminism need not be inconsistent with a strong and loving man-woman relationship, as in Pamela Sargent's bittersweet "If Ever I Should Leave You" (_Worlds of If:_ 22, January/February 1974), a story showing also that fresh, humanly appealing variations can still be written even on so overworked a theme as time-travel. Pointing out that male as well as female writers were increasingly writing of women "in various decision-making capacities, such as President of Mars, founder of an experimental ocean research station, . . . a bodyguard, an astrogator, and geologist-miners," reader Lola L. Lucas concluded (in "Brass Tacks," _Analog:_ 95, June 1975) that "SF is not blissfully free of sexism, but it is steadily improving. . . . The war hasn't been won yet, but the skirmishes are looking better and better." The traditional stereotypes and inequalities, by which women had figured merely as "voluptuous scenery, mindless prizes, or pneumatic sex objects" were becoming "as unacceptable as dandruff."

In any discussion of women's liberation, in or out of science fiction, we must sooner or later move from the individual and personal to the sociological and political dimensions of the question. That transition in science fiction has been most systematically accomplished by Ursula LeGuin in her fine novel *The Dispossessed* (1974), whose male protagonist, having grown up on a planet where both private property and sex discrimination have been abolished, visits a neighboring world that still knows the burden of both. Shevek's home world, Anarres, is shown in a series of flashbacks, which detail both the voluntaristic, antipropertarian society in which Shevek grew up and the way his own personal character evolved in such a society. The host world, Urras, is presented in the great satiric tradition of *Gulliver's Travels;* just as Lilliput and Brobdingnag are both based upon eighteenth-century England, the one satirizing England's pretentiousness and the other its grossness, so the major nations on Urras satirize the Soviet Union and the United States of the twentieth century.

So meticulously egalitarian is the culture of Anarres that it has an artificially invented language, in which masculine and feminine inflections are not possible. One cannot describe one's spouse as "my" wife or husband; Shevek refers to Takver, the woman on Anarres who with him plays the comparable role, as "the partner." Coming from that kind of cultural background, he attends a reception given by his Urrasti fellow-scientists of the American-style nation and is surprised to learn afterward that all the women attending were his colleagues' nonscientist wives. Asking whether all the scientists on Urras are men, Shevek draws from his hosts the standard male chauvinist responses—women "can't do the math; no head for abstract thought; don't belong"—in a conversation that LeGuin sets forth with biting sarcasm. In turn, his disclosure that about half the Anarresti scientists are women is received by his hosts with surprise and aversion.

LeGuin is careful, however, not to spoil the effect of the book by portraying Shevek's home world as the perfect society; *The Dispossessed* is subtitled *An Ambiguous Utopia*. Anarres's antiproperty ideology is anarchist rather than socialist, and Shevek therefore rejects the overtures of the Soviet-type Urrasti nation's agents whose homeland practices the socialist forms of coercion. However, Anarres practices almost unknowingly its own forms of coercion; despite its formal commitment against regimentation of any kind, most crucially in its emphasis on the voluntary nature of work, it has other sanctions for forcing its citizens into line. Tocqueville warned that the abolition of all the old authoritarian structures in a society of equals might only clear the way for the more effective tyranny of public opinion. It is so on Anarres; the individual maverick is shamed into conformity by being accused of "egoizing." Shevek, struggling for full human autonomy, is a stranger and an alien not only in the class-structured society of Urras, but upon his home planet as well.

Moreover, Anarres is a planet poor in natural resources. Part of the glue holding its anarchistic society together is the common effort its people must make to cope with their barren environment. The affluent corruptions of richly endowed Urras are contrasted with the mean crabbedness that pervades frontier Anarres. *Both* worlds, in fact, are perceived as Utopian from the perspective of Earth, which in this future knows neither Anarres's freedom nor Urras's affluence. "My world, my Earth, is a ruin," the Terran representative on Urras— who is a native of long-overpopulated India and a woman— explains. "There are no forests left on my Earth. The air is grey, the sky is grey, it is always hot. . . . We made a kind of life in the ruins, on Terra, in the only way it could be done: by total centralization. . . . Total rationing, birth control, euthanasia, universal conscription into the labor force. The absolute regimentation of each life toward the goal of racial survival." Women, in that barracks society, are apparently no more unequal than men.

Upon both Urras and Anarres, in contrast to the ravaged planet that is the ultimate mother-world of both, there is still hope. A pro-Anarres underground exists on Urras; perhaps its members can be a vanguard for liberation, including women's liberation. But for the ruined Earth, the Terran ambassador tells Shevek, it is too late: "We forfeited our chance for Anarres centuries ago, before it ever came into being." Did Ursula LeGuin's theretofore confident voice falter at that point? Or should these words be taken as a hopeful prophecy, affirming that today's Earth still has its chance to combine (Urrasti) abundance with (Anarresti) idealism?

Chapter 8

Paradise and Iron
After Utopia, What?

Reduction of labor costs is only a part of the point. Another highly desirable feature of automation in relation to labor is that machines are easier to control than people.

—John I. Snyder, president of United States
Industries, Inc.

If we could take some of the money that we are spending in trying to ease the pain of our assembly-line personnel, and apply that money for some research to get the men out of there entirely, we would be far better off in the long run.

—Dr. J. J. Brown, Aluminium, Ltd.

(both as quoted in Robert Bendiner, "The Age of
the Thinking Robot, and What It Will Mean to Us,"
The Reporter: April 7, 1955)

201

Soldier-robot X-120, unemployed because there are no more people to exterminate, tries his hand at art by way of consolation. But he was not built for creativity.

"Rust," by Joseph E. Kelleam. *Astounding Science-Fiction*, 24 (October, 1939), p. 133.

AS HE STANDS IN THE MOONLIGHT by the bedside, looking down upon his creator "with yellow, watery, but speculative eyes," Frankenstein's monster is the perfect proletarian. Homeless, roving, cut off from the bourgeois ties of family and place, he is not merely an exploited victim of the productive process; he is *himself* a product. Mary Wollstonecraft Shelley, writing her classic novel in 1816, might not have put it quite that way, since the industrial revolution had as yet hardly begun. The story as she told it is a fable of individual sin and revenge, not an allegory of social oppression and struggle. Not until another century of industrial progress had gone by would the next logical step in fiction be taken, that of applying to the creation of artificial human beings the same techniques of mass production that were liberating and degrading real people.

On January 26, 1921, Karel Čapek's play *R.U.R.* opened in Prague. An instant success there, it was carried the following year to London and New York. The play (spookily staged for the Theater Guild by Lee Simonson) introduced the English-speaking world to the word *robot,* which in the playwright's native Czech connotes both *forced labor* and *worker.* Čapek's Robots are not the handiwork of a mad scientist who pours bubbling test tubes and slams home switches in a darkened laboratory. Instead, the curtain rises on a modern business office whose windows look out on rows of factory chimneys. At an American-style desk sits Harry Domin, the General Manager of R.U.R. (Rossum's Universal Robots), briskly dictating letters to a Robot secretary. Enter the heroine, ushered in by another Robot. Shortly Domin offers to conduct her on a tour of his plant, a far cry from the home workshop whence sprang Doctor Frankenstein's hand-crafted creation: "I will show you the kneading trough. . . . In each one we mix the ingredients for a thousand Robots at one operation. Then there are the vats for the preparation of liver, brains, and so on. Then you will see the bone factory. After that I'll show you the spinning mill . . . for weaving nerves and veins. Miles and miles of digestive tubes pass through it at a time." Doctor

Frankenstein's motive for his impious action had been much like Faust's: "I will pioneer a new way, explore unknown powers and unfold to the world the deepest mysteries of creation." The capitalists and engineers of R.U.R. conceive the purpose of their invention quite differently. "In ten years Rossum's Universal Robots will produce so much corn, so much cloth, so much everything, that things will be practically without price," the firm's General Manager tells his guest. "There will be no poverty. All work will be done by living machines. Everybody will be free from worry and liberated from the degradation of labor. Everybody will live only to perfect himself."

As might be expected, that is not at all the way it works out. Just as Frankenstein's monster (not without justification) had turned upon its maker, so these factory-produced Robots turn upon mankind. "Robots of the world!" proclaims Radius, their dynamic leader, at the end of Act III, "the power of man has fallen!" To the thunderous offstage tramping of thousands of marching Robot feet, the curtain falls. An ironic epilogue discloses that the victorious Robots have begun to die out, the formula for their manufacture having been lost. However, two of the last experimental models had been given sexuality. "Go, Adam, go, Eve," the sole surviving human tells them, "the world is yours."

Both kinds of artificial humans—Karel Čapek's assembly-line model and Mary Shelley's home-brewed version—soon became commonplace in science fiction. But a mutation took place along the way. "Any one who has looked into human anatomy will have seen at once that man is too complicated, and that a good engineer could make him more simply," R. U. R.'s General Manager Domin explains. "To manufacture artificial workers is the same thing as to manufacture gasoline motors"; in both cases the manufacturer seeks to lower his production costs to the utmost. The next logical step—which, however, the Rossum company does not take—would be to manufacture both products out of the same kind of materials, rather than start with something as complicated and messy as the inventor Rossum's artificial protoplasm. In science fiction, the Čapek "Robot," a synthetic biochemical organism, has come to be called *android* ("similar to or resembling man"); the word *robot* has ordinarily been applied to a creature not of artificial flesh, but of metal, operated not by vat-grown muscles and nerves, but by power packs and electronic circuitry.

Children's fantasy first made this transition away from the Frankenstein biological model, in the person of Tik-Tok the Clockwork Man, a character in L. Frank Baum's Oz books, who is wound up from the back with a key. Another early "robot," as thus mechanically defined, is the steel-clad girl-automaton that is brought to life in the great German silent film *Metropolis* (1925). Whether "robot" or "android," the man-made man soon became a fixture in American popular mythology. In countless movie retellings of Mary Shelley's story, Doctor Frankenstein tempts the wrath of the Creator by artificially creating life; and in endless pulp-magazine rewrites of *R. U. R.*, humanity faces attack by hordes of clanking, intelligent machines. Modern history added its own sinister twist to these powerful mythic themes. Prior to its violent downfall, Karel Čapek's R. U. R. corporation had designed and manufactured some of its Robots as soldiers, selling them impartially and at a handsome profit to warring nations. As the world in 1939 again fell under the thrall of war, soldier-robots again marched through the pages of science fiction, sometimes displacing their human creators entirely. "It was only a short step from killing men in yellow uniforms to killing all men," muses robot soldier X-120 in Joseph E. Kelleam's quietly melancholy story "Rust" (*Astounding:* 24, October 1939). "Did we do right?" His companion, L-1716, replies with the robot equivalent of a shrug: "We were made so."

However, not all stories of robot and man presented the former as a threat. In several short stories published during the early 1940s, Isaac Asimov worked out his "Three Laws of Robotics," by which robots and humans are able to live together in harmony; and in two novels written in the 1950s, *The Caves of Steel* (1953, serialized in *Galaxy:* 7, October,

November, December 1953) and *The Naked Sun* (1957, serialized in *Astounding SF:* 58, October, November, December
1956), Asimov paired a human and a robot as a highly effective crime detection team. In a lighter vein, "Lewis Padgett"
(Henry Kuttner) wrote of the inebriated inventor Galloway
Gallegher, who, in "The Proud Robot" (*Astounding:* 32, October 1943), gets drunk and sings duets with the mechanical
creation he had originally designed as a beercan-opener.
(Sadly, technological progress has in the meantime done away
with the beercan.) And quite touchingly, in the title story of
his fine collection *I Sing the Body Electric* (1969), Ray Bradbury
wrote of a robot baby-sitting "grandmother" whose role is
altogether benign.

But the animated machine, whether conceived as a menacing monster or as a friendly partner, inhabits a somewhat
different social universe from that of *R. U. R.* By sheathing
their robots in steel, the science fiction writers accidentally
covered up the political reality that Čapek's biochemical
Robots had been designed to symbolize. *R. U. R.* had obvious
reference to the then-recent Bolshevik revolution. "Rossum's
Universal Robots, Inc." is a classic business enterprise, insen-
sately and even suicidally devoted to making the maximum
profit for its stockholders. The ultimate rebellion of its mass-
produced workers is a parable on what *any* workers may do to
a system by which they have been regimented and dehuman-
ized. But the machine-robot is a parable of quite another kind;
a metaphor not for exploitation, but for displacement. The
menace and promise of a technology that could at one stroke
free man from drudgery and deprive him of his living was a
subject for debate far outside the orbit of pulp science fiction.
Arthur Pound, for example, discussed that question in a series
of "Iron Man papers" for the venerable *Atlantic Monthly;* these
were collected into a book, *The Iron Man in Industry,* published
in the same year that saw the American stage première of
R. U. R. In the 1920s and 1930s this problem was often
described as "technological unemployment." Nowadays we
call it "automation."

II

Automation presents a fundamental challenge to a civilization that since the dawn of human history has been founded on human labor. In particular it challenges any cultures as work-haunted as those of Western Europe and North America. When R.U.R.'s General Manager Domin preaches that the Robots will liberate humanity from "the degradation of labor," Mr. Alquist, the head of the corporation's Works Department—whose life will be spared at the end of the play by the Robot revolutionaries because "he works with his hands like the Robots"—objects: "Domin, Domin. What you say sounds too much like Paradise. There was something good in service and something great in humility. There was some kind of virtue in toil and weariness." Domin's reply is that of any progress-minded technocrat, whether capitalist or socialist: "Perhaps. But we cannot reckon with what is lost when we start out to transform the world."

The conflict expressed by Alquist and Domin in *R.U.R.* was further acted out in "Paradise and Iron," by Miles J. Breuer (*Amazing Stories Quarterly:* 3, Summer 1930). Visually, this seemed a straightforward adventure story. On the magazine's front cover, a man in a conventional business suit and hat, armed only with a knife, battles an animated, self-propelled motorcycle that has squid arms and searchlight eyes. Interior illustrations by H. W. Wesso showed a scoop bucket going after a group of people in evening dress, a prospector machine climbing over a scrap heap in search of recyclable items, an animated lasso capturing the hero, and another view of him hacking away futilely with an axe at one of those robot motorcycles. But these menacing images are also figures of allegory. Dr. Breuer's narrative took his readers into a totally automated "City of Smoke," whose swinging beams and derricks, as in a Charles Sheeler cubistic painting, lend an eerie sense of movement to a scene from which animate life is absent. Coexisting with this robot-operated "City of Smoke," however, is a "City of Beauty," whose nonworking human citizens have been given total leisure to create art. Together, these two cities constitute a new Athens that has no need of slaves.

These citizens, however, are functionally useless. Nominally they take turns "supervising" the machines, but in actual fact there is nothing to do during these tours of duty except stroll aimlessly or recline in easy chairs. The humans do not run the machinery; they do not even understand it. (The equipment in the Supervision Building all turns out to be fake, with dials and gauges that are not connected to anything.) "They were just passing the day in utter boredom, waiting for evening to come"—and if all of us are similarly liberated from labor, Dr. Breuer implied, such may become the fate of mankind. As it dawns on the machines that the people are not really necessary, the robot rebellion begins.

The machines need not attack man directly to bring him down; it would be sufficient if they corrupted him into Sloth, of all the seven deadly sins the easiest to commit. Once the sources of energy had become "so inexhaustible, and the amount of work necessary to make them available so slight, that half an hour's labor a day sufficed to earn a man his living," what would there be to do with the rest of his time? Not much, according to writers Fletcher Pratt and Laurence Manning in their somber story "City of the Living Dead," published in the same year as Breuer's "Paradise and Iron" (*Science Wonder Stories:* 1, May 1930). "For some people, art filled the vacant hours. But as the scientists grew in knowledge, the Machines they made executed the arts better than the artists themselves." At the same time, the Machines were doing away with all occupations that provided adventure, on the ground that "adventure is always the outcome of some lawless act." There remained only endless, purposeless leisure. "Men became connoisseurs of odors, of clothes. . . . But even here the Machines followed us, doing things better than we."

At last the government steps in with its Adventure Machines. Unlike the real thing, this kind of adventuring is absolutely safe. All the citizen has to do is submit to surgery, by which his or her sensory nerve endings are permanently connected to a vast library of recorded adventures. The one most suited to the individual's psyche is switched on, and by direct electrical stimulus he or she experiences whatever life story he or she has chosen, in full color, sound, touch, taste, and kinesthesia (muscle sense). Glowing reports of the results lead thousands to sign up for such programming; mankind has at last accomplished the goal so crudely foreshadowed by radio and TV and 3-D movies—total envelopment and escape. Fed and cared for by the Machines, these ultimate consumers are now free—or bound—to pass "the rest of their days in a series of pleasing and thrilling experiences that always ended happily"; or, if they prefer, they may "float as disembodied spirits down the endless corridors of an artificial Nirvana." The shelves of the Adventure Houses fill up with silent human forms swathed in silver wires (even Children's Adventures are available), and "the world's population, which had been rising ever since the apes first descended from their trees, began to fall."

It is not quite the ideal solution to the world's crowdedness envisioned by today's advocates of Zero Population Growth, for there is a catch: once undergone, the operation is all but irreversible. The vicarious adventurer cannot return to the real world. "But nobody wished to return," explains the one functioning inhabitant of the City of the Living Dead, who sits by a switchboard changing dreams when they end for a few among its tenants who had been his friends, plays out solitaire gambits on a chessboard, and laments the happy adventure-world from which he was wrenched by the last surviving surgeons, who fitted him with a metal mask-face and bionic sensors so that someone might be there to tend the eternal Machines.

Authors Pratt and Manning did not explicitly say so, but even this one remaining human functionary in the City of the Living Dead is not really necessary. Such machines, which in the story draw their power from the practically limitless geothermal energy of the earth's core, might just as well run and

maintain themselves. If muscle power could be displaced by
technology, so eventually might brains; Rossum's Universal
Robots could as well be marketed by a computer as by a
bustling human general manager who dictates business
letters.

Government itself, in another of Miles Breuer's stories,
"Mechanocracy" (*Amazing Stories:* 7, April 1932), has become a
literal, rubber-and-glass machine, "merely a little more auto-
matic and more complex" than the machines men had long
used to help them run their offices and banks. Unfortunately,
along with routine bureaucratic functions, the Government
Machine has inherited also the state's authority to kill. The
story begins with its hero receiving a formal notice: "Quentin
Smith Lakeman, the Government regrets your personal feelings and sympathizes with your relatives, but finds it necessary
to condemn you at once to euthanasia." Even though there no
longer exists a working class to oppress, and even though the
state as such has withered away, tyranny has not ceased;
enlightened Marxists would do well to ponder this paradox
disclosed by American science fiction.

It may seem strange that a literature preaching the decad-
ence of purposeless leisure should have appealed to readers
during the Great Depression, when so many millions were
suffering enforced leisure without the compensating benefit
of machine-made luxuries. But Franklin Roosevelt did not
conceive "a new deal for the American people" as an opportunity to lift from their backs the age-old burden of toil. Quite
the contrary, he told them in his inaugural address on March
4, 1933: "Our greatest primary task is to put people to work."
Accepting his major premise, Roosevelt's Republican opponents early in the game developed a rhetoric of "Get those
bums off welfare." Mirroring this national consensus in favor
of gainful employment, the science fiction of the 1930s again
and again presented the alternative to working for a living as
psychologically and morally disastrous.

In "Emissaries of Space" by Nat Schachner (*Wonder Stories
Quarterly:* 4, Fall 1932), the atom is unlocked, "and because the

atomic motor produces such extravagant power, the human race will at last be released from the curse of excessive toil"— only to fall into a false Golden Age "founded . . . on idleness and selfishness and the avid pursuit of empty pleasure." To prevent a recurrence, atomic experimentation has to be forbidden! Two decades later, the story's author had not mellowed; Schachner's book *Space Lawyer,* published in 1953 but based on stories that appeared in *Astounding* in the early 1940s, ends with the loss of an inexhaustible supply of cheap energy as a comet containing that source crashes into Jupiter. Just as well, muses the crusty old tycoon who throughout this series of tales has been the hero's adversary: "What d'ye think would happen if men didn' t have to work any more?"

The young hero flounders:

> "Why—I suppose they'd have more time to improve their minds, seek out the secrets of the universe, enrich their culture, write, paint—"
> "Superbunkum!" snapped the old man. "They'd lose all incentive, get bored, stop thinking and striving, and degenerate into pigs. Young man, within a hundred years they'd be slinking through cities they wouldn't know the use of, and staring helplessly at machines they didn't know how to handle."

This little curtain speech has echoes from an earlier story that has haunted the imagination of two generations of science fiction readers, "Twilight" by John W. Campbell (writing as "Don A. Stuart," in *Astounding:* 14, November 1934). Since its first appearance, this quietly told story has frequently been anthologized; it remains in print in the *Science Fiction Hall of Fame* (1970). It has also frequently been imitated. A time traveler ventures seven million years into Earth's future, and finds there a civilization that has fulfilled the technocrats' dreams. Machines, not men, do all the mining and smelting, lighting and weather control, street cleaning and repair. Automated freighters ply between the cities of Earth and between this and other planets. The time traveler enters an empty restaurant, and at the touch of a button it serves him food; he enters a hangar, and an aircar whisks him to San Francisco. There at last he finds the people—bewildered, forlorn little creatures who "wander through the vast cities their ancestors built, knowing less of them than the machines themselves."

So long has their automated environment been in existence, taken for granted, that the knowledge which created it is gone: "Do we know the legends of our first ancestors? Do we remember . . . the secret of chipping a flint till it had a sharp-cutting edge? They were now in similar straits." And the race is dying; as in "City of the Living Dead," the spark of speculation and adventure is gone. The time traveler, hailing from a more venturesome era, wakens a long-unused mechanism and sets it the task of building "a machine which would have what man had lost. A curious machine." Then he returns from the far future, overshoots his own time, and is found by the roadside in 1932. A motorist picks him up, and the visitor from the future, with ironic appropriateness, tells his story of the hopeless outcome of all man's strivings to that most onward-and-upward of American types, a realtor!

III

"The men who created and continued the [science fiction] magazines through the 1930s at least were, by and large, enthusiasts of science. They . . . believed that science, technology in particular, gave men the tools with which to remedy the ills of society and advance it toward some (ever-more-distant?) perfection." So writes the scholarly critic of science fiction, Thomas D. Clareson, in *SF: The Other Side of Realism* (1971). It is a judgment many a regular reader in the 1930s would have accepted. "The reader of such magazines as *Astounding* is ready, willing, and able to foresee vast improvements in the future of the human race," wrote Seymour Kapetansky in a thoughtful fan letter (*Astounding:* 24, October 1939). "He is an incurable and narrow-minded optimist, because he believes that whatever will come, will be right." Why, then, had the pessimistic theme of "Twilight" at once received so favorable a reception—so favorable that a sequel, "Night," in which man is gone from the universe and even his machine-cities are closing down, appeared within a year (*Astounding:* 16, October 1935)? Why did literary critic Bernard DeVoto, in an editorial "Doom Beyond Jupiter" (*Harper's,* September 1939), blast pulp magazine science fiction not for its technocratic utopianism, but rather for its defeatism and despair? Puzzled by such discrepancies, a graduate student (Albert I. Berger) put the question to John Campbell himself, in the course of a ninety-minute interview at the *Astounding/Analog* editor's office on January 28, 1971, some six months before Campbell's death. The editor's answer, so far as the story "Twilight" itself was concerned, was succinct: "That's what happens to civilizations."

"What keeps human societies going?" the young interviewer asked.

"Competition," Campbell said.

"Work ethic," the interrogator prompted him.

(There is a pause in the tape.) "Yes—the ethics of evolution is 'try.'"

As Campbell's story "Night" expressed it in 1935, "Evolution is the rise under pressure. Devolution is the gradual sinking that comes when there is no pressure—and there is no end to it." By that reasoning, however, all human progress must be self-negating; man's very success in conquering nature spells his doom, since the conquest would remove the environmental conditions—the "pressure"— which had made that success possible. Yet Campbell, most of the time, did not see this dilemma as insoluble. Did he still feel as optimistic about the future of man as he had in the 1930s? his 1971 interviewer asked.

"All science fictioneers are fundamentally optimistic," the veteran editor replied.

"You still think the future is basically bright?" persisted the student, fresh from the recent political confrontations of the 1960s.

"Yup, I do."

"What reinforces your optimism?"

"Three billion years of experience," said Campbell, and then in his characteristic debater's fashion, he took the offensive: "How long has the life-force in you been going on?"

"Twenty-three years," the young inquirer replied.

"No. Three billion years."

The subject was tactfully changed, and the editor went on to reminisce about the atom bomb.

If the logic of the machine pursued to its conclusion results at worst in human extinction (quietly as in Campbell's "Twilight" and "Night," or violently as in *R. U. R.* and "Rust") or at best in hideous stasis (as in Pratt and Manning's "City of the Living Dead"), then man might resort to a drastic preventive measure: smash the machines before they take us too far. In the Pratt and Manning story, the metal-masked human attendant who sits among all those wire-wrapped dreamers is discovered by a visitor from a simple Arcadian society shut away in a far-off mountain fastness, who in their folk religion have abjured the Demon Power and his agents, the Machines. The society of Samuel Butler's classic satire *Erewhon* (1872) came to the same conclusion; the victors in an Erewhonian civil war long ago "wrecked all the more complicated machines, and burned all treatises on mechanics, and all engineers' workshops—thus, so they thought, cutting the mischief out root and branch."

E. M. Forster in *The Machine Stops,* written in 1909 quite frankly as a rebuttal to H. G. Wells, solved the problem (or allowed it to solve itself) by having the future civilization's automated technology spontaneously fall apart. More deliberately, in another John Campbell story titled "The Machine" (*Astounding:* 14, February 1935), a robot intelligence that operates the entire planetary economy shuts itself off and throws man upon his own naked resources for his own good—although the Machine is aware that in the short run this means starvation, freezing, and cannibalism. But such conditions will force man to resume his upward march, the

"Human beings have created what they call civilization, which is actually merely a material barrier between themselves and their environment, so vast and unwieldy that keeping it going occupies the entire existence of the race."

"Co-Operate—Or Else!", by A. E. Van Vogt.
Astounding Science-Fiction, 29 (April, 1942), p. 79.

Machine tells its wretched, shivering human hearers: "You
will not die—weak fragments of you will die. . . . You are
older than the Machine. . . . You are older than the ground
upon which you stand; older than the sands of the ocean
beach in which you bathe. You are older than the river that
carries the hills away to the sea. You are life."

This is a desperate remedy for an admittedly desperate
disease. Since the same radical therapy would presumably
have to be repeated whenever humanity achieved the stagnation of affluence and leisure, would an "upward" march
under such conditions amount to anything more than a tread-
mill? Not surprisingly, many science fiction writers, rejecting
any such Luddite solution, celebrated the triumph of an ongo-
ing future technology regardless of the plagues it may inflict
on us along the way. Or, like Ray Bradbury, they rejected the
machine selectively rather than wholesale.

They focused in particular upon the automobile, which has
been fair game for the satirist in science fiction even since Dr.
Keller's "The Revolt of the Pedestrians" first appeared in 1928
(see chapter 1). For example, in "The Great God Awto," by
Clark Ashton Smith (*Thrilling Wonder Stories:* 15, February
1940), an archeologist of a future civilization conjectures that
the automobile, in the long-ago twentieth century, was deified
as "an abstract principle of death and destruction," to which
human victims were sacrificed in the same fashion as were the
devotees crushed under the ancient Hindu god Jagannath's
("Juggernaut's") sacred chariots. Again, "The Drivers," by
Edward W. Ludwig, a story written and published in the gas-
gulping, tail-finny 1950s (*If: Worlds of Science Fiction:* 6, February 1956), portrays a future culture in which all American
young men are coerced—or are shamed by their girlfriends—
into enlisting in a "Drivers' Corps." Membership in that quasi-
military organization entitles them to transform highway
slaughter into a dangerous but perfectly legal game, with
medals awarded for properly accredited kills—a logical-
enough extrapolation from the present-day pastime known as
"chicken." Science fiction writers in the socialist countries also

have done this kind of satire. "Vampire Ltd." by Czech writer Josef Nesvadba (reprinted in Darko Suvin's excellent anthology *Other Worlds, Other Seas,* 1970), introduces a car that runs on human blood, which it taps from the driver's foot through the gas pedal.

Ray Bradbury thus spoke from an established and specific tradition in science fiction when he told insurgent students at the peak of the radical 1960s not to burn their draft cards: "Burn your auto licenses instead. Don't kill the cops—shoot the works out of every third car you see. . . . The car is destroying many more lives than the Vietnam war" (quoted in *Chicago Sun-Times,* October 4, 1970). Bradbury practices what he preaches. Although a resident of Los Angeles, a city whose tribal deity is indeed the Great God Awto, he has never learned to drive one. Yet (as noted in chapter 2) he admired, and still admires, the massive but meticulous engineering that went into the Apollo moon shots. Rejecting the technology of Detroit, he embraces that of Cape Kennedy. Moreover, Ray Bradbury's proposed alternative to the car in a sprawled-out metropolitan civilization is not walking, but free public rapid transit, financed by extra charges on people's utility bills. To reject the entire technology of the future, in effect he argues, is to reject the gifts of Prometheus, as well as the curse of Frankenstein.

IV

Ray Bradbury made his debut as a professional writer in 1941; Robert A. Heinlein sold his first story two years earlier. Both authors quickly carved out major places for themselves in the magazine field, Heinlein primarily in John Campbell's *Astounding* and *Unknown,* Bradbury in *Weird Tales* and in the colorful pages of *Planet Stories.* They were also among the first science fiction writers to break out of the pulp ghetto, and many an outsider to science fiction still derives much of his or her first impression of the field from these two writers. Yet in many ways they were poles apart. Bradbury's nostalgic, romantically night-sided vision, which by the later 1940s was beginning to reach such outlets as *Harper's* and the *New Yorker,* contrasted sharply with the matter-of-fact rationality in the stories Heinlein was selling at about the same time to the *Saturday Evening Post.*

Robert Heinlein set much of his early work (including his *Post* stories) in a carefully worked out "History of the Future," whose predominant mood is expectantly utopian. Heinlein's future history was scrupulously dated; in particular it listed the precise times when new inventions, from transatlantic rockets to synthetic foods and weather control, were to be introduced (or, in some cases, abandoned as obsolete). In his later development as a fiction writer, Heinlein found that he had to abandon this framework as too rigid. But he continued—until Southern California mindlessness overcame him, in *Stranger in a Strange Land* (1961)—to create human cultures yet to come whose plausibility of detail rests upon intricate and sophisticated technologies. If these societies are oppressive machine-wielding tyrannies, as in his first long story, "If This Goes On——" (*Astounding:* 24, February 1940 and 25, March 1940), they are overthrown by revolutionists wielding better machines. If they allow for considerable personal freedom, as in Heinlein's book-length Utopia "Beyond This Horizon" (written under the name of Anson Macdonald and serialized in *ASF:* 29, April and May 1942), they fulfill fan-reader Seymour Kapetansky's credo of 1939: "With the forward march of civilization will come less work and more educated play for the average man."

To be sure, Heinlein's history of the future has its ups and downs. His forecast for the 1950s, for example, named that era "The Crazy Years"—a period of "considerable technical advance . . . accompanied by a gradual deterioration of mores, orientation, and social institutions, terminating in mass psychoses." Some might now say he was only a decade off! Again, around the turn of next century, Heinlein predicted a resurgence of imperialism marked by the introduction of slave labor into a colonial economy on Venus, the outright annexation of

Australia to the United States, and the reign of an American fundamentalist religious dictator. But these, in Robert Heinlein's world view, were to be only temporary setbacks. He dated "the first human civilization" from 2075, and although in the following century he foresaw further "civil disorder," he prophesied that it would be "followed by the end of human adolescence, and beginning of first mature culture."

The beginning of maturity, however, may also be the beginning of stodginess. One trouble with Utopia, which by definition is a society that has solved all its problems, is that living in it can be very dull. In "Poker Face" (*Astounding:* 27, March 1941), Theodore Sturgeon wrote of a man from just such a predictable, automated, riskless, routine future. He has gone back via time machine into the barbarous and turbulent twentieth century, to track down a fellow citizen of that insipid utopia who has "gone native" in the earlier society. By the time he has flushed out his quarry, in a sleazy back-room poker game, the hunter has also succumbed to the attractions of barbarism:

> "Do you realize that never before had I seen color, or movement, or argument, or love, hate, noise, confusion, growth, death, laughter?" . . .
> "Colors," I murmured. "Noise, and happy filth, and sorrows and screams. So they got you—*too!*"

Robert Heinlein was acutely aware of this problem of the zestless utopia. In one of his early stories, "Coventry" (*Astounding:* 25, July 1940), he seemed at the outset to be writing in the antiprogressive vein of Theodore Sturgeon's "Poker Face" and of John Campbell's "The Machine." But it soon became apparent that Heinlein was up to something quite different. As the story opens, its central character has just been cast out of a peaceable, but somewhat humdrum, future society— which he denounces for its blandness:

> You've planned your whole world so carefully that you've planned all the fun and zest right out of it. Nobody is ever hungry, nobody gets hurt. Your ships can't crack up and your

crops can't fail. You even have the weather tamed so it rains
politely, after midnight. Why wait till midnight, I don't know—
you all go to bed at nine o'clock!

He then storms off to a reservation that his society has
prepared for just such rugged individualists as himself. Unable to persuade a zoo to sell him a string of burros, our hero
loads up a tanklike vehicle powered by solar energy and drives
off into the hills, animated by "a feeling of Crusoe-like independence." It never occurs to him that this vehicle is the end-
product of a technology vastly more complicated than that
symbolized in the ship that got Robinson Crusoe to his island.
As he checks off his inventory, he imagines himself showing
off his equipment to a kindred spirit from the adventurous
past, Jack London—a knock-down, weatherproof cabin, for
example, light enough for one man to set up in five minutes,
but strong enough to stand the assaults of a grizzly bear. "And
London would scratch his head and say, Dave you're a wonder. If I'd had that in the Yukon, it would have been a cinch!"

Within the Wild West reservation to which Dave is going,
however, unpleasant surprises are in store. Although he has
"read all the classics: Zane Grey, and Emerson Hough, and so
forth," this housebroken offspring of a tame civilization has
never in his life fired a rifle, dressed a second time in once-
worn clothes, or eaten real rather than synthetic meat (when
he finally does, he promptly throws up). His notion of "living
off the land" is to use his six months' supply of freeze-dried
food and vitamin concentrates until he has had time to stir up
the chemicals for hydroponic farming. Moreover, this would-
be pioneer has no notion of the orneriness he will encounter
among real, live pioneers!

Some fiction writers, after the manner of Jack London in
The Sea Wolf or Kipling in *Captains Courageous,* might have
made out of such experiences the education and toughening
of a dude. Instead, Heinlein played them for laughs, making
them the occasion for the hero to learn acceptance of his
civilized identity: "He was no more able to discard his past
history than he would have been able to discard his accus-

tomed body." Or, to generalize: we have eaten from the forbidden tree, and we are stuck with the technology that is one of the fruits thereof. We may pine for a lost Eden where no machines intrude, or dream of another beyond the skies, a theme often picked up and transformed by the authors of interplanetary and interstellar tales, as noted in chapter 3; but here below we have the exacting task of trying to fashion paradise out of iron.

V

"Human beings have created what they call civilization, which is actually merely a material barrier between themselves and their environment, so vast and unwieldy that keeping it going occupies the entire existence of the race." It sounds like a line out of Lewis Mumford, but it is spoken by a blue "ezwal," a "rearing, monstrous shape of frightful fangs and claws," as it and its human antagonist go parachuting down toward the surface of an unknown planet in A. E. Van Vogt's story "Co-operate—Or Else!" (*Astounding:* 29, April 1942). The subsequent adventure together of man and ezwal is a variation on a favorite Van Vogtian theme, namely, conflict in outer space between human explorers and intelligent monsters (see chapter 6). Imitations of the earliest Van Vogt stories' basic plot line—the unfriendly Thing that gets loose inside a spaceship—can still be viewed on the endless TV reruns of *Star Trek.*

Television, in this case and as usual, waters down everything it touches. But the pulps in the pre-TV era had their own built-in intellectual limitations. The climax of the first published story by A. E. Van Vogt, "Black Destroyer" (discussed also in chapter 1), as the critic Richard Mullen has pointed out ("Blish, Van Vogt, and the Uses of History," *Riverside Quarterly:* 3, August 1968), betrays a "tendency of commercial science fiction to bring ideas of the most complex kind down to the level of physical combat." The ideas are there, nonetheless; and they are a far cry from the rationalist, technophile humanism of Robert Heinlein. On the roster of the starship *Beagle* in "Black Destroyer" is a Japanese archeologist-historian named Korita. As the crew explores the ruins of a fallen planetary civilization, Korita lectures them—at times word for word!—out of Oswald Spengler's *The Decline of the West.*

According to Spengler, whose pessimistic philosophy of history was widely quoted (if not read) during the modern West's first years of Caesarism, decline and fall is something that happens to *all* civilizations. Machine technology would be, in that case, only a symptom of cultural decay, not a primary cause. If Spengler was right, man can escape his historic destiny neither by embracing his machines nor by smashing them; in either event he is bound to go down. In the positivist tradition of Hugo Gernsback, however, Van Vogt exempted from this universal doom the particular future society he was writing about. As historian Korita in "Black Destroyer" recounts the breakdowns of other, older cultures—Chinese, Egyptian, Classical, and "West European American"—he adds: "Modern historians agree that, nominally, we entered the same phase fifty years ago; though, of course, we have solved the problem."

Some science fiction writers were less ready than Van Vogt to grant the "of course." James Blish, whose first stories appeared in the pulps in 1940, took Spengler very seriously indeed. Eventually, in his *Cities in Flight* series, as we have seen (chapter 3), Blish projected Spengler's model of historical rise and decline upon the entire galaxy; the cycle is terminated only by the end of the universe itself. Other authors, albeit consciously "progressive," may in that wartorn era have been unconsciously more Spenglerian than they knew. One alert reader (Wynne M. Trenholme, in *Astounding:* 25, June 1940, p. 152) thought he detected, both in the revivalist attack on space travel in Isaac Asimov's "Trends" (see chapter 2) and in the evangelical dictatorship in Robert Heinlein's "If This Goes On—," the "Second Religiousness" that Spengler believed is part of the winter phase of a declining civilization.

Rivaling *The Decline of the West* as a model for a philosophy of history in those troubled times was the equally sweeping vision of Arnold Toynbee, the fourth, fifth, and sixth volumes of whose *Study of History* were published in 1939. The science fiction community had some familiarity with the ideas of Toynbee, thanks to L. Sprague de Camp, who skeptically but quite accurately presented Toynbee's philosophy of history— along with those of Spengler, Pareto, Sorokin, Hegel, Mumford, and Marx—in a factual article "The Science of Whithering" (*Astounding:* 25, July, August 1940). Jack Williamson, at the age of thirty-three a seasoned professional whose work had appeared in the pulps for more than a dozen years, wrote one frankly Toynbeean story, "Breakdown." It was *Astounding*'s cover story for January 1942—coincident with those dark early days of war when even the invincible Americans were suffering disaster in the field.

The setting for "Breakdown" is the future metropolis of Sunport, which rises in the year 2145 from the parched Southwestern desert, whence man in 1978 had first blasted off into space. The city's upper levels at night are a vista of "tapering, graceful pylons of soft and many-colored fire," set off by broad parks and reflected in a hundred pleasure lakes. Gliders float overhead, "colored eggs of crystal light." This is the playground of Sunport's hereditary caste of a million engineers, entitled to wear the royal purple. In the levels beneath them toil eighty million lesser citizens, required to wear "labor gray"; these masses are held down by the police, who wear wine-colored uniforms, and the military, clad in black and orange. Over this rigidly graded society (a type of culture uncomfortably common in science fiction) rules sixty-year-old Boss Harvey Kellon, by title only the executive secretary of the Union of Spacemen, Managers, and Engineers, but in fact a caesar. He has the toga and the baldness that go with the part, the latter discreetly concealed under a toupee.

But the empire over which Kellon presides is in decay. When man conquered space, the engineers had been, to use Toynbee's term, a creative minority. Exploiting and institutionalizing their conquest, they have become a "dominant minority," and have made Sunport as much a petrifact as the pyramids of ancient Egypt, despite its colorfully lighted upper façades. The commerce of Mars and Venus continues to enrich their pleasure time, but the Saturn docks rust from long disuse; the retreat from empire has begun.

When a "creative minority" fails in this fashion, according to Toynbee, it loses the moral allegiance of the "internal proletariat," whose members mentally secede from the empire and start looking for a new cause to which they can give their hearts. That happened two thousand years ago when the masses of ancient Rome abandoned the Empire for the Church, and in this world of the future it is happening again. Hiding out in the drainage tunnels (that is, the catacombs) of Sunport, a subversive figure known as The Preacher leads the disaffected in a Gray Crusade, singing the "Battle Hymn of God" as they loot a library:

> Burn the books and break the gears,
> Kill Antichrist and engineers!

Caesar Kellon does not yet understand what is happening. Thinking to squelch the rebellion by picking off its leader, the Boss has the Preacher arrested by his secret police. Then Kellon confronts his adversary like a good Gernsbackian technocrat:

> I don't understand you. . . . Do you want the future to forget the power of science? Do you want to turn men back into naked savages, and wipe out civilization?

Unabashed, the Bible-quoting revolutionary replies:

> The science you revere is your false prophet. Your machines are the very Beast of the Apocalypse. . . . Babylon the great is fallen, is fallen!

Preacher Eli Catlaw is presented to the reader as an unsympathetic figure, and "bad guys" in pulp stories generally lose. Nevertheless, his prediction turns out to be correct. Catlaw's capture touches off a riot and a bombing; the admiral of

Kellon's space fleet defects to the Preacher; and Kellon's lovely mistress, Selene du Mars, deserts him for the admiral. All this action is much condensed, as was typical with stories published in 1942. A present-day science fiction writer would probably open these events out into a long, thickly textured novel on the model of Frank Herbert's *Dune* (1965); whether such expansion would improve Williamson's vivid, swift-paced story is primarily a matter of literary taste. As it stands, "Breakdown" reads like the synopsis of a potentially first-rate movie, although science fiction has usually suffered such ill treatment at the hands of Hollywood that I hesitate to make the suggestion.

"Evidently it isn't sinful to use machines—when they're guns," the Caesar of Sunport bitterly reflects as he flees for his life. In the course of his flight, he finds the "philosopher-historian" Charles Melkart, a small, stooped man in a red wool skullcap, working on the last pages of a manuscript and oblivious to the tumult outside. "Charles—do you know what is happening to Sunport?" Kellon cries. The aged scholar has a long-winded answer: "I've known for thirty years. Old Giovanni Vico had a glimpse of it, in his 'law of cycles' . . . Spengler and Toynbee glimpsed it. . . . But it remained for me to reduce the laws of the rise and fall of human cultures to the exact science that I call *destiny*."

The garrulous old pedant is beginning to sound like Archimedes at the siege of Syracuse, waving away from his carefully inscribed mathematical circles the intruding Roman soldier who was about to kill him. "Can you sit here writing a book, while the Preacher's fanatics are burning libraries in the park?" Kellon demands. "Who will be left to read your precious book?"

"Nobody, I'm afraid. It is tragic that cultures must reach the point of breakdown before they can breed men able to understand them."

Science fiction has come a long way at this point from menacing androids or clanking machines as reasons for man's downfall. Civilizations do not require a high technology to

make them wither, grow bored, and die. Nor is their fall a
mere matter of biological senescence, as Spengler suggested.
Arnold Toynbee used the term "challenge-and-response,"
which implies that the breakdown of a civilization is a failure
not of science, but of the will. "Men want to merge themselves
in things greater than their individual lives," Melkart explains.
They can't do that in Sunport any more; all it has to offer is
the pursuit of power and pleasure. The Preacher offers them
a crude way of satisfying their deep self-transcendent need.

As the city crashes in destruction, however, another and
perhaps better answer appears. Caesar Kellon has an
estranged son, who has long since rejected the struggle for
privilege and advantage in Sunport to do "impractical" scientific research. Out of that research, just at this moment of
crisis, has come a starship. The boss ends up, incognito, as one
member of a work party—democratically drawn from all
social classes—that digs the younger Kellon out of the rubble
of his bombarded laboratory. And then the good ship *Nova*,
with the chastened father reconciled to and working for the
son, lifts off for the stars. Once again there is meaningful
work to be done, both for people and for their machines.

This is the same American-style resolution of a social (or
personal) problem that occurs so often in the interplanetary
and interstellar stories we surveyed in chapter 3: to begin
again as an immigrant to a New World, to travel far in search
of an ever-receding Far West—even though, out there on the
frontiers of the galaxy, the entire cycle may be fated to play
itself out all over again. In a sequel to "Breakdown" titled *Star
Bridge*, which Williamson wrote in collaboration with James E.
Gunn (1955), the free society founded by the junior Kellon
has evolved into a stagnant, star-spanning tyranny. Like Sunport in its last days, this galactic society is neatly color-coded—
blue for Commerce, green for Transport, orange for Power,
gold for Communications, black for Security. And, to drive
home the irony, its precious coins that circulate throughout
the universe are called *kellons*.

The historical philosophy that the fictional Charles Melkart voiced in *Astounding* in 1942 has continued to echo through more recent science fiction as well. "We have not had the good fortune to be born in an era when our society offers us something transcendental to live for," says a citizen of still another declining empire that has spread out from little Earth to span the stars, in one of Poul Anderson's "Dominic Flandry" stories, *A Knight of Ghosts and Shadows* (1974). Therefore, the Long Night must inevitably come down over human civilization. In the Anderson story, its all-enveloping darkness swallows up the personal relationships as well: a son betrays his father, and the father orders the death of his son. But Poul Anderson's bitter denouement is just as arbitrary as the happier ending of Jack Williamson's "Breakdown." Whether to confront a societal/personal crisis where you are, or—like Bunyan's pilgrim—to fly from the City of Destruction, is a choice whose wisdom or folly depends upon where you stand along the arc of history. And where that is, as Charles Melkart might have said, is very difficult to know at the time.

Chapter 9

By the Waters of Babylon
Our Barbarous Descendants

I walked some miles of Hadrian's Wall, away at the back of beyond in Northumberland. . . . It is an empty country still, much of it; Pictish hill forts still scowl almost within bowshot of the Roman masonry. To the men of the legions, garrisoned here generation upon generation, it must have seemed— even toward the end—that indeed Rome was immortal. . . . Yet in the fullness of time, when the common faith of the Roman world had lost its virtue, the Picts came over the wall.

—Russell Kirk, *The Intemperate Professor* (1965)

Artist: Edd Cartier

"Over 90% of stories submitted still nag away at atomic, hydrogen and bacteriological war, the post-atomic world, reversion to barbarism, mutant children killed because they have only ten toes and fingers instead of twelve. . . . The temptation is strong to write: 'Look, fellers, the end isn't here yet.' "---H. L. Gold, editorial in *Galaxy Science Fiction*, 3 (January, 1952).

"Tomorrow's Children" by Poul Anderson and F. N. Waldrop. *Astounding Science-Fiction*, 39 (March 1947), p.

A N OLD MAN IN A MANGY GARMENT OF GOATSKIN and a boy
wearing a ragged piece of bear hide trudge along a
narrow woodland trail. An occasional piece of rusty iron,
glimpsed through the forest mold, mutely hints that this was
once a railroad embankment. Emerging from the forest into
sand dunes by the sea, they find two other skin-clad, sun-
burned boys cooking crabs and rock-mussels over a fire. The
roar of surf mingles with the bark of seals, sunning themselves
on some jagged rocks a hundred yards from shore. The
pungent steam that rises from a fresh-cooked crab's cracked
legs stirs the old man's memory. Sixty years since the last
mayonnaise was made, he reflects; "In those days it was served
in every restaurant with crab."

Rambling on, in the long-winded, self-absorbed way of old
people that forever bores and offends the young, aged Granser declares that he has seen this very beach crowded with
swimmers and sunbathers, on a pleasant Sunday afternoon
back in the year 2013 when four million people lived in San
Francisco. There had been a big restaurant up on the cliff,
where you could get anything you wanted to eat, but if you
ordered crabmeat it was scarce and expensive; the encroach-
ing population had come near fishing the beach out. Times
have changed; the fishermen and the pollution are long gone,
"and now crabs are accessible the whole year around. Think of
it—catching all the crabs you want, any time you want, in the
surf of the Cliff House beach!"

So begins Jack London's cautionary tale "The Scarlet
Plague," first published in 1913 just as the proud towers of
Europe's Edwardean culture were about to fall. In this story,
civilization, with its monorail trains and dirigible airships and
wireless, its books and medicine and money, has vanished.
The plague, itself a product of civilization in that it was
incubated in man's crowded cities, has swept around the
planet before burning itself out. Eight billions of human
beings have been reduced to a few tribal handfuls. And the
end of the decline is not yet. "If only one physicist or one
chemist had survived!" the old man exclaims. Like the former

professor he is—the first plague victim he ever saw was a
student, stricken during one of his own lectures at Berkeley—
Granser tries to tell the heedless youngsters by the fire about
the alphabet, gunpowder, and steam. He warns them against
the quackeries of the medicine men who have already
appeared in this new primitive society. But he knows his is a
losing cause. In another generation, boys like these will be
perforating their noses and ears and wearing ornaments of
bone and shell; they will hang human scalplocks at their
waists. The fallen civilization will have to go all the way back
down to the bottom before the historical process can resume.

A quarter-century after Jack London uttered that prophecy, the distinguished poet and story-writer Stephen Vincent
Benét took up the same melancholy theme. "By the Waters of
Babylon" (first published as "Place of the Gods," *Saturday
Evening Post:* 210, July 31, 1937) shifts the locale of the coming
barbarian society from San Francisco to New York. The medicine men who were emerging in Jack London's future have
triumphed in Benét's. The island of Manhattan is tabooed as a
Dead Place: "The north and the west and the south are good
hunting ground, but it is forbidden to go east." In the story
John, son of John, tribesman of the Hill People, sets forth on a
journey comparable to the vision-quests of young American
Indian braves back in the days before the coming of the white
man. The waking dream John has by the medicine fire before
he goes, and the omens he sees along the trail, convince him
he must break the taboo against visiting the great Dead Places.
Just the same, when he comes to the great river Ou-dis-sun
(Hudson), he sings his death-song before rafting over to New
York. There beside a heap of stones and shattered columns
with the broken inscription UBTREAS, down near where
Wall Street used to be, John finds a white, tie-wigged marble
image of a god. "His name was ASHING, as I read on the
cracked half of a stone," John relates. "I thought it wise to
pray to ASHING, though I do not know that god."

As times change, prophecies change. Jack London in outwardly peaceful 1913 had forecast the destruction of civilization by epidemic disease. But in 1937, with Spain, China, and Ethiopia in smoking ruins, Stephen Vincent Benét surmised that its downfall would come by war. His hero refers back to "the time of the Great Burning when the fire fell out of the sky." H. G. Wells, as he detailed the process of collapse in *The Shape of Things to Come* (1933), attributed it to both causes. War would disrupt Western civilization's depression-weakened ties, and plague would do the rest.

This relatively late work by Wells was cast not in the form of a novel, but of a history textbook purportedly written in the future. Completing his task soon after New Year's Day in 2106, the imagined historian describes how "the last war cyclone" started in 1935 between Japan and China, with the United States inevitably drawn in, and then how it spread to Europe in 1940 when Poland and Germany went to war over Danzig. (It did not take any special genius to make the second forecast; well before the advent of Hitler, an American journalist, Frederick Palmer, had tabbed the Polish Corridor as the place "where the next European war will start" (*Harper's:* 151, November 1925). However, H. G. Wells's fictional World War II does not follow the course of the actual Nazi blitzkrieg of 1940. Instead, it rages to an inconclusive "suspension of hostilities," after which the exhausted and bankrupt belligerents are finished off by starvation and disease. National governments come unstuck, and municipal authorities—a self-appointed "Duke" or "Mayor," a "Town Council," here and there a "Workers' Soviet"—organize health services and barter economies as best they can.

While Europe reverts to a kaleidoscope of local, quarreling fiefdoms like those of the early Middle Ages, America goes through a similar process: "The authority of the Federal Government of the United States shrank to Washington, very much as the Eastern Empire shrank to Byzantium." Internationally, the Catholic Church splits, with one pontiff reigning in Rome and the other, having somewhat the better apostolic

claim, in Dublin. In a chapter titled "Europe in 1960," written
in deadpan parody of standard history textbook style, Wells
described a bucolic society in which peasants hitch oxen to
broken-down automobiles to haul their goods to market, cat-
tle-raisers battle potato-growers for possession of Hyde Park
and Kensington Gardens, and in a broken-down textile factory in Lyons "a wild cat crouches among the spindles of a
spinning-machine and spits at the unwanted intruder." The
old structure of nations and empires "was still standing—a
hollow shell in 1933," Wells summed up; "in 1960 it had
gone."

Pulp writers picked up and elaborated these themes of
London, Benét, and Wells. The New York World's Fair of
1939, for example, with its congenial Gernsbackian "World of
Tomorrow" theme, prompted the local organizers of the first
World Science Fiction Convention held in New York that
same summer to seek a publicity tie-in with the fair; but a few
dissenters saw the fair and all it symbolized as only a last
utopian fling before the world dashed over the brink to
destruction. Even mere natural catastrophe, perhaps of a
different sort from the rampaging micro-organisms of Jack
London's "The Scarlet Plague," might intervene before the
Time Capsule that had been ceremoniously buried under the
World's Fair site in 1938 was even unearthed. In "The Day of
the Cold," by Sam Weston (*Astounding:* 24, January 1940), the
capsule, with its mementoes of the advanced civilization of
1939—for example, a letter from Professor Albert Einstein—
is dug up by fur-parka-clad primitives of a new Ice Age.
Suffering a worse fate than that of Jack London's old Granser,
who is merely teased and ignored, the one man who might
have understood what the movie reels and telephone handset
are really for is brutally murdered. The killer wastes no
sympathy either on his victim or on the more knowledgeable
ancestors who left these artifacts behind. "They could read,"
he smugly tells his cavemate, "but they died just the same in
the cold. Maybe we can't, but we're here."

II

In the grim year 1939 it did not take a fantastic imagination to dream of Dead Places created in a Great Burning. All one had to do was watch the newsreels. Jon, son of John, was followed in science fiction by a host of other pilgrims to dead or holy places. In "The Priestess Who Rebelled" by Nelson S. Bond (*Amazing Stories:* 13, October 1939), the colossal stone faces of George Washington, Thomas Jefferson, Abraham Lincoln, and Theodore Roosevelt that were sculpted with dynamite out of the eternal granite of Mount Rushmore have become the high gods Jarg, Taamuz, Ibrim, and Tedhi, and their dwelling place in western South Dakota has become a shrine to which young novitiates must go in pilgrimage.

Unlike Stephen Benét's young traveler, the pilgrim in Bond's tale is a proud, sun-bronzed girl; for when the men in this future went off to war, making a mess of civilization as they dropped their bombs, the women back home decided enough was enough and reorganized the postwar society on matriarchal lines. However, like a true twentieth-century male chauvinist, Bond assumed that matriarchy would be a barbarian reversion rather than a step forward. So did his heroine; the priestess *does* rebel, as soon as she has gazed upon the presidential statues and realized her tribe's well-kept secret: that the gods, in reality, were male.

Quite different is the social reorganization that takes place in a war-shattered Europe, in L. Ron Hubbard's grim and powerful novel "Final Blackout" (serialized in *Astounding:* 25, April, May, June 1940). Assuming, as Wells had in *The Shape of Things to Come*, that World War II would end not in blitzkrieg, but in stalemate, Hubbard told his story from the viewpoint of a British soldier known only as "the Lieutenant," born in an air raid shelter during a raid, who has lived to see the airplanes vanish from the skies as the industrial society that had produced them falls to pieces. As with Wells, the social disintegration of Europe begun by war is finished off by

starvation and disease: "Death crept silently over the wastes of
grass-grown shell holes and gutted cities, slipping bony fingers
into the cogs of what organization had survived. From the
Mediterranean to the Baltic, no wheel turned."

Down in the ruins, however, some semblance of the war still
goes on. The Lieutenant commands a motley assortment of
Englishmen, Poles, Spaniards, Frenchmen, Finns, and Italians, "uniformed in the rags of twenty nations, friend and foe
alike"—much like those "formidable middle-aged rascals in
patched and shabby and supplemented uniforms," who in H.
G. Wells's vision were expected to be roaming over Europe in
"fragments of unpaid armies" during the 1950s. One
hundred sixty-eight enlisted men and five noncoms are all
that remain of a brigade that at full strength numbered
6,000—and that has had 93,000 replacements; the hard and
unkillable core.

These men do not so much fight as forage. Early in the
story they surprise and defeat a Russian outfit that still has
horse-drawn artillery, going into battle not for any grand
strategic reasons, but simply for the unusual reward of roast-
ing juicy horse steaks over their campfires. The original ideologies that had started the fighting no longer exist; England
has gone through seven governments since the war began,
Germany through eighteen. A British Communist leader
occupies the Tower of London, but over the Kremlin floats
again the banner of the Tsar!

Sailing against the English Leftist regime in an assemblage
of former war vessels that had lately been used as fishing
boats, the Lieutenant's forces topple the home government
with surprising ease, and then set about the painful process of
rebuilding. Banditry and thieving are suppressed; a barter
traffic is established between the Lieutenant's administration
and the individual who styles himself King of Scotland. There
remain "still enough printed data to supply the working background of a very elementary kind of civilization," but full-scale
reindustrialization seems out of the question. No matter, the
Lieutenant decides; "machines only make unemployment and

ultimately politicians out of otherwise sensible men." When
the inevitable Americans arrive—they have stayed out of the
war and escaped devastation, but kept their military forces in
shape by fighting in South America and China—the Lieutenant refuses their offer of technical know-how and economic
aid. To enable England to continue at its newly stabilized
medieval level, he assassinates the English puppet leaders of
the client government the Americans want to impose, willingly
paying the price of British independence with his life.

By the time the last serial installment of "Final Blackout"
appeared on the newsstands in May 1940, the Nazi invasion of
the Low Countries was under way, and none of the British
troops who crowded on board the channel boats at Dunkirk
had any intention of marching against the Tower of London.
Hubbard's (and Wells's) prediction that World War II would
end in stalemate was nullified by the speedy fall of France in
the third week of June, and any likelihood of Englishmen
someday battling Russians—plausible enough during the
short Russo-Finnish War of 1939–40, in which the sympathies
of the West had clearly been with Finland—ended just one
year later when Hitler's legions invaded the Soviet Union. In
the meantime a blizzard of letters commenting on "Final
Blackout" had descended upon *Astounding*'s "Brass Tacks"
letter column. Author Hubbard had created a far more interesting hero than the raygun-toting Boy Scouts who still
appeared too often in the pulps of those days, and he evoked
strong reader response—all the way from an admiring poem
(quite bad) titled "The Lieutenant" by H. K. Pruyn (*Astounding:* 27, June 1941), to Charles Hidley's comment that "the
Lieutenant, despite Hubbard's obvious sympathetic feelings
for his character, was, to me, one of the most despicable I ever
encountered" (*Astounding:* 25, August 1940). "These 'Final
Blackout' letters are but a few of many," editor John W.
Campbell reported. "They vastly interested me, because the
readers dispute the actions of the character with the author—
which means the author made that character live!"

The readers disputed not only the actions of Hubbard's

character, but also his political philosophy, which they variously labeled feudal, militaristic, authoritarian, and even Fascist. "I prefer the happy, though jumbled, freedom I now enjoy," Charles Hidley objected. But that, said Campbell, was not the real issue: "Hubbard wasn't arguing forms of government. Feudalism *did* spring from bandit-soldiers. Hubbard's point was that it would" (comment on a letter by Joseph W. Wilson, *ASF:* 26, September 1940). John D. Clark, a regular reader and occasional science fiction writer, agreed; "a person who holds an author responsible for his characters' political beliefs possesses . . . a remarkable amount of gullibility," Clark wrote (December 1940).

However, it may not be possible to tell this kind of story without arguing forms of government, because of an author's prior assumptions as to what is historically possible. "His initial premise that a devastating war has been raging for years until all Europe is in ruins is absurd," wrote reader Ray St. Clair (October 1940); absurd because the masses would rebel and overthrow all the old governments long before such a collapse could happen. That sounds like the classic Marxist interpretation of World War I and the Russian Revolution, as indeed it was; the devotees of science fiction, no less than the people involved in more pretentious branches of literature, were affected by the leftward intellectual currents of the 1930s. (Science fiction author and editor Frederik Pohl has described, with empathy and candor, this end-of-Depression, beginning-of-war involvement of young science fictionists with Communism, in his personal memoir, *The Early Pohl,* 1976.)

"Logical science-fiction inevitable points to the necessity of socialism, the advance of science, and the world-state," argued Donald Wollheim in the English science fiction fan magazine *Novae Terrae* for January 1938 (as quoted in Sam Moskowitz, *The Immortal Storm: A History of Science Fiction Fandom,* 1954). "These aims . . . can best be reached through adherence to the program of the Communist International." Faithful adherence to that program was inherent in Ray St. Clair's critique of

"Final Blackout." St. Clair was particularly displeased with Hubbard's depiction of the future British Communist party as stupid and corrupt, and he offered in rebuttal the present effective performance of Communism in the Soviet Union— and in the Red army, which, St. Clair noted, had recently "smashed the Mannerheim Line in Finland—a feat pronounced impossible by all the other generals in Europe."

These lines were of course written during the Russo-German truce of 1939–41, a time when the U.S. Communist party was distributing a pamphlet which said that "The Yanks Are Not Coming" to fight in another of Europe's imperialist wars. Ray St. Clair took the same hard-lining view: "It is particularly bad that Astounding should print pro-war propaganda of this kind because most of your readers are young men of draft age who may be called upon to shed their blood in a foreign land for the defense of the British Empire. . . . I hope that you print this letter, but I have my doubts; we are in times now when it takes courage to speak out."

But John Campbell loved nothing better than a good roaring argument, and he did print St. Clair's letter—adding a caption: "Ye Gods! The utter desolation of 'Final Blackout' called pro-war propaganda!" Anti-Communist readers rose to the bait. One of them (S. Murray Moore III, in "Brass Tacks" for December 1940), contemplating service in the United States Army as a second lieutenant, ominously remarked that he could "think of no greater pleasure than to have St. Clair in a platoon under my command."

The unfortunate example of the Mannerheim Line drew particularly sarcastic comment from readers. "Mr. St. Clair could hardly have picked a worse example to prove the prowess of the Red Army than their heroic defense of Russia against the invading hordes of Finnish capitalists," Caleb Northrop wrote (December 1940). "The fact that, after months of trying, with an absurdly vast preponderance of man-power, artillery, airplanes, and tanks, they finally broke through the Finns' modest little strip of barbed wire and blockhouses does not prove them mighty warriors." As for St.

Clair's contention that members of the Soviet Communist party were both able and incorruptible, Northrop reminded *Astounding*'s readers that, unfortunately, they had heard that argument before, prior to the Moscow purge trials of 1937. "Then it transpired that a lot of these wonderful men . . . were in fact spies, wreckers, slimy traitors, vile Trotskyist-Rykhovist-Bukharinist-leftist-rightist deviationists, and had to be liquidated. Now again we hear what wonderful men the survivors are."

Finally, Northrop argued, the author of "Final Blackout" was not really a Fascist sympathizer. He was "a kind of philosophical anarchist, with a naive belief that the military are a superior and altruistic lot who can be trusted to set things to rights" when the corrupt civilian politicians have brought society to disaster. "On the fallacy of this last belief, at least," Northrop temperately concluded, "Mr. St. Clair and I can get together."

III

Although Spengler's *Decline of the West* had not yet appeared when Jack London wrote "The Scarlet Plague," London clearly implied a similar, basically antiprogressive philosophy of history. "All things pass," the story's senile, bare-shanked philosopher concludes. "Only remain cosmic force and matter, ever in flux, ever acting and reacting and realizing the eternal types—the priest, the soldier, and the king." Still, even from that bleak perspective, the rout of civilization ought logically to be followed one day by a rally. In *The Shape of Things to Come*, the rally comes with impressive speed, for H. G. Wells could never stray very far from the vision of a World State, which was his lifelong holy grail. By the 1960s, as his future historian's narrative continues, internationally organized technicians and airmen are already taking over oil wells, power stations, landing fields, and mines, thereby creating a skeletal planet-wide government; by 1978 it has a World Council. Unlike the decline and fall of the Roman

Empire, which spread over so many generations that nobody could fully grasp what was happening, this new collapse and its ensuing Dark Ages turn out to be mercifully brief: "People who could remember the plentiful and relatively stable times between 1924 and 1928 were still only at the riper end of middle age in 1960" (if they survived), and in their old age they could be participants in the first true World State.

The Indian-like culture in "By the Waters of Babylon" is evidently destined to take longer to recover, but by the end of Benét's tale it has at least taken the first step. Although he concedes that "perhaps in the old days they ate knowledge too fast," John, son of John prophesies that one day the rest of his people will cross the great river to the Place of the Gods, and study the books and tools that remain there: "We must build again," the story concludes.

The same theme of rebirth out of a new barbarism characterized much magazine science fiction. Nelson Bond's tawny young priestess Meg reappeared on the cover of *Astounding* for February 1941, with Daiv, the male consort she had met in the first story; she stands resplendent in deerskins while he paddles their raft toward a vine-shrouded Statue of Liberty. The new story, "Magic City," details their adventures together in the ruins of New York, which their society superstitiously believes to be the special abode of the great god Death Himself. But at the story's end, as they pore over a cache of medical books they have found in what used to be the library of St. Luke's Hospital, they are learning that Death is not to be fought with charms and incantations, but with "boiled water . . . , and fresh air, and cleanliness." "In these books it tells the ways in which to do battle with Him," says Daiv. "These magics are called by strange names—serum, and vaccination, and physic. But the way of each is told in these books. One day we shall understand all the mysteries, and Death's hand will be stayed."

Such an attitude, basically positivist and technocratic, was in full accord with the spirit of Gernsbackian science fiction. It was in accord also, some might have added, with the spirit of

America; with the nation's traditional "can do" attitude and with its founding fathers' historical optimism. Thomas Jefferson would have been mortified at the thought that his graven image might some day be worshiped by savages as the high god Taamuz. "I will not believe our labors are lost," he wrote to his old colleague and antagonist John Adams on September 12, 1821—at a moment when the outlook for liberty and enlightenment in Europe was in fact quite bad. "We have seen, indeed, once within the records of history, a complete eclipse of the human mind continuing for centuries," Jefferson conceded. However, should it start to happen again, "should the same northern hordes, allured again by the corn, wine, and oil of the south, be able again to settle their swarms in the countries of their growth, the art of printing alone, and the vast dissemination of books, will maintain the mind where it is, and raise the conquering ruffians to the level of the conquered, instead of degrading these to that of their conquerors."

In a similar spirit, some readers of the tales about future barbarism that appeared in American science fiction magazines reacted negatively to the idea that humanity could fall so low as the authors prophesied. "For the life of me I can't see why our social-science fictioners so often throw the world back to primitivism," wrote Richard Rafael after reading Bond's "Magic City" (letter in *Astounding*: 27, May 1941). "Can't they imagine a non-machine culture without talking in terms of the hairy apes?" Reader Rafael gave short shrift to Meg and Daiv: "Why must we always have Rousseau's Noble Savage, with his biceps, his stone ax and his mate, crawling around the ruins of mighty Nyawk or Chikgo? After all, don't you think a post-Euro-American Age would at least start in on the level of, say, Rome?"

The science fiction writer L. Sprague DeCamp (known more recently for his judicious biography of H. P. Lovecraft, 1975) shared Richard Rafael's skepticism. "I've been wondering for a long time just how far down our civilization *could* lapse; to the 'Final Blackout' level, the 'Magic City' level, or what?" DeCamp wrote in response to the Rafael letter ("Brass Tacks" for July 1941). "I doubt whether we could really get back to the good old stone hatchet. Reason: too much printed matter floating around, which would be virtually impossible to destroy entirely, even without Time Capsules." Sprague DeCamp had earlier expressed the same Jeffersonian optimism in a humorous novel, *Lest Darkness Fall* (first published in *Unknown:* II, December 1939; first hard-cover publication 1941). This was a tale of renaissance made retroactive. Hurled backward in time to a point just after the fall of Rome, when Western civilization has begun to crumble, a twentieth-century American undertakes single-handedly to prevent the Dark Ages from happening at all.

DeCamp's Martin Padway (Latinized as Martinus Paduei) is obviously modeled on Mark Twain's *Connecticut Yankee in King Arthur's Court.* But DeCamp avoided one major implausibility that can be found in Twain's classic. Padway is not an omnicompetent genius—able, as does Sir Boss at Camelot, to conjure up modern machine tooling and metallurgy out of thin air. (How, for example, would an ordinary car driver tell a preindustrial mechanic who had never seen an automobile how to build one?) Instead, DeCamp's hero has the bare minimal skills necessary to survive in that turbulent society at all: he is a graduate student in archeology who, when he finds himself in sixth-century Rome, is able to comprehend spoken vulgar Latin!

To operate as a free agent, a matter of some importance if he expects any leverage upon the future, Padway acquires sufficient working capital by "inventing" distilled liquor and double-entry bookkeeping. Then our hero proceeds to introduce some improvements that the handicraft industry and subsistence economy of that era might actually have been able to assimilate: a semaphore system, a simple telescope, the sterilization of bandages by boiling, and—above all—printing: "Not even the most diligently destructive barbarian can extirpate the written word from a culture wherein the *minimum* edition of most books is fifteen hundred copies," Padway

muses. "There are just too many books." By the end of the
story these modest innovations have changed the course of
history; they have prevented the coming of the Dark Ages,
and with them a thousand years of superstition, starvation,
and disease.

As in this imagined past, so in a possible future. "In my
version of Our Barbarous Descendants, I think I'll allow the
intrepid explorers of the ruins of mighty Nawk-on-the-Huzn
guns at least," DeCamp declared in his "Brass Tacks" letter.
"You can have guns, clocks, schooners, and large-scale gov-
ernmental organization without a highly integrated and
mechanized industrial civilization. It's been done." Other
readers, however, were not so sure. Bob Camden (*Astounding:*
28, December 1941) disagreed with DeCamp's rationalist
judgment that the persistence of books would be the salvation
of man: "Once civilization loses her grip on him, he slips fast
and far. The printed page would do little to retard him. . . .
Even without a wholesale destruction of books, it would take
only one generation for the greater masses to forget how to
read."

DeCamp's fellow writer and lifelong friend, P. Schuyler
Miller, also disagreed with DeCamp (and Jefferson) on this
point: "Illiteracy would spread faster, I think, than the loss of
books; if our culture reached a stage where reading was not
useful, and where all available time and effort were needed to
keep alive, reading might be lost even with some books on
hand" (letter in "Brass Tacks" for October 1941). Miller did
not add that such a stage might well be reached *without* a loss
of machine technology, given certain trends in that technology (e.g., television) as reinforced by some of the doctrines
taught in American colleges of education; that, indeed, a
highly mechanized civilization might be able to coexist with
mass functional illiteracy. Such a world is the setting of "Null-
ABC" by H. Beam Piper and John J. McGuire, published in
the educational wasteland of the 1950s (*Astounding:* 50, February 1953). Piper and McGuire described a world of the future
that has helicopters, antibiotics, video telephones, and depart-

ment stores—but in which 90 percent of the people can neither read nor write. It is a tricky question, not answerable in simple Gernsbackian terms, whether or not such a society should be classified as "barbarian."

The barbarism envisioned in 1941, however, was far more raw and primary. The really critical factor, Miller argued in his letter to *Astounding,* would not be the loss of books or of the knowledge of previous culture, but "the practical physical result of any very radical backward change in our economy." If, for example, the present food distribution system broke down, so that a "wave of hungry urbanites spreads from every city . . . in search of anything that will keep them alive," not even the harshest of martial law might suffice to keep the population from crashing back to the level that the continent had been able to support at the time when the Indian ruled the land. "Cultures do backslide," Schuyler Miller insisted. "The question is, as I see it, whether . . . we have reached too high a pinnacle to hit bottom before we can stop ourselves, and whether we would immediately climb back and continue climbing." Despite Stephen Vincent Benét's hopeful conclusion, "We must build again," Miller warned, "there are plenty of precedents for a people hitting bottom and staying there."

IV

It was the fall of 1941 by the time this debate drew to a close, and the rampaging events abroad gave the question a more than academic urgency. Leaking through the wraps of secrecy, the atomic bomb was already becoming a part of the discussion. "Next month, Anson MacDonald [Robert A. Heinlein] presents a story about an irresistible weapon—'Solution Unsatisfactory,' and that title is the Editor's," Campbell wrote in his magazine's "In Times to Come" column for April 1941. The solution was unsatisfactory because a weapon which could be easily duplicated and against which there could be no real defense seemed to pose an intolerable political choice—total tyranny or total destruction.

"MacDonald suggests that the weapon will come—and

come in about three years," Campbell went on. "Personally, *I'm most desperately afraid he's absolutely correct.*" Then he asked his readers for their suggestions as to how to get a satisfactory solution that did not involve either a ruthless, worldwide police state with power to suppress any potential user of the weapon other than itself (and in that case, Heinlein asked, *quis custodiet ipsos custodes?*) or, alternatively, " a chaos ending only when the simplest industrial facilities—even the one-man shop—have been wiped out." Stephen Vincent Benét's war of the gods, with "fire falling out of the sky and a mist that poisoned," began to seem terrifyingly near.

In the foreground of that imagined war of the gods, always, was the existent war going on among men. It was a grim time to be reading Edward Gibbon's classic *Decline and Fall of the Roman Empire,* as young Isaac Asimov had recently been doing. On August 1, 1941, Asimov was on a New York subway train en route to a story conference with Campbell. Above ground, on the other side of the planet, Germany's gray legions were storming past Smolensk, fifty-five miles due north of the village where Asimov had been born—a world-shaking event that was personal enough in import to prompt dark meditation about cycles of decline and fall. Understandably distracted by the Nazi invasion of the Soviet Union, and what its apparent success implied, Asimov was having difficulty getting on with his science fiction writing. At the same time he did not like to walk into John Campbell's office without an idea. What he came up with on that subway ride was a story to be written against the background of the slow fall of a galactic empire, in effect a projection of Gibbon out upon the stars. When this idea was broached, "Campbell caught fire," Asimov reports, and together that day they worked out the plan for what was to become the immensely popular *Foundation* series.

"In telling future-history I always felt it wisest to be guided by past-history," the author has since written (in *The Early Asimov,* 1972), and the decline and fall of the Roman Empire seemed terrifyingly relevant at a moment in modern history when nation after nation of Western civilization seemed to be crashing in ruins. But this was to be a decline and fall with a difference. Like the aged philosopher-historian Charles Melkart in Jack Williamson's "Breakdown" (discussed in chapter 8), the savant Hari Seldon in Isaac Asimov's "Foundation" (*Astounding:* 29, May 1942) has discovered the rigorous laws by which the course of history can be predicted. And exact prediction, in science, generally implies some possibility of control.

Seldon, like Melkart—or like Gustave DeWindt in H. G. Wells's *Shape of Things to Come,* whose imagined book that blueprints the coming Modern State is published in 1942, while the "last war cyclone" is already whirling mankind into barbarism—comes on the scene when his society is already on its downward plunge. Seldon might even have accepted Melkart's pessimistic judgment that "cultures must reach the point of breakdown before they can breed men able to understand them." But it is not yet too late, in Asimov's declining galactic empire, for men consciously and rationally to *shorten* the oncoming Dark Age. Hari Seldon and his associates assemble a corps of scholars and technicians (the "Foundation" of the title) and establish them on a planet out at the end of the galaxy, safe from the Galactic Empire's convulsive death-throes, where they and their children's children will function as the nucleus—"chrysalis," to use Arnold Toynbee's term—for a renascent civilization.

As story follows story in this series, the Foundation wins victory after victory over the Empire's barbarian successor-states—and, in an episode paralleling the East Roman Emperor Justinian's effort to reconquer Italy for Byzantium, over the sinking Empire itself. The stories are told from the point of view of a people who believe that the stars in their courses are fighting for them, and despite the backdrop of decline and fall, the immediate message of the "Foundation" stories is one of technocratic and political optimism.

However, even Asimov—as witness his very popular story "Nightfall" (*Astounding:* 28, September 1941)—could surren-

der at times to a mood of tragic, deterministic cyclism. Moreover, the first two of Asimov's "Foundation" stories appeared
in *Astounding* in the same year with Jack Williamson's "Breakdown"; with Joseph E. Kelleam's "The Eagles Gather" (April
1942), a tale of a talk-fest and shoot-out among four unemployed mercenary soldiers from an interstellar war, thrown
out of work by the collapse of civilization's energy supply (as
one of them explains, "When the war lords ran out of uranium, they sent me home"); and with Ross Rocklynne's "Jack-
daw" (August 1942), in which highly evolved alien visitors, for
whom war is unimaginable, search the ruins of an obviously
war-devastated Earth, trying vainly to deduce what might
have happened. In 1942, as always in science fiction—outside
the Soviet Union, whose vision of the future has always
demanded a happy ending—optimism and pessimism
remained in uneasy dialectical tension; and it was not always
possible, as at the end of Williamson's "Breakdown," to thwart
history's decree by escaping out among the stars.

The tension was acted out with unusual vividness in "There
Shall Be Darkness" by C. L. Moore (*Astounding:* 28, February
1942). Moore borrowed her plot from another Stephen Vincent Benét short story, "The Last of the Legions" (*Saturday
Evening Post:* 210, November 6, 1937). That tale by Benét is
narrated from the standpoint of a centurion in a proud
Roman infantry outfit, the XX (Valeria Victrix) Legion, which
is pulling out of Britain after a stay of 358 years—well aware
that "when the eagles go, Britain falls," and that "afterwards,
there follow darkness and the howling peoples." Catherine
Moore transformed Stephen Benét's Roman legionary hero
into a brooding Scotsman named James Douglas; perhaps he
is descended from the Pictish hordes who came over Hadrian's wall after the legions had left. Douglas commands the
last Terrestrial Patrol on Venus; like the Valeria Victrix in the
Benét story, it has been called home after three centuries as an
army of occupation.

The civilization-wrecking barbarians in Moore's version of
the tale come not from the outer lands beyond the Rhine and

the Danube, but from the outer worlds beyond the asteroids. Even Benét's imagined Greek character Agathocles, with his sardonic comment as a son of an older, previously fallen civilization to the effect that now it is Rome's turn, reappears as a Martian trader named Ghej (Martian civilization, as noted in chapter 3, was commonly assumed in science fiction to have been older than Earth's), who prophesies by retrospection in the same fashion as Agathocles: "I know about Rome and America and the other great fallen empires of Earth."

C. L. Moore, however, gave her version of "The Last of the Legions" a sharp turn in an optimistic direction. At the story's climax, its Earthman hero and the native Venutian guerilla leader, who during most of the story has been trying to assassinate him, are brought together by the old Martian trader, who informs them both that "the barbarians have come." They promptly bury the hatchet and together smash the first invasion. It is as if the commander of Benét's XXth Legion, before marching off to Rome, had effected an alliance between the Romanized Britons and the Gaelic tribes beyond the Wall, and then helped them to repulse the first landings by the Angles, Jutes, and Saxons. Moreover, Moore's Earthman hero has a native Venutian mistress, Quanna, from whose point of view part of the story is told. Eventually he takes her back to Earth with him; Benét's centurion, in contrast, knows no such consolation as he follows "a hairy general to an unknown battle, over the rim of the world." Different races and cultures may be able, Moore's story implied, to adjourn their conflicts and work together against the onrushing cultural darkness; and if a dominant people's time in history is over, they may be able at least to pass the torch of civilization on to a younger folk.

In her serial "Judgment Night," however (*Astounding*: 31, August 1943; 32, September 1943), Moore voiced second and colder thoughts. A galactic empire as vast as Asimov's goes thundering into civil war, from which neither last-minute alliances nor encyclopedic Foundations can save it. "You and your people had gone too far already along the road all

humans go," the representatives of humanity are told at the
end of the story. "Every nation digs its own grave," says the
envoy of an aloof, godlike, nonhuman species, "and we are
weary of mankind."

V

From the wars out among the stars, the writers with whom
John Campbell had worked since taking the helm at *Astounding*
in 1938 now turned their attention to the war here on
earth. L. Ron Hubbard, the author of "Final Blackout" (but
not yet of Dianetics), got a commission in the Navy; so did L.
Sprague DeCamp, the author of "Lest Darkness Fall."
DeCamp and Robert Heinlein went to work on top-secret
technology for the Naval Air Experiment Station in Philadel-
phia, and Isaac Asimov was recruited to join them there. Jack
Williamson, after brooding through a series of stories (under
the pseudonym of Will Stewart) that projected balance-of-
power politics out into the Solar System—with an oriental
empire on Venus, a Martian Reich, an Anglo-American capitalist Earth, and a Union of Soviet Satellites of Jupiter—
chucked it all and at the age of thirty-four became an Air
Corps weatherman (at a larger annual income, incidentally,
than he had ever earned in his previous fourteen years as a
prolific and successful science fiction writer). Theodore Sturgeon took a job in Puerto Rico as a bulldozer operator, out of
which experience he fashioned the exciting tale "Killdozer!"
(see chapter 6); Henry Kuttner joined the Medical Corps;
Lester del Rey, turned down for military service, went to work
as a sheetmetal worker for McDonald Aircraft. When they all
came back after the war, the situation in which they wrote had
radically changed. The question before the house was no
longer whether the next major war would throw the human
race back into barbarism, but whether it would survive at all.

In the first postwar years, a spate of atomic doom stories hit
the pulp magazines, especially *Astounding*, such as "The
Nightmare" by Chandler Davis (*Astounding*: 37, April, May

1946); "Tomorrow's Children" by F. N. Waldrop and Poul Anderson (Anderson's first published story, incidentally) (*ASF:* 39, March 1947); "Thunder and Roses" by Theodore Sturgeon (*ASF:* 40, November 1947); and "That Only a Mother," the first story by Judith Merril (*ASF:* 41, June 1948). But such war parables, well done though many of them were, generated a backlash against this kind of theme. "People are getting atomic warfare thrown at them from all angles these days," one Canadian reader complained. "I for one am heartily sick of it. You are no longer a prophet crying in the wilderness." Science fiction readers, of all people, *least* needed to be warned how dangerous nuclear energy was. "I've been reading enough of this type of story to have a reasonable idea of what ravening energies lie in the heart of the atom, and I want a bit of pure escapism" (W. N. McBain, letter in "Brass Tacks," *ASF:* 42, September 1948). Obligingly, editor Campbell replied: "We have specified to our authors that the 'atomic doom' stories are not wanted, for precisely the reasons you give."

In 1950, when *Astounding*'s supremacy in the science fiction field was challenged for the first time since the days of Hugo Gernsback and T. O'Conor Sloane, Campbell's new competitor Horace Gold pointedly declined to publish in his new magazine *Galaxy* any stories on the gloom-and-doom theme. "The shape humanity is in is cause for worry, I believe, but not the kind of paralyzing terror that clutches science fiction writers in particular, every time they think of it," Gold explained (editorial in *Galaxy:* 3, October 1951). "Over 90% of stories submitted," he complained in another *Galaxy* editorial (January 1952), "still nag away at atomic, hydrogen and bacteriological war, the post-atomic world, reversion to barbarism, mutant children killed because they have only ten toes and fingers instead of twelve. . . . Look, fellers, the end isn't here yet."

The dreadful alternative to nuclear destruction, however, as posed by some of the stories published in *Galaxy* in its first few years, seemed to be a regimented, nominally peaceful, but

sociologically insane hell-on-earth: the book-burning world of
Ray Bradbury's "The Fireman" (see chapter 5); the automated, dismally lowbrow civilization of "The Marching
Morons" by C. M. Kornbluth (*Galaxy:* 2, April 1951); a stable
society in which total schizophrenia is the norm, in "Beyond
Bedlam" by Wyman Guin (August, 1951); or a world literally
ruled by Madison Avenue, in "Gravy Planet" by C. M. Kornbluth and Frederik Pohl (see chapter 10). This theme of
worldwide future tyranny draws science fiction writers again
and again. Sometimes they seek to exorcise the horror of that
future by invoking earlier prophets, such as Henry David
Thoreau (in "'Repent, Harlequin!' Said the Ticktockman," by
Harlan Ellison, *Galaxy:* 24, December 1965), or Alexis de
Tocqueville (in "Above This Race of Men" by Robert F.
Young, *Amazing:* 49, January 1976). Brave and wise as are the
words of Tocqueville and Thoreau, their invocation in stories
like these betrays science fiction's ingrained nostalgia at its
most desperate; for many of these ugly future societies, like
that of George Orwell's *1984,* seem depressingly invulnerable
to being overthrown. If the expectable civilized future must be
bleak as one of these, then perhaps a homely, human barbarism such as that depicted by Jack London and Stephen
Vincent Benét would actually be an improvement. If, for
example, the grim civilization of *1984* were one day to collapse to the cave-dweller level, would its Julias and Winston
Smiths be markedly any worse off?

In any case, the threat of atomic destruction was not to be
assuaged by the hopeful words of Horace Gold's editorials.
The problem was now built into our future history. Gold
himself, in his repudiation of the nuclear war theme in fiction
he was willing to buy, hedged somewhat; Fritz Leiber's dark
prophecies "Coming Attraction" and "Appointment in
Tomorrow" (*Galaxy:* 1, November 1950; 2, July 1951) were set
in a world following just such a war. Gold even published a
tale or two in the classic tradition of barbarian reversion à la
London and Benét. The opening lines of "Bridge Crossing,"
by Dave Dryfoos (May 1951) recalled the beginning of "The

Scarlet Plague": "In 1849, the mist that sometimes rolled through the Golden Gate was known as fog. In 2149, it had become far more frequent, and was known as smog. By 2349, it was fog again."

Meanwhile, "mainstream" fiction had taken up the atomic doom theme also, as in Philip Wylie's *Tomorrow!* and Pat Frank's *Atlas, Babylon.* Eventually, the subject found its way to the motion picture screen in films like *On The Beach* and *Doctor Strangelove.* Campbell and Gold might quibble, but the subject would not go away; and Anthony Boucher, who edited *Astounding*'s other effective new competitor in the 1950s, *The Magazine of Fantasy and Science Fiction,* was quite willing to gaze into—and beyond—the nuclear fires. In 1955 (vol. 8, April), Boucher published the memorable tale "A Canticle for Leibowitz," by Walter M. Miller, which fused the newly typical post-atomic-war theme with the older, previously explored subject of reversion to the Dark Ages. Miller's story dealt the technocratic materialism of Hugo Gernsback—and of H. G. Wells—a punishing blow. It assumed that the only social institution able to survive the holocaust of a nuclear war would be the same one that had survived the raids of the Goths and Vandals: the Roman Catholic Church. Sequels to "Canticle," gathered up with the title story in a critically well-received book (1959), would carry the parallel with post-Roman history still further. A future Texarkana and a future Laredo emerge as quarrelsome early-Renaissance-style city-states, and the cycle continues on to modernity. At the end of the novel, a new civilization, possessing spaceships, news media reporters, and twenty-lane highways, succumbs to *another* nuclear war!

For a literature supposedly committed to a positivist, onward-and-upward philosophy of history, science fiction seems drawn in spite of itself to historical cyclism; the Nicholas Van Rijn and Dominic Flandry stories by Poul Anderson, which also began to appear in the 1950s, are a case in point. Nor need a future downswing in such a cycle be precipitated by grand catastrophe. Civilization might fall, argued Gordon R. Dickson in "The Iron Years" (*Fantasy and Science Fiction:* 47,

October 1974), neither from external natural causes such as plague nor by the self-inflicted apocalypse of nuclear war, but simply because "all the prosaic, predictable things"—crime, inflation, and so on—"had come to a head at once," beyond any possibility of rational human control.

Science fiction may have found historical cyclism congenial by analogy with the logic of science itself; if planetary orbits, star formation, and organic life all follow rules of periodicity, why not human history as well? But science fiction also may have picked up a moral judgment from some of the philosophers of history (Vico, Ibn Khaldun, perhaps Toynbee), namely, that periodic social collapse and barbarian reversion are necessary for the rejuvenation—perhaps indeed for the survival—of mankind. Robert Abernathy, in "Heirs Apparent" (*F&SF:* 6, June 1954), hinted that such a cultural recycling might be history's eventual drastic solution to the Cold War.

In a village in a remote corner of Russia, after a devastating Soviet-American nuclear exchange under which both governments have broken down, a surviving Communist party activist and an American flyer who was shot down in the fighting work together through a stormy Russian winter, combining Marxist dialectic and Yankee know-how in an effort to keep one small shred of civilized society going. "You and we, the Americans and Russians—we fought our war for the control of Civilization, and very nearly wrecked it in the process," the American lectures the Russian (who is nominally his captor). "But on both sides we were and are on the side of Civilization. That's what counts now." What neither man yet knows is that industrial civilization, of either the capitalist or socialist variety, is already a lost cause.

Out on the vast Asian steppes, the Nomad culture that Europe had met and beaten back in the Middle Ages has begun to return (is something similar also happening on the trans-Mississippi high plains? the American wonders). Nomad brigands attack and destroy the fledgling town, on the logical ground that a settlement big enough to be seen from the air would only attract whatever roving bombers remain at large. The Communist leader, Nikolai Bogomazov, unable to believe that his orderly world of five-year-plans is dead forever, resists and is cut down by a Nomad horseman's saber blow; the American handyman, Leroy Smith, and the dispossessed Russian villagers prepare to trudge off in the general direction of Europe. "Down by the river the last sparks were dying" from their town's smoldering ashes, the story concludes. "Somewhere far off in the steppe shuddered a mournful cry that Smith did not know—perhaps it was the howl of a wolf." When Chairman Mao quoted the old Chinese proverb, "The East Wind shall prevail over the West Wind," this somber pastoral scene was not at all what he had had in mind! "In the West the light faded, and night fell with the darkness sweeping on illimitable wings out of Asia."

Chapter 10

The Dwindling Sphere
The Finite Limits and the Spirit of Man

There are parts of Asia Minor, of Northern Africa, of Greece, and even of Alpine Europe, where the operation of causes set in action by man has brought the earth to a desolation almost as complete as that of the moon. . . . The earth is fast becoming an unfit home for its noblest inhabitant, and another era of equal human crime and human improvidence . . . would reduce it to such a condition of impoverished productiveness, of shattered surface, of climatic excess, as to threaten the depravation, barbarism, and perhaps even extinction of the species.

—George Perkins Marsh, *Man and Nature* (1864)

Not at a crisis of nervousness do we stand now, not at a time for the vacillations of flabby souls; but at a great turning point in the history of scientific thought, at a crisis such as occurs but once in a thousand years. . . . Standing at this point, with the vista of future achievements before us, we should be happy that it is our lot to live at this time and to participate in the creation of the tomorrow.

—V. I. Vernadskii, 1932 (as quoted in A. P. Vinogradov, ed., *Chemistry of the Earth's Crust:* I, 1968)

257

"And now began a grim game of hide-and-seek. Hargry was evidently determined to smash the entire city to the ground and thus destroy all hiding places."

Fourth episode of "The Man Who Awoke," by Laurence Manning. *Wonder Stories,* **58 (June, 1933), p. 58.**

M YSTERY LURKS AT THE FIELD OF VISION'S EDGE. When the eye turns to look upon it directly, it draws back into the dark. We have seen and mapped and explored, driving the unknowns before us as we moved. No longer may we expect Utopia to turn up on some yet-uncharted continent here on Earth; Austin Tappan Wright's beautifully wrought *Islandia* (1946) was doubtlessly the last in that historic line. No longer may an Edgar Rice Burroughs send Tarzan and his friends in quest of ancient hidden cities in Africa; no longer, in a brutally modernized Tibet, may a James Hilton find his Shangri-La; no longer may a Howard Phillips Lovecraft people the inner fastnesses of Antarctica with frightful nonhuman entities from the stars. No longer may Ray Bradbury's thin, fragile-boned Martians with their yellow coin eyes flit through the porcelain cities' dusk; and not yet, except speculatively, can we count on transcending the speed of light to look for similarly elusive beings on planets orbiting other suns. Nor is it yet certain we can thwart the flow of entropy to hunt for them by time machine.

But the oldest and simplest of all literary gambits for thrusting into the unknown is well within the reach of present or near-future technology. If we may not yet journey wide-awake to the far shores of space and time, perhaps we may sink into sleep and get there anyhow. The idea has deep roots in myth (the Seven Sleepers, Rip Van Winkle, Frederick Barbarossa), and it lent itself easily to the purposes of science fiction. Thus the hero of *Looking Backward,* by Edward Bellamy (1887), put into hypnotic trance in a subterranean sleeping chamber and then forgotten for over a century, awakens to discover that Utopia has arrived in—of all unlikely places—Proper Boston. H. G. Wells used the same device in *When the Sleeper Wakes* (1899); the pioneering feminist writer Charlotte Perkins Gilman used it in her utopian novel "Moving the Mountain" (serialized in *The Forerunner,* 1910); the Marxist literary critic Granville Hicks used it in *The First to Awaken* (1940); the comedian Woody Allen used it in his antic motion picture *Sleeper* (1975). The pulps of the 1930s used it regularly. Dr.

Sloane, editor of *Amazing Stories* between 1929 and 1938, may have doubted the practicability of interplanetary travel (see chapter 2), but he had no ground for quibbling at the possibility of suspended animation. Similarly, Hugo Gernsback, during his tenure at *Wonder Stories,* published "The Man Who Awoke," by Laurence Manning (*Wonder Stories:* 4, March 1933), which probed the future Rip Van Winkle fashion; it was the first in a popular series, which indeed can be found in print in paperback today.

Not all of these sleepers wake up to find themselves in Utopia. H. G. Wells's protagonist certainly didn't; and Laurence Manning's hero is somewhat disconcerted when he does not find himself in the supermechanized metropolis so many of his contemporaries had been forecasting. Instead, he emerges from his burial chamber into a grove of tall trees—a forest that stretches to the tip of Manhattan Island. Its inhabitants, however, are not the postcivilization barbarians we observed in chapter 9. They have aircraft, television, and decent medical care. But they use their technology sparingly, and they live off the products of the forest they have grown and tended. They bake with flour ground from nuts, and pick mushrooms grown on felled logs; they run their airships on wood alcohol and lubricate them with pine pitch. This ecologically cautious tribe is mightily unimpressed with "the false civilization of Waste" from which the reanimate hero says he has come. For what ought they to thank the people of his era? the Chief Forester asks him:

> "For exhausting the coal supplies of the world? For leaving us no petroleum for our chemical factories? For destroying the forests on whole mountain ranges and letting the soil erode into the valleys? Shall we thank them, perhaps, for the Sahara or the Gobi deserts?"
>
> "But the Sahara and the Gobi were deserts five thousand years before my time."
>
> "I do not know what you mean by 'your' time. But if so, all the more reason you should have learned a lesson from those deserts."

"In the 1970s," comments Isaac Asimov (in *Before the Golden Age,* 1974) "everyone is aware of, and achingly involved in, the energy crisis. Manning was aware of it forty years ago, and because he was, I was, and so, I'm sure, were many thoughtful young science fiction readers." If pulp science fiction was "escape literature"—a term Asimov obviously resents—it was a most peculiar kind of escape. From a science fictionist's point of view, Asimov often argues in his science column for *The Magazine of Fantasy and Science Fiction,* the true escapist is the person who still, forty years later, has not really acknowledged that an ecology-energy crisis exists—or who, having once acknowledged it, lost interest as soon as the media directed his or her attention toward something else.

Granted, few science fictionists of the 1930s and 1940s grasped the complexity of the problem. "We were all very high on ecology in those days," Leigh Brackett has reminisced, "but it was all so simple." They were not, however, so simple as to assume that to be pro-"ecology" you had to go back to nature and scrap your technology altogether. The Gernsback-Campbell machine mystique in science fiction was usually too strong to allow for a Greening of America unless the civilization were to collapse as a whole. That technophile bias associated with Campbell and Gernsback was, however, compatible with the "conservation" ethic that long preceded the more recent "ecology" bandwagon; an ethic variously expressed in the poetic New Deal documentary films on soil erosion (*The River, The Plow That Broke the Plains*) and in the activities of those civilized Proper Bostonians of the Appalachian Mountain Club, who hacked hiking trails through scrubby Eastern forests and condemned the wasteful practices of the lumber and paper companies. The argument of Stuart Chase's *Rich Land, Poor Land* (1936), with its vivid portrayal of the earth butchery surrounding a small smelter town, was carried directly into science fiction in tales like "Sterile Planet" by Nat Schachner (*Astounding:* 19, July 1937). For his first two and a half pages, before even beginning to tell his readers a story, Schachner preached an ecological sermon to them:

Deaf to all warnings, heedless of the future, [man] had
denuded the forests, plowed up the soil, meddled recklessly
with the delicate balances of nature. This, in his vanity, he had
called the march of civilization; and an outraged earth struck
back. . . .

The matted roots of the trees, the tangled bottoms of the
prairie grasses no longer held the rain in their intertwined
fingers, to soak slowly and gently into fertile loam. Instead, the
falling waters ran off in quick, scouring torrents, digging huge
gullies in the land, bearing countless millions of tons of crop-
bearing soil into the oceans. Then drought came, and heat, and
dust storms, that lifted the dried and powdered remnants to
the heavens, scattered them afar, leaving naked to the
parching sun the sterile sands beneath. . . . The deserts were
on the march!

Men fell back before their resistless sweep, huddled in the
few remaining well-favored places, fought one another for a
foothold, harried and maimed and slew for the too-scanty
food. The strong drove out the weak; the cunning evicted the
simple; the ruthless slaughtered the mild, and gained for
themselves temporary possession of the few oases that were left
on all the earth.

I showed this Biblically cadenced passage in 1971 to a very
bright, very radical young professor who was strongly committed to the "new" ecology movement; at that time he was
urging everyone he encountered to read *The Closing Circle*,
Barry Commoner's powerful indictment of industrial pollution. This activist entirely agreed, as a matter of course, with
Schachner's sentiments; but, he added, "that's only science
fiction." One can well imagine the fury of Isaac Asimov, had
he also been present, upon hearing that fatal word "only"!

Schachner carried his extrapolation far beyond the "dust
bowls" that warned of the finiteness of our planetary
resources in the 1930s (much as energy shortages sound a
similar warning today). In Schachner's story the oceans themselves shrink into their beds, leaving the Continental Shelf
exposed. Mankind divides; the remnants of civilized man, in
possession of the remaining subsurface reservoirs, wall them-

selves into fortress cities and drive the remainder out into the Deeps, where some foul ocean water still lingers, there to revert to savagery. The oasis cities evolve into smug, self-satisfied, hierarchical states, locked within their protective force fields except for quick and well-guarded forays into the deserts to acquire needed minerals. They shut out the new barbarians, who subsist as best they can out in the former ocean beds, on the plausible ground that to admit these millions of unfortunates would only deplete the cities' own carefully rationed resources. Schachner's extrapolation, as so often in his work, was not only material but political; he made his urban oligarchs rationalize this exclusion on what amounted to racist grounds. The "haves" of the oases learn to perceive the "have nots" of the Deeps, not as fellow humans with whom they have refused to share, but as "monstrosities spawned by the fetid swamps of the ocean bed . . . beings without a spark of human intelligence or human emotion."

As the story proper gets under way after this long prologue, the inevitable rising of the have nots against the haves is about to begin:

> The hungry hordes drifted stealthily by night from the farthest deeps. . . . A million brawny savages, driven by famine, . . . in whose fumbling brains lingered the tradition of the ancestral expulsion from the oases, in whose savage breasts burned an ineradicable hatred for the fortunate inhabitants of those segregated Paradises, . . . climbed up the steep Continental shelf . . . toward the city of selfish plenty.

In the pulp shoot-out that follows, the hero—a young engineer who is a scion of New York City's hereditary aristocracy—finds himself accidentally locked outside the city's impenetrable force barrier. Previously blocked by the Manhattan power elite in his plans for ecological renewal, he decides to throw in with the savages. He does not, however, reject his own civilized training and "go native," or assume that it is morally superior to suffer and starve; instead, he undertakes to reclaim the ravaged land. Dig the salt away and

dump it on the deserts, he tells the Deeps men, for the fertile
ooze underneath can be farmed. The story ends not with a
shudder of ecological despair, like so much of the earth-doom
writings of later years, but on a triumphant note of "can do,"
more appropriate to the New Deal years when it was written:
"What man had destroyed in his selfishness and greed, man
could restore with sacrifice and courage."

II

Despite Manning's and Schachner's precedents, there were
not many stories of this specific type in the pulps during the
1930s and 1940s. When writers considered the energy question, they were usually more concerned with the social impact
of *unlimited* energy (see chapter 8) than with the social con-
strictions that might be forced upon man by a diminishing
stock of natural resources (except in an occasional story set in
the *very* far future, in which the hourglass has just about run
out of sand). They wrote—most prophetically—about the
dangers inherent in atomic power; not only as a war weapon
(see chapters 1 and 9), but also, as in Lester del Rey's powerful,
well-characterized, scientifically plausible novella "Nerves"
(Astounding: 30, September 1942), about the danger of an
uncontrolled nuclear reaction in a factory where the atom is
used for peaceful purposes. Had they reflected upon the
scarcity crisis predicted by Schachner and Manning, most of
them would probably have assumed that the release of plentiful nuclear energy would end that crisis for all time. As a
matter of fact, the hero of Manning's "The Man Who Awoke,"
in a sequel that takes him on a further sleep-jump into the
future (*Wonder Stories:* 4, April 1933), learns in his next awak-
ening that man in the meantime has learned how to unlock
the power of the atom. The material shortages faced by the
forest people he met in his first reanimation have therefore
ended; instead, man faces a challenge of political and social
control.

Occasionally, however, a writer in that era recognized that

the planet after all *is* finite; that problems of the kind Manning and Schachner described are never really solved, only postponed. Willard E. Hawkins, as he sat in a barber's chair in 1939 having his hair cut, had a flash of satiric inspiration, which he turned into a short story titled "The Dwindling Sphere" (*Astounding:* 25, March 1940). Its theme is expressed by a little boy as he watches the mighty machines that dig up ordinary rock and dirt and convert them into all man's requirements for food, clothes, and housing: "What are we going to do when this hole gets so big it takes up the whole world?" By the end of the story it is quite clear that that is exactly what is going to happen. As in Hans Christian Anderson's classic fable of the emperor's new clothes, nobody pays any attention to a wide-eyed child who sees reality exactly for what it is.

Another example from the early 1940s of this kind of concern with the finite limits was voiced by John B. Michel, a science fiction fan politically radical enough to have had an "ism" named after him ("Michelism," a special variant on the sectarian socialist politics typical of New York City in that era; it was derived partially from Technocracy). Written in collaboration with pulp editor Robert W. Lowndes, Michel's effective tale "The Inheritors" (*Future Fantasy and Science Fiction:* 3, October 1942) linked the familiar "next war" warning—as in "Final Blackout" and so on—with an ecological theme. Modern warfare, like any other industrial process, pollutes its environment. Carrying this axiom forward, Michel and Lowndes extrapolated a future in which the physics and chemistry of industrialized battle have rendered the surface of the planet uninhabitable; it has become "a great bare plain, misty, green, vapours swirling in endless writhing strings," broken only by "small, jagged ridges covered with a green slime from which pale streamers arose in slow ascent to the invisible sky." Cowering in redoubts under the surface of the earth, the surviving humans learn at the story's end that evolution has meanwhile produced an entirely new, hostile, alien life-form, adapted to the poisonous wastes of No Man's

Land. "I wonder if it'll wipe itself out in wars the way we did," one of the remnant of humanity asks—an extraordinary question with which to end a story published in flag-waving, Hitler-defying 1942.

A less lethal, or at least a cleaner, environment for the learning of hard ecological lessons was the ancient, dried-out Martian sea bottom so often described in the vivid stories of Edgar Rice Burroughs, Stanley Weinbaum, Leigh Brackett, and Ray Bradbury. In P. Schuyler Miller's memorable short story "The Cave" (*Astounding:* 30, January 1943), the severe shortage of water on desert Mars has dictated a radical revision of the biological struggle for survival. "No Martian would ever dispute the theory of evolution—it is the very core of his existence that all beasts are brothers," muses one small, beaked, black-furred nomadic wanderer that finds itself trapped in a cave during a sandstorm with divers other life-forms—including a brutal and uncomprehending Earthman. "They were all *grekka* here—all living things, united in the common battle for existence against a cruel and malignant Nature." Little noticed at the time it appeared, this story foreshadowed a major theme in science fiction two decades later. The noun *grak* (pl. *grekka*) reappeared in Robert Heinlein's *Stranger in a Strange Land* (1961) as the verb *to grok,* and in that cultic novel by Heinlein and in Frank Herbert's comparably popular *Dune* (1965), the idea of an ethic derived from water sharing on a planet acutely short of natural resources is crucial to the story.

In Schuyler Miller's modest fable, the truce in the cave is broken by the insensitive Earthman Harrigan, to whom all the other creatures present are mere animals, even if some of them can talk and build houses and keep herds; "hell," he exclaims, "parrots [can] talk and ants keep cattle." Harrigan opens his canteen, but he would never dream of sharing; and so the other beings in the cave kill him. The Earthman's fate is an object lesson: Harrigan did not share his water because, fundamentally, he could not share the Martian creatures' reverence for the delicate web that encloses all life. This is the same moral universe as that of *A Sand County Almanac,* by Aldo Leopold; of *The Desert Year,* by Joseph Wood Krutch; of *Silent Spring,* by Rachel Carson—and of Loren Eiseley, who once confessed (in an address printed in *The Key Reporter:* 28, Spring 1963) that he personally was "just primitive enough to hope that somehow, somewhere, a cardinal may still be whistling on a green bush when the last man goes blind before his man-made sun. If it should turn out that we have mishandled our own lives as several civilizations before us have done, it seems a pity that we should involve the violet and the tree frog in our departure."

On this our own planet, unlike P. Schuyler Miller's Mars or Frank Herbert's Dune, there was plenty of water, even if most of it was not very clean. The resource most acutely in need of conservation on Earth was people. After depression and world war came the postwar baby boom, and science fictionists quickly saw its ecological significance. More conventional "mainstream" culture critics during the godly Eisenhower years were prone to point to surface symptoms; to denounce, for example, the ostentatious vulgarity of Detroit-built cars rather than to worry about the fact that there were now so many more drivers. Some writers for middlebrow magazines (e.g., *Harper's*) seemed indeed to *welcome* the population surge, as a sign that America had not lost its lusty youthful vitality. But when Frederik Pohl and Cyril M. Kornbluth wrote their deservedly famous satire on the advertising agencies, *The Space Merchants* (1953, serialized as "Gravy Planet" in *Galaxy Science Fiction:* 4, June, July, August 1952), they made it clear that the future world they described is intolerably overcrowded: "It was getting on toward ten o'clock, and the consumers whose living quarters were on the stairs [of Manhattan office buildings] were beginning to drift there for the night." Moreover, the authors argued that the economic logic of such a world would positively require just such overcrowdedness. The underground opposition to the stuff-'em-with goodies regime that rules this wretched society does not consist of the traditional kind of political radicals, who had been as prone to a rhetoric of "progress," "productivity," and "development" as any of their capitalist opponents. Rather, the "connies" (short for "conservationists") are given to such acts as blowing up strip-mining machinery just as it is about to rape the topsoil. Ecology was not yet a catchword of student activists and trendy professors when this story first appeared; once more—but in a way this time that Hugo Gernsback might not have understood—the extravagant fiction of today had anticipated the cold fact of tomorrow.

And the facts of tomorrow got colder and colder. Belatedly, the mass media began to take alarm instead of satisfaction from the fact that the United States was growing at a rate comparable to that of India. By the end of the 1960s we were hearing of Zero Population Growth as a goal, and many Americans seemed to be arranging their personal lives accordingly. Science fictionists, far from relaxing into the complacency of "we told you so," redoubled their efforts, and population-explosion stories became one of the more popular forms.

An early signal was "The Census Takers," by Frederik Pohl (*Fantasy and Science Fiction:* 10, February 1956), which succinctly described a future society in America which takes it for granted that the official census enumerators, as part of their job, will kill off every three-hundredth person they count. (Those designated as surplus are impersonally referred to, in chilling bureaucratese, as Overs.) In 1965, British writer Brian Aldiss published *Earthworks,* a novel which forecast a future so desperately overcrowded that the only humanly endurable solution the hero and heroine can imagine for the population explosion is deliberately to start a global nuclear war. In 1966, Harry Harrison produced a realistic novel, *Make Room! Make Room!,* in which New York City as of 1999 has 35 million inhabitants; the story was afterward made into a fairly successful movie, *Soylent Green.* A year later Harrison followed up his novel with a laissez-faire version of Pohl's "Census Takers," titled "A Criminal Act" (*Analog:* 78, January 1967); in the society depicted in that short, stark melodrama, the birth of a surplus child automatically licenses any citizen to murder either of the parents. If this act is successful—or if the hunted in self-defense is able to kill the hunter—the population balance is considered restored. The climax in this literary trend came in 1968 in the form of a bulky blockbuster of a novel about a hideously overpopulated civilization, by another English writer, John Brunner, titled *Stand on Zanzibar.* The subject continues to challenge science fiction writers to some of their best efforts. In a compact, overcrowded, life-denying urban environment, suggests Michael Bishop in "The Samurai and the Willows" (*Fantasy and Science Fiction:* 50, February 1976), the only inhabitants spiritually able to prevail against its inhumanity may be persons conditioned by the long cultural heritage of an urban ghetto; in the story, a working-class Afro-American and a transplanted Japanese.

III

A session on science fiction at the 1968 annual meeting of the Modern Language Association brought writers like Isaac Asimov, Robert Silverberg, and Frederik Pohl before an audience of English professors, many of whom had not been accustomed to taking either science or science fiction very seriously. Pohl, who had succeeded Horace Gold as editor of *Galaxy* and its companion magazine *Worlds of If,* took the opportunity this occasion afforded for a bit of ecological preaching:

> Our air is despoiled to the point where the big debate [among scientists] is whether our massive discharge of carbon dioxide will melt the polar ice caps and drown us all, or our equally massive discharge of particulate waste . . . will screen off so much heat that we freeze. There is a third school which says that these two processes will cancel each other out, so that the air remains about the same in temperature, but is contaminated to the point of being a sort of smoggy, toxic poison gas which will strangle us. These are the optimists.

Nathan Schachner had envisioned a future fully as desper-

ate in his "Sterile Planet," three decades previously. But
Schachner, writing in the late 1930s when the American birth
rate in particular seemed to have leveled off, in many of his
stories for *Astounding* had imagined an essentially *under*popu-
lated future Earth, composed typically of walled-in city-states
separated by many miles of untamed wilderness. However,
from the late-1960s vantage point out of which Frederik Pohl
addressed the staid MLA (as reported in the scholarly journal
of science fiction, *Extrapolation:* 10, May 1969), the population
question was inescapable. "Out of every 100 pounds of living
matter on the face of this planet—whether it is whales, or
porpoises, or redwoods, or bacteria—two pounds are human
flesh," Pohl continued: "This, in turn, has its inevitable consequences, in terms of the degradation of the environment, at
least as we perceive it. I mean it's goodbye to beef steaks and
all that sort of thing. It is quite certain that we will have
inevitable mass famine affecting hundreds of millions of people in our life time, and by inevitable I mean to say it is
inevitable: meaning we can no longer avoid it."

We can no longer avoid it. Science fiction had often put its
direst predictions upon an "or else" basis, leaving a loophole
for optimism: *if* we take preventive steps, in sufficient time,
the disaster may yet be averted. To say that Israel may repent
in the nick of time and be spared, as its ancient prophets
preached again and again, is a vastly different thing from
saying—as other prophets have—that the Almighty's patience
is exhausted, and that the only thing left for us to do is to
prepare for the worst. Over most of science fiction's history,
testimony like Pohl's would have been dismissed by outsiders
as sensationalism—indeed, as mere "science fiction." But in
this crisis, as Pohl was careful to point out, the story-writers
were echoing cries from within the scientific community,
including the prestigious American Association for the
Advancement of Science; and the general media of news and
opinion, for a while at least, took respectful notice of those
cries.

So conservative an organ as the *Chicago Tribune,* for example, whose normal approach was to consider any new idea half-baked until proven otherwise, ran a straightforward editorial based on an address by Indiana geologist Lawrence Rooney at the University of Michigan: "The Party's Over." "He means that our civilization is doomed," the paper explained (*Chicago Tribune:* April 17, 1970). "We are not going to find the minerals to provide a high standard of living for 30 billion people," Rooney was quoted as saying. Meanwhile, minerals were going to become exceedingly profitable for those engaged in exploring for and developing them; but that boom, the geologist prophesied, "will be bittersweet, like the sale of coffins during an epidemic." The newspaper's own conclusion was more cautious, but melancholy nonetheless: "We have neither the scientific self-confidence nor the dogged optimism to say that Dr. Rooney is wrong."

Radical student activists of that time routinely included the rape of the Earth among the atrocities against which they demonstrated. On this issue, therefore, coupon-clipping, business-suited Republicans and long-haired, patch-garmented youths quite unexpectedly found themselves on the same side. Indeed, when some demonstrators at Northern Illinois University (sixty miles from Chicago) that same spring chained themselves to trees that were about to be cut down—to make room for construction of a *life sciences* building, a horrid irony!—the *Chicago Tribune* ran a boxed editorial on Page One, titled "Right On, Kids!" The paper offered to pay the fine of the first person arrested, and urged the Loop business community to dig into its pockets to help the rest. For once, science fiction seemed to be swimming in the middle of the stream of opinion. "The seamless web of our world has come apart at the seams we didn't know it had," wrote Frank Herbert, the author of *Dune,* in his introduction to a collection of stories all on environmental themes, titled *Saving Worlds* (Roger Elwood and Virginia Kidd, eds., 1973). "And the ecologist and science fiction writer are merely saying: 'Hey! Look there!'"

Some notes of hope mingled with the cries of alarm. The

distinguished American historian Barbara Tuchman (in "The United States and China," *Colorado Quarterly:* 21, Summer 1972) surmised that the Nixon détente with both Russia and China might be "a kind of approaching recognition that we are all really in the same boat, in danger of being overturned by environmental disaster; that the enemy is not so much each other as it is the common enemy of all: unrestrained growth and pollution." Many science fiction writers in the West, however, were not yet ready to draw such hopeful conclusions as Tuchman's. Perhaps, as some of the post-future-war stories in the pulps had hinted (see chapter 9), on the far side of our collapsing present civilization a better future may await us. But the short run, in much prophetic science fiction of the late 1960s and early 1970s, seemed dark indeed. On the second page of *There Will Be Time,* a novel by Poul Anderson (1972), in an episode set in 1971, an old man who has been told by a time traveler what the next few years are going to bring is shown watching his grandchildren at play, his "pleasure in their company interrupted by moments of what looked like pain." At last, addressing the author, he exclaims: "Oh, God, the young, the poor young! Poul, my generation and yours [about a quarter-century younger; Anderson in real life began to write in 1948] have had it outrageously easy. All we ever had to do was be white Americans in reasonable health, and we got our place in the sun. But now history's returning to its normal climate here also, and the norm is an ice age."

As for warning people of what is to come, so that they may change their life-styles to prevent disaster, it turns out that the time traveler in this story has already tried that course of action and failed. "Environment was very big for awhile," he admits. "Ecology Now stickers on the windshields of cars belonging to hairy young men—cars which dripped oil wherever they parked. . . . Before long, the fashionable cause was something else, I forget what."

This was not quite Poul Anderson's own last word on the subject. Science fiction, he told a University of Arizona panel in February 1975, having faithfully sounded the alarm against the many possible ecological dooms, "will work out of this into human survival of these problems." However, survival in this instance requires awareness; and the trouble with crying "Wolf!" (as the old fable itself pointed out) is that when the wolf finally does come nobody will believe you. Outside the specialized world of science fiction, members of which remained able to disagree temperately about some very fundamental issues (*e.g.,* civil rights and Vietnam), the 1960s nationally were a time of hyperinflated rhetoric. As epithets like "off the pigs" displaced more conventional political discourse, the language of the conservation advocates became tinged with the same kind of verbal inflation. Moreover, it was easy enough to refute the more hasty and ill-considered of the warnings; Lake Erie, for example, did *not* die of pollution in the mid-1970s as ecology-minded journalists had confidently predicted it would (although, to be sure, it is still polluted). As the political passions of the 1960s dampened down, most of the communications media, assuming a short attention span in their audience, tactfully changed the subject. Instead of hearing about clean air and energy conservation, as Americans had for a short time during Gerald Ford's first year in the White House, the citizens were told instead that they must put up with the stench and increase their coal production. The tragedy in such a case is that no problem goes away merely because people stop paying attention to it. Nor, for that matter, is a prophecy necessarily proved untrue by its intemperate tone.

But science fiction, as evidenced in the continuing appearance in its magazines and paperbacks of stories like "To Walk With Thunder," by Dean McLaughlin (*Amazing:* 47, August 1973)—a most acute portrayal of the political economy of air pollution—refused to change the subject. As they considered the problems of our dwindling sphere, many of its writers would have accepted the insight of Soviet biogeochemist Vladimir I. Vernadskii: man has come to have an impact on the biosphere as profound as that exerted by natural forces, so that it behooves him to act as responsibly toward his environ-

ment as if in effect he *were* a process of Nature, comparable to
mountain-making revolutions and ice ages.

America's apparent unwillingness to cope seriously with a
deteriorating environment, like its apparent abandonment of
manned space flight after the completion of the Apollo program (chapter 2), struck science fictionists very much as a
failure to respond to a Toynbeean challenge. It is now or
never, declared Norman Spinrad in 1975 (guest editorial,
"Energy and Survival: the Fork in the Road," *Analog:* 95, July
1975); unless the steps are taken soon to establish a clean and
abundant fusion steady-state energy system, by the 1990s the
world will have fallen into an economic depression which will
last "as long as we endure as a species"—a depression caused
not by "banking system failures, currency manipulations, or
swings of the business cycle," but rather by "the irrevocable
depletion of the Earth's fossil fuel energy resources before an
alternate and enduring replacement has been developed and
deployed." Unless the fork leading to a different future be
consciously taken in the present, Spinrad argued, in another
generation it will be too late; "we will never be able to power a
high industrial technology again."

Despite these Cassandra tones, Spinrad was still hopeful; by
writing and publishing such an article at all, he and *Analog*'s
editor Ben Bova tacitly assumed that people can be rationally
persuaded to put forth the necessary effort to save themselves. Reviewing a sober essay in futurology by Italian systems analyst Roberto Vacca, titled *The Coming Dark Age* (1973),
Grant Carrington urged any reader of science fiction who
worked for a large organization to buy a copy of Vacca's book
"and give it to the highest person in management you can
reach. Send a copy to your congressman. . . . The world you
save may be your own" ("The Future in Books," *Amazing:* 49,
July 1975). Still more overtly political, *Amazing*'s editor in
September of 1975 urged readers to organize a letter-writing
campaign to Congress advocating that freon-powered spray
cans be banned, lest we deplete the ozone in the upper
atmosphere (and end the world, as that editor put it, "not with

a bang, but with a psssst!"): "There are over twenty thousand of you who buy this magazine each issue—and another five to ten thousand who buy it occasionally and may be reading this editorial. If each of you writes a letter to one representative, we'd get action. We'd get it *now*."

This was a radically different perception of the science fiction reader's social role from that which F. Orlin Tremaine had expressed in the mid-1930s, as he renamed *Astounding*'s letter column "Science Discussions" (see chapter 1). But the conclusion to this appeal by *Amazing* editor Ted White inadvertently gave away the fatal flaw in all science fiction considered as serious prophecy, the stereotype that had plagued it ever since its gaudy-covered, raw-paged pulp magazine days: "As the newsweekly boys are in the habit of saying, 'This isn't science fiction—this is *real*.'"

IV

By the mid-1950s, Frederik Pohl has estimated, there were in existence thirty-eight different periodicals all more or less describable as science fiction magazines. Then came Sputnik—and soon thereafter the number dwindled to seven! By a perfect irony, the kind of magazine that Hugo Gernsback had invented fell into economic doldrums just as the extravagant fiction he had heralded was turning into the cold fact of tomorrow. Pulps founded in the magazine explosion of 1939–40, which had managed to survive the wartime paper shortages, now went under, including *Super Science, Startling,* and the widely lamented *Planet Stories.* New magazines, nourished in the postwar affluence—*Fantastic Universe, Science Fiction Plus,* and others—also died. *Thrilling Wonder Stories,* which traced its origins back to 1929 as *Science Wonder Stories* (one year before *Analog*), suspended publication in 1954, and in that same year the oldest science fiction outlet of them all, *Weird Tales,* folded its tents and stole away.

Ignoring the economics of the situation, which swept away surviving non-science-fiction pulps as well, it would be tempting to see all this as cause and effect: man breached the hidden reality of space and the atom, and then retreated in terror from his former daydreams. However, the attrition of the magazines did not accurately measure what was happening to science fiction on the whole; outside the dwindling pulp ghetto, this variety of literature was moving on to new heights of prestige and acceptance. Four science fiction writers— Alfred Bester, Robert Bloch, Robert Heinlein, and Cyril Kornbluth—appeared on the lecture platform at the University of Chicago, and their remarks were duly compiled (by Basil Davenport of the *Saturday Review*) into a book, *The Science Fiction Novel: Imagination and Social Criticism* (1959). Major hard-cover publishers, notably Simon & Schuster and Doubleday, stocked regular science fiction lines—Doubleday's evolved into a book club. Commercial TV launched *Star Trek* during prime time. The absolute volume of science fiction being published in America in, say, 1970 was greater than ever before—but most of it was appearing in paperbound books rather than in magazines.

Pohl, in an essay "The Publishing of Science Fiction" (printed in R. Bretnor, ed., *Science Fiction Today and Tomorrow* (1974), clearly explained the economics of that last-named change. With a date on its cover and spine, a magazine on the rack is assumed to get stale, like bread on a supermarket shelf. But a paperback, undated, can be left on that rack indefinitely; if it is not noticeably worn by browsers it may still sell. Such a development was, of course, not peculiar to science fiction. The post-Sputnik era saw the decline of *all* types of magazines; not only the ragged-edged pulps, but also the big, mass-circulation "slicks"—*Collier's, Life, The Saturday Evening Post*—followed one another to oblivion. Fiction in particular has suffered; indeed, science fiction is about the only brand of all-fiction magazine that has survived at all. The magazines containing short stories and serials that used to crowd the newsstands are gone for the most part, displaced by magazines dealing in fact (or pretended fact) rather than fiction; "true" stories and "how-to" articles, in every field from car repair to *kung fu*. The academic quarterlies with their elite handfuls of readers, like the mass magazines written for the millions, have also moved away from the story, replacing it with reams of literary criticism. And if the old-time pulpster often wrote to put groceries on the table rather than to create Art, academic authors often write for an equally pragmatic purpose: to add a line to their list of "publications," to please their deans and keep their jobs.

Paradoxically, therefore, the science fiction magazine, which began as an outcast from American literature, has become one of the few places where the craft of imaginative writing can still be practiced, enjoyed, and paid for. "The animal called short fiction is almost extinct outside the sf field," wrote editor Edward L. Ferman for the twenty-fifth anniversary number of *The Magazine of Fantasy and Science Fiction* (vol. 47, October 1974). "And I am self-servingly convinced that the science fiction magazines are the best vehicles for presenting short fiction." Editor-publisher Donald A. Wollheim agrees; the mass-produced paperback collections of original stories, he believes, "present very impressive fronts, featuring some quite notable authors, but . . . almost universally the stories therein give evidence of haste and lack of critically responsible editorial control" (Wollheim, introduction to *The 1974 Annual World's Best SF*). Or, if there *is* critically responsible editing, it is of a kind that favors the same narcissistic, self-pitying, plotless stuff that passes for serious writing out in the non-sf literary "mainstream."

"A magazine, simply by virtue of its frequent and regular publication—by its *continuity*—has a unique commitment to the writers and the readers of science fiction," editor Edward Ferman argues. More bluntly, he might have added that the magazines are a more competitive market than the paperback anthologies; there are far fewer magazines than there were at the height of the pulp era, and there are many more people trying with some degree of seriousness to write science fiction. Still, if they are harder to break into than they used to be, the surviving science fiction magazines are also places where new talent *can* break in, make its first mistakes, get its seasoning. A beginner can warm up on short stories rather than spend him- or herself on the all-or-nothing gamble of an elephant-sized novel, and those stories may turn out better than the novel would have anyhow. Furthermore, the beginner can expect the courtesy of being taken seriously by the editor. The late John Campbell claimed he read everything that came in to the "slush pile" of unsolicited manuscripts, and the manuscript readers for the magazine he founded and its competitors continue to wade conscientiously through the mass of paper trash that rolls into any editor's office, hoping to find the occasional nugget of gold.

In addition to the able new writers who entered the field in this fashion in the late 1960s and early 1970s, the magazines drew the "old-timers" back into their pages as well. It would have been impossible, in the kind of economy America has lately known, to make a living solely by writing for science fiction magazines—as had been possible (modestly and by very hard work) in the last years of the New Deal. Science fictionists in recent years have been paying for the groceries with TV scripts (Harlan Ellison), popularized science (Isaac Asimov), movie scenarios (Leigh Brackett), literary criticism for the elite British media (Brian Aldiss), or stories for the "girlie" magazines—which have their own staunch literary defenders and pay better than the pulps ever did (Fritz Leiber). Nevertheless, when *Fantasy and Science Fiction* scheduled its quarter-century anniversary number in 1974, Theodore Sturgeon—whose earliest story dates from 1939, before that magazine yet existed—practically demanded that a new story under his byline be included. Other veterans of the pulp era returned to the magazines, some of them after long absences; they liked to keep their hand in, and they felt they owed the medium that had nurtured them a great deal. Then too, some of their experiences with Hollywood and TV had been so traumatic—see Harlan Ellison's savage, and unhappily *not* fictitious, account of his experience with the frenetic collective idiocy of television production, acidly titled "Somehow, I

Don't Think We're in Kansas, Toto" (*Amazing:* 49, July
1975)—that they may have resumed writing magazine stories
for the same reason a screen actor or actress sometimes takes a
turn on the less-well-paying legitimate stage, namely to keep
in contact with what they consider to be the "real thing."

Both for neophyte writers and for timeworn veterans,
therefore, the recent economically decrepit condition of the
science fiction magazines—despite the flourishing of the field
as a whole—was a cause for concern. "For some people at
least," mourned editor Ted White (editorial in *Amazing:* 46,
January 1973), "the day of the sf magazine is over. I hope this
turns out to be untrue." The post-Sputnik attrition continued;
Worlds of If, the companion to *Galaxy* which from its foundation in 1950 had enjoyed a most distinguished career, and
Vertex, which was launched as recently as 1973 as an avant-
garde, slick-paper publication, both folded in 1974. *Galaxy,* to
be sure, reached its silver anniversary a year later, and its
former editor Horace Gold claimed it was "solidly established
enough . . . to endure at least another quarter of a century"
(Gold, "Looking Aft," *Galaxy:* 36, October 1975). *Galaxy* was,
however, beginning to skip issues, which in the pulp era would
have been a symptom of trouble. *Fantasy and Science Fiction*
seemed in no immediate danger, and *Analog* in its late forties
seemed in the pink of fiscal condition. The announcement in
1976 that a senior writer would lend his prestige to a new
periodical, to be titled *Isaac Asimov's Science Fiction Magazine,*
encouraged all would-be contributors. But the adoption by
Analog in 1975 of Lester del Rey as its regular book
reviewer—a task del Rey had performed with distinction for
the defunct *Worlds of If*—had an ominous resemblance to the
earlier scrambling movement of New York's best news col-
umnists from one paper to another when the majority of that
city's dailies started to close down.

Amazing, the senior survivor in the 1970s, was plagued by
severe problems of financing and distribution. Authors began
to complain of delays in being paid, an economic danger
signal uncomfortably reminiscent of the threadbare, penny-

pinching years of Hugo Gernsback and Farnsworth Wright. Within the Science Fiction Writers of America, the medium's professional guild, there was talk of boycotting the publisher of *Amazing* and *Fantastic* until it mended its parsimonious ways (SFWA *Bulletin:* 10, October 1975). However, sympathy was mingled with the censure. As *Amazing* began to count down toward its fiftieth anniversary in 1976, long-term readers crossed their fingers and hoped that the onetime "aristocrat of science fiction" would make it—which, skipping an issue and going quarterly in the process, it did (June 1976). Meanwhile, however, the authors' boycott of its publisher went ahead; sales to *Fantastic* and *Amazing* would no longer be counted as credentials for membership in the Science Fiction Writers of America, the president of that organization announced (SFWA *Bulletin:* 11, October 1976).

Amazing's youngish editor Ted White—the most fan-oriented of his generation of editors and the most willing to argue creatively and constructively with his readers (see editorial in *Amazing:* 48, August 1974, esp. p. 127)—responded to the historical situation in which he found himself in two seemingly contradictory ways. On the one hand, his two magazines carried, earlier and more often than their competitors, stories marked by New Left clichés, kinky sex, and four-letter-word dialogue of the kind that also entered polite "mainstream" literature in the course of the 1960s. On the other hand, toward science fiction's own pulp heritage White was in some respects an arch-traditionalist. He sought, for example (editorial in *Amazing:* 48, May 1975), to revive the use of the awkward word *scientifiction* (instead of *science fiction*)—a term coined originally by Hugo Gernsback and in general disuse since the demise of *Wonder Stories*. And *Amazing*'s golden anniversary number (vol. 50, June 1976) faithfully reproduced in miniature Frank R. Paul's cover for the magazine's initial issue in April 1926—wrecked square-rigger, ice skaters, the planet Saturn, and all.

Thus again, science fiction displays its perennial paradox: its effort to foretell the future takes the form of nostalgia for the past (in this case, for science fiction's own past). Arnold Toynbee had a term for such a dialectical process; he called it Archaism-and-Futurism. Science fictionists, most of them not familiar with Toynbee's work, regularly applied something like the Toynbee "challenge-and-response" thesis to imagined world crises, from thwarting a Martian invasion to developing a new source of energy when the sun goes out; "The ethics of evolution," said John Campbell, "is 'try.' " How ironic, therefore, that such intuitive and unconscious Toynbeeans as the science fiction writers should themselves fall so often into a state of mind that Toynbee himself believed was a sign that a society is in trouble. For in Toynbee's grand historical scheme, Archaism-and-Futurism—a longing for Utopia (in the future or in heaven) combined with a veneration for antiquity—does not come upon the scene until a civilization is actually in the process of disintegration. (Toynbee, however, also believed in the possibility of self-transcendence and renewal, and that too is a perennial theme in science fiction.)

V

"Though the pulps were looked down upon, their influence on science fiction was not entirely bad," Jack Williamson has written (in *The Early Williamson*, 1975). "The pulp editors demanded strong plots and clear writing; they required distinctive characters and consistently motivated action and positive themes. Every writer, I think, needs to know what they taught, and it's a misfortune for the young person learning to write today that they are gone." But they *are* gone; science fiction has its own version of the much discussed generation gap. "There was . . . a time—fast fading—for which those of us from the 1950s and afterward are forever barred," wrote Algis Budrys in one of his book review columns (*Fantasy and Science Fiction:* 50, January 1976). "We are not pulp writers, even those of us who wouldn't mind a bit. We are their heirs, even those of us who do." Those who did mind—those who felt cramped by the old pulp ghetto's social and literary con-

ventions, and who aspired to write (or at least read) fiction
acceptable to schoolteachers and formal critics; perhaps even
to create Literature, with a capital L—welcomed the "New
Wave" that washed over the little world of science fiction in
the 1960s. This represented an effort to incorporate avant-
garde "mainstream" literary techniques, and also (in many
instances) deliberately to break down the long-established
barrier between "science fiction" and "fantasy."

The New Wave originated in England, where science fiction
had never been so ghettoized as in the United States (H. G.
Wells, for example, was always reckoned there as a legitimate
member of the literary community, whatever one thought of
his social and political views and practices). The movement
was incubated in the skillfully edited British science fiction
magazine *New Worlds,* which for a time enjoyed not only
critical acclaim, but even public subsidy; can one imagine even
the most soft-hearted of New Deal cultural bureaucrats ever
bestowing a grant upon *Weird Tales* or *Astounding Stories?* The
New Wave quickly acquired a transatlantic following, and for
a time it had a rejuvenating effect upon the remaining magazines on this side of the pond. Younger—and some older—
American writers adopted its methods and themes, and in
counterpoint to Ted White's proposed revival of the word
"scientifiction" came proposals to abolish the term "science
fiction" altogether.

Like most of the other cultural vogues of the 1960s, the
New Wave passed more quickly than it had come. *New Worlds*
itself, like many another magazine, is no more. For one thing,
this attempted reform of science fiction was vulnerable to the
charge that it was itself, unknowingly, a mode of archaism and
nostalgia. Many of its stylistic innovations would have been
startling half a century ago, but had long since ceased to be
novelties anywhere except in science fiction. The New Wave,
declared the *Times Literary Supplement*—as quoted by Old
Wave exponent Donald A. Wollheim, in his introduction to
The 1974 Annual World's Best SF—"amounted to little more
than a dreary rechauffé of surrealist work of the 1920s and

1930s, which had largely petered out in the mainstream." In science fiction, argued the *TLS* reviewer, stream-of-consciousness or other "techniques which confuse or disrupt the sense" usually will not work: "When something strange is afoot, in a strange time or on a strange planet, only a measure of clarity will let us know what is supposed to be going on."

Thematically, some New Wave writing had picked up the anti-science, anti-technology mood of the 1960s counterculture—and of some of the liberal arts professors who at about that same time began jumping on the science fiction bandwagon. And that, for people who had learned their craft from the likes of *Astounding*'s John Campbell, simply would not do. Jack Williamson has gone so far as to argue that "the desperate pessimism of the 'new wave' generation of science fiction writers should bear some of the blame" for the broader crisis of faith that characterizes the whole temper of our times. "I even wonder," he writes, "about the final effect of all those low-budget science-horror films that end with a pious proclamation about 'things man was not meant to know' "—although that kind of proclamation, one must say in all fairness, long antedates the New Wave; it is, after all, a major moral theme in the story of Doctor Frankenstein.

Williamson in his own long writing career, which began in 1928, has successfully adapted to all the changes that have taken place in science fiction, making the transition from the crude *Amazing Stories* of Hugo Gernsback to the far more sophisticated *Amazing* of Ted White. The generation gap in science fiction is nowhere more evident than in the fact that some of Williamson's younger contemporaries, who began their work in the 1950s and 1960s, have since decided that they must quit the field. Thus in an essay titled "Rage, Pain, Alienation and Other Aspects of the Writing of Science Fiction" (*Fantasy and Science Fiction*: 50, April 1976) Barry Malzberg announced that after ten years and two million words of science fiction writing he would do so no more. "It is true that I must leave science fiction," Malzberg declared. "As the vise of the seventies comes down upon all of us in every field of the

so-called arts, there is almost no room left for the kind of work
which I try to do." Similarly Robert Silverberg, after twenty
years of serious, conscientious science fiction writing, also
decided to stop writing it. "I'm troubled about sf as a lasting
. . . artform, because many of its concerns are transient,"
Silverberg explained in an interview (*Amazing:* 49, January
1976). He lamented his own hackwork as a young writer for
Amazing in the mid-1950s, and he foresaw in the paperback
market of the later 1970s a similar demand for what he called
"yard-goods." (*Amazing*'s editor noted, however, that Silverberg had "announced his first retirement from sf in 1959;
conditions changed. Perhaps they will change again.")

Robert Silverberg, significantly, did *not* wish—in the manner of Asimov and Heinlein before him—to exchange the
specialized readership of science fiction for a wider audience:
"I don't want to do stuff that's so accessible that millions and
millions of people all over the world read it, because all
important fiction, literary art, has been an elite art." Disagree-
ing, *Amazing*'s interviewer Darrell Schweitzer reminded him
of the vulgar popularity of Shakespeare in his own day.
Silverberg after some argument conceded the point, and
noted that the same might be said also of Dickens but, he
added, "I don't think you can reach everybody at once."
Surely, in such a testament, the poison of academic respectability has done its fatal work; science fiction has become self-
conscious enough to be ashamed!

Both of these writers acknowledged in spite of themselves
that science fiction retained some hold on their intellect and
emotions. "I feel most comfortable with science fictional
ideas," Silverberg told the *Amazing* interviewer when
Schweitzer asked him if he could "write and sell a straight
mainstream novel just as well." "I want to make it clear," Barry
Malzberg declared, "I *love* this field. My debt to it is incalculable," and he spelled out some of that debt in an impressionistic
essay, "Down Here in the Dream Quarter," which appeared in
Amazing's golden anniversary number. "Fifty years and forever, yet into darkness, I am one of Hugo's children," Malz-

berg ended. "Me too." Alongside the nostalgia of hope (of, for example, frontier renewal among healthy new barbarians or in colonies out among the stars), there can be a nostalgia of despair: "In their grievous, distracted, foolish way," Barry Malzberg mused, "Hugo's children may be the last custodians of . . . the America of our past . . . the only alternative to the mindless and electrical future."

Perhaps, however, there exists a middle way between Algis Budrys's lament for an irrecoverable pulp past and Robert Silverberg's quest for a new and equally constricting ghetto of elitism. Most of their colleagues and competitors (in the Science Fiction Writers of America, for example), young as well as old, were not giving up the struggle; and for such writers, the relevant question was not where have all the flowers gone, but rather what do we do next? Specifically, "What will be next after the New Wave?" someone asked Poul Anderson, in the authors' symposium at the University of Arizona in February 1975. In partial dissent from the *T.L.S.* and Donald Wollheim, Anderson replied that the New Wave had taught science fiction writers a great deal; many of its techniques and insights, including its "sense of tragedy," had "become a part of everybody's equipment." However, he predicted, the next development in science fiction would take place where it had all started: at science's own far frontiers of discovery. No necessary archaism here, for a great deal had been happening lately along those frontiers, disclosing a strange new world of quarks and quasars and black holes: "Everything in science once again [is] up for grabs." The editor of *Fantasy and Science Fiction* put it a different way; advertising "The Anvil of Jove," a novella by Gregory Benford and Gordon Eklund (*Fantasy and Science Fiction:* 51, July 1976), he described it as "a story that blends the best qualities of traditional sf (carefully extrapolated future technology, big concepts, suspenseful problem-solving) with the good prose and complex and interesting characters we've come to expect in more contemporary sf."

To judge from that and other recent magazine stories, the thrall of despair has begun to lift from science fiction also. "In

spite of pollution, in spite of the baby boom, in spite of the
spreading nuclear arsenals, I still believe our civilization has at
least a fair chance to survive," Jack Williamson affirmed in
1975. "If we attack our problems with reason and with hope,
instead of surrendering to panic or despair, it ought to be an
even better chance. I think the world still needs . . . faith in
man and his reason." Faith has always been the substance of
things hoped for, the evidence of things not seen; and fantasy,
according to J.R.R. Tolkien, "certainly does not destroy or
even insult Reason." Nor does it "blunt the appetite for, nor
obscure the perception of, scientific verity," Tolkien wrote, in
1964. "On the contrary. The keener and clearer is the reason,
the better fantasy will it make."

Vault of the Beast
Science Fiction in the Library

*"I know I made it—but I don't know what it is. It just stands there and does
nothing, but anything that involved must do something."*

"The Mechanical Mice," by Maurice A. Hugi, *Astounding
Science-Fiction,* **26 (January 1941), p. 61.**

TWO KINDS OF PEOPLE collect and preserve science fiction: fans, who buy it as it comes on the stands and dicker with used-book dealers for older specimens of it, and university librarians, who have a healthy pack rat's instinct to accumulate *everything*. To amass a complete personal collection of the magazines I have discussed is becoming more and more difficult as time passes. The cheap second-hand magazine stores in decaying urban areas, where collectors in the Depression years could pick up a back-numbered pulp for a nickel or a dime, are long gone, casualties of expressway development; and the hucksters who turn up at science fiction conventions with magazine back copies carefully encased in plastic know to the full, and then some, the market value of their wares. Thus the university librarians have become indispensable to the student of science fiction.

Unfortunately, owing to the pulp magazines' traditional ill repute, university libraries got into this area of acquisition late in the game. Rare indeed is the library that has, for example, a complete run of *Weird Tales;* and rarer still is one the greater part of whose collection of magazines is in mint condition. Moreover, the concern for acquisition of science fiction has so far not extended to its preservation; these old pulps self-destruct in about fifty years even if left to themselves, and many have suffered extensive physical deterioration long before they were filed away on library shelves. I was fortunate enough to be able to use the excellent collection in the Swen Franklin Parson Library at Northern Illinois University, and more recently the materials housed in special collections at the library of the University of Arizona. The staffs of both these libraries have been most obliging.

To find one's way around in this material, the indispensable research tool for the early years is Donald B. Day, *Index to the Science-Fiction Magazines, 1926–1950* (Portland, Oregon: Perri Press, 1952). This was a real labor of love, done without modern compilation techniques, by hand. It lists authors, including cross-references to pseudonyms—a most important and bewildering matter when dealing with the pulps; titles of stories; and magazines, by name (frequently changed), volume, number, and page size. It identifies for each issue the name of the cover artist. I have found the work extraordinarily accurate on the whole; it did mislist a story of my own, "Ounce of Prevention" (*The Magazine of Fantasy and Science Fiction:* 1, Summer 1950) under the name "Philip" Carter, but that was not Day's fault—the mistake was made by the magazine, which at that time was edited in Berkeley and published in New York, a circumstance positively inviting that kind of trouble.

For the years since 1950, Erwin S. Strauss compiled for the M.I.T. Science Fiction Society a further *Index to the Science Fiction Magazines, 1951–1965*. As befits a publication emanating from M.I.T., this one sets up the data—by magazine contents page, by story title, and by author—in the form of a computer printout. The same format is continued by the New England Science Fiction Association in its *Index to the Science Fiction Magazines, 1966–1970*. By the time these bibliographic tools appeared, science fiction had long since burst its magazine boundaries, and a different sort of reference work was called for. Donald H. Tuck responded admirably with his *Encyclopedia of Science Fiction and Fantasy*, of which the volume from A through H has appeared (Chicago: Advent Publishers, 1974), with others in preparation.

Books preserve science fiction in more permanent form than pulp-paper magazines. Commercial book publishers were, however, slow to become aware of the potential gold mine awaiting the digging, and the chain pulp publishers of the Depression years were ordinarily not geared for the production of books. (An interesting exception is Ziff-Davis of Chicago, which published *Amazing Stories* from 1938 until 1965; largely at the urging of Raymond A. Palmer, *Amazing*'s editor, it posthumously published Stanley G. Weinbaum's *The New Adam* in 1939 as a hard-cover novel. Thus *Amazing*, the most juvenile and "pulpy" of the science fiction magazines at the time, ironically became the sponsor of the first pulp-originating science fiction novel with aspirations toward serious literature.)

The first anthology of science fiction stories from a general publisher, *The Other Worlds* (New York: Wilfred Funk, 1941), was unfortunate from a science fictionist's point of view, for it defined science fiction as *pure* fantasy: "The first requirement of a good fantastic story . . . is that it should not be even remotely possible." That definition automatically rules out the Gernsback-Sloane-Campbell kind of science fiction in its entirety. The collection includes excellent early pieces by Theodore Sturgeon and Lester del Rey, but both stories were pure supernatural fantasies, first published in *Unknown;* it has good representation of the *Weird Tales* ghost story tradition, such as "The Considerate Hosts," by Thorp McClusky, and "School for the Unspeakable," by Manly Wade Wellman. But its sampling of what is more recognizably science fiction, by the standards of what was already available in the magazines, is wayward, to say the least.

Donald A. Wollheim had considerably better luck with *The Pocket Book of Science-Fiction* (New York: Pocket Books, 1943). Wollheim, seasoned by the editing of two short-lived pulps, *Stirring Science Stories* and *Cosmic Stories,* included along with stories by recognized "mainstream" writers (Ambrose Bierce, H. G. Wells, Stephen Vincent Benét) also such items as "A Martian Odyssey," by Stanley G. Weinbaum, "Twilight," by "Don A. Stuart" (John W. Campbell), and "Microcosmic God," by Theodore Sturgeon, all three of which have proved durable enough for inclusion in the Science Fiction Writers of America anthology edited by Robert Silverberg, *Science Fiction Hall of Fame* (New York: Doubleday, 1970). Wollheim also edited the *Portable Novels of Science* (New York: Viking Press, 1945), which anthologized longer pieces by H. G. Wells, "John Taine" (Eric Temple Bell), Olaf Stapledon, and H. P. Lovecraft. On the whole, however, Publisher's Row stayed away from pulp science fiction until after World War II.

The gap was filled for the time being by specialty houses,

most especially Arkham House (Sauk City, Wisconsin). Arkham was originally founded by August Derleth and Donald Wandrei for the purpose of preserving in hard covers the complete writings of Howard Phillips Lovecraft, who alone among the pulpsters of that era enjoyed a special coterie reputation. That work is still not finished; Arkham is still in the process of selecting, editing, and publishing Lovecraft's letters. Meanwhile, however, it branched out and began to print collections of stories by other members of the Lovecraft circle and of the *Weird Tales* school. Science fiction began to appear in these Arkham House books through the back door; there were, for example, several "thought-variant" stories from the Tremaine *Astounding* of the mid-1930s in Donald Wandrei, *The Eye and the Finger* (1944). In 1946, Derleth took the plunge into science fiction—Arkham House published *Slan,* by A. E. Van Vogt. The following year it published a book in its more typical *Weird Tales* vein, but one which in retrospect has special distinction: it was *Dark Carnival,* the first hard-cover book by Ray Bradbury.

Immediately after the war several science fiction specialty or hobby publishers appeared, gambling that among the people who had read favorite stories in the magazines at 15¢ to 25¢ a copy, a smaller but sufficient market existed for books at $3 per copy. Thus, the Fantasy Press of Reading, Pennsylvania, published the space operas of E. E. Smith and Jack Williamson; Prime Press, of Philadelphia, issued Lester del Rey's excellent first collection, ". . . *and Some Were Human*" (1949); Shasta Publishers, in Chicago, printed the early stories of Robert Heinlein; and Gnome Press, Inc., of New York, published C. L. Moore, Isaac Asimov, and Arthur C. Clarke. By this time, however, the regular "mainstream" publishers had begun to get wind of what was going on. August Derleth, while still maintaining his limited-editions operation at Arkham House, also edited science fiction collections like *Strange Ports of Call* (New York: Pellegrini & Cudahy, 1948), *The Other Side of the Moon* (1949), and *Far Boundaries* (1951). He was joined by Groff Conklin, who skimmed the cream off the magazines of the 1930s and 1940s in several large anthologies for Crown Publishers, notably *The Best of Science Fiction* (1946), *A Treasury of Science Fiction* (1948), and *Omnibus of Science Fiction* (1952). These included such outstanding stories, mentioned in this book, as "The Piper's Son," "No Woman Born," and "The Scarlet Plague." A kind of baptism into the Establishment was achieved when Random House published *Adventures in Time and Space,* edited by Raymond J. Healy and J. Francis McComas. Drawing heavily on Campbell's *Astounding* of the early 1940s (e.g., "Nightfall," by Isaac Asimov, "Requiem," by Robert Heinlein, "Black Destroyer," by A. E. Van Vogt), this one remains in print as a standard item; even very small libraries are likely to own a copy.

With the back numbers of the magazines skimmed— although it remains possible to do a viable anthology from the 1930s, as Isaac Asimov showed in his outsized collection *Before the Golden Age* (Doubleday, 1974)—the publishers in their quest for science fiction readers' dollars turned to a "best-of-the-year" format, modeled on the O'Brien and O. Henry annual short story collections. Everett F. Bleiler and T. E. Dikty led the way with *The Best Science Fiction Stories: 1949* (New York: Frederick Fell, 1949); *The Best Science Fiction Stories: 1950;* and so on. Judith Merril in 1956 launched her thoughtfully edited series *SF: the Year's Greatest,* whose annual editions concluded with authoritative critical essays well worth the scholar's attention; see, for example, Judith Merril, ed., *9th Annual Edition, the Year's Best SF* (New York: Simon & Schuster, 1964; paper, Dell, 1965, pp. 370–78). Donald Wollheim and Terry Carr in the mid-1960s entered the field with their *World's Best Science Fiction* series; subsequently they split up, Wollheim editing one such line of annual anthologies, Carr another. In the mid-1970s, Lester del Rey launched *Best Science Fiction Stories of the Year.*

Meanwhile, the anthologists were collecting stories from the files of individual magazines. Anthony Boucher started a series, *The Best From Fantasy and Science Fiction,* published in hard covers by Doubleday and in paper by Ace Books; H. L.

Gold began a *Galaxy Reader* series; John W. Campbell did an *Astounding Science-Fiction Anthology;* Ted White edited *The Best From Fantastic* (New York: Manor Books, 1973); Leigh Brackett, paying tribute to a defunct magazine with which in the 1940s she had enjoyed "the happiest relationship possible for a writer," put together *The Best of Planet Stories, #1* (New York: Ballantine, 1975). And so it goes. The bewildering variety of stories, impossible to find individually under a vague umbrella of *The Best* or *The Greatest,* obviously posed a problem for bibliographers. W. R. Cole tried to meet it with *A Checklist of Science-Fiction Anthologies* (Brooklyn: privately printed, 1964), which indexed such collections by title; by the book's editor, followed by a contents page; by story titles; and by authors. Would that other forms of popular culture were as well looked after, from a researcher's point of view, as science fiction! (Such study books are not always well done, however; an attempt to carry this indexing process past the point where Cole left off, Frederick Siemon's *Science Fiction Story Index, 1950–1968,* received a scathing, knowledgeable, back-of-the-hand review from Lester del Rey in *Worlds of If:* 24, April 1972, even though it was published by the American Library Association.)

There is great unevenness of quality, inevitably, both within and between these story anthologies. One way to control such quality is to *vote* the stories in, as with Isaac Asimov, ed., *The Hugo Winners* (2 vols.; New York: Doubleday, 1962 and 1971). Such a basis for selection is of course subject to criticism of the same sort as that directed at the Academy Awards, upon which the Hugo competition is modeled. Another winnowing device is to leave the judgment up to the authors' professional peers; the Science Fiction Writers of America ballot annually for the stories that in due course appear in the Nebula Awards anthologies, each of which is ordinarily edited by that year's president of SFWA. Some outstanding collections have resulted. But in even the best such compendia there is a smorgasbord quality that inevitably puts some readers off, and editors and publishers for the past three decades have sought for unifying principles of some other kind.

Hence the one-author anthology, such as *What's It Like Out There? and Other Stories*, by Edmond Hamilton (New York: Ace Books, 1974), or *The Best of Fritz Leiber* (New York: Ballantine, 1974). Hence also the "theme" anthology, in which all of the stories are about robots, or time travel, or trips to the moon, or matriarchs, or telepathy; or they are all written by practicing scientists, or Soviet citizens, or British New Wavers, or Frenchmen. There were also the complete novels and serials, as distinguished from short stories, that could be turned into individual books. Henry Holt and Company gingerly tested the water as early as 1941 by publishing *Lest Darkness Fall,* by L. Sprague DeCamp, an expanded version of a story that had first appeared in *Unknown;* a specialty house, Prime Press, reprinted it in 1949. Simon & Schuster took over *Slan* from Arkham House and then issued another Van Vogt science fiction adventure, *The World of Ā,* in 1948; that novel had first appeared in *Astounding Science-Fiction* 35, August; 36, September, October 1945. Ray Bradbury wove together his Mars stories from *Planet Stories* and *Thrilling Wonder* (and the slick-paper magazine *Collier's*), with some new material, into an episodic novel that appeared as *The Martian Chronicles* (Garden City, New York: Doubleday, 1950).

Sooner or later, however, as the magazine files were picked over so often that individual popular stories were reprinted again and again—and as the walls of the pulp ghetto began to crumble—it was inevitable that the book publishers would turn to *new* science fiction, not deriving from the magazines. Isaac Asimov could not find a major magazine market for his important transitional novel *Pebble in the Sky;* it found a home with Doubleday (1950). Cyril Kornbluth, putting together a short story collection, *The Explorers* (New York: Ballantine, 1954), which reprinted tales that ranged back to his teen-age fan days, opened with a new one written specifically for that anthology, entitled "Gomez;" it is one of his best. Kornbluth's friend and collaborator Frederik Pohl commenced a series of collections of never-previously-published stories, *Star Science Fiction Stories* (1953 *et seq.*) and *Star Short Novels* (New York: Ballantine, 1954). Eventually, novels appeared in book form that had never previously been serialized, and authors began submitting stories directly to anthology editors rather than to magazines. I placed one short story, "Constitution in E Flat," that had been bounced by all the then-extant science fiction magazines, in a collection of stories primarily by beginning writers (David Gerrold, ed., *Generation* [New York: Dell, 1972]); it was a small sign of changing times.

Comment *about* science fiction begins in the letter columns of the early pulp magazines; much of it was juvenile, gushy, ego-inflated, or unsuccessfully humorous, but a residue of shrewd and apposite criticism remains. It is a major source for this book, as should be apparent from chapter 1 onward. Serious book reviewing at first was sketchy and intermittent; there were not very many science fiction books available for review. C. A. Brandt, the scholarly author of the column "In the Realm of Books" in the Sloane-edited *Amazing Stories* (1929–1938), frequently filled up that gap by discussing books about *science,* from the Gernsbackian motive of informing the readers about the other of the Two Cultures. In two of the wartime pulps edited by Frederik Pohl, *Astonishing Stories* and *Super Science Stories,* book reviewing for the first time began to merit the term "literary criticism," and it was in those magazines that the custom began of paying attention to science fiction on the stage and screen also.

The real turning point in science fiction criticism, as in so much else having to do with the field, came at the end of the Second World War. The two or three pages of book reviews in *Astounding* expanded into a lengthy column, "The Reference Shelf," conducted with skill and intelligence by P. Schuyler Miller until his death in 1974. (A measure of the intellectual freedom in science fiction is that on occasion a Miller book review strongly disagreed with a Campbell editorial!) Miller's tradition is ably carried on in *Analog* by Lester del Rey. *Galaxy,*

Fantasy and Science Fiction, and *Amazing* all ran book reviews; those of Algis Budrys in particular—sometimes to the irritation of the fans, who may prefer "book reports" (that is, synopses of books they might want to read)—stand up as first class critical essays. The volume of book reviews has become so large that it also, like the stories, now requires critical indexing, a task admirably accomplished by H. W. Hall, ed., *Science Fiction Book Review Index, 1923–1973* (Detroit: Gale Research Company, 1975).

The science fiction writers who began work in the pulp era have become highly reminiscent about it. Lately they have taken to getting out collections of their own earliest work, with connecting autobiographical commentary; some examples are *The Early Asimov* (Doubleday, 1972; published as two paperback volumes by Fawcett, 1974), *Early Del Rey* (Doubleday, 1975); *The Early Williamson* (1975); and *The Early Pohl* (1976). With appropriate historical discounting for the haze and distortions of memory, these are very valuable sources indeed, not only about their subjects, but about the other persons, notably editors, with whom these authors had dealings in their youth. Another useful kind of source is the "I knew him when" memoir, such as "James Blish: Profile," which Blish's 1945 roommate, Robert W. Lowndes, contributed to an all–James Blish number of *The Magazine of Fantasy and Science Fiction* (vol. 42, April 1972). Single-author issues of that magazine—an all–Poul Anderson number (vol. 40, April 1971), an all-Robert Silverberg number (vol. 46, April 1974)—contain not only biographical, but also, most helpfully, bibliographical information. (Lest we become too mustily academic in this inquiry, let it also be noted that these special issues of *Fantasy and Science Fiction* also contain *stories* by these writers! The Poul Anderson number, for example, carried Anderson's Nebula Award-winning "The Queen of Air and Darkness.")

Full-dress biography of these writers has barely begun. H. G. Wells, as an accepted "mainstream" figure, was so treated early, in studies such as Bernard Bergonzi, *The Early H. G. Wells* (Toronto, 1962), and W. Warren Wagar, *H. G. Wells and the World State* (Yale, 1961). Of particular interest is a Ph.D. dissertation on Wells by a practicing pulp science fiction writer who became a professor of English, Jack Williamson, titled *H. G. Wells: Critic of Progress* (Baltimore: Mirage Press, 1973). Another important study is *The Life and Thought of H. G. Wells* by the Soviet scholar Julius Kagarlitski (London: Sidgwick & Jackson, 1966). Of the pulp writers per se, Howard Phillips Lovecraft has thus far received the fullest treatment; see L. Sprague De Camp, *Lovecraft* (Doubleday, 1975). Masters' theses have been written on Asimov, Bradbury, and so on, but most of them remain unpublished; an exception is "The Magic That Works: John W. Campbell and the American Response to Technology" by Albert I. Berger, done for a master's degree in history at Northern Illinois University and published in the *Journal of Popular Culture* (5, Spring 1972, 867–943).

More such work is appearing constantly. The academicians in the Science Fiction Research Association are as active, in their own way, as the authors in the Science Fiction Writers of America; like SFWA, the SFRA gives annual awards to the best work in its field. Scholarly journals, like Thomas Clareson's *Extrapolation,* Leland Sapiro's *Riverside Quarterly,* and Darko Suvin's *Science Fiction Studies* have drawn upon both "outsider" and "insider" criticism. An example of this kind of work is Thomas Clareson, ed., *SF: The Other Side of Realism* (Bowling Green: Popular Culture Press, 1971); an instance of the critical study of a single writer is Alexei Panshin, *Heinlein in Dimension* (Chicago: Advent Publishers, 1968). In a special category is Jack Williamson's compendium *Teaching SF,* published by the author at Box 761, Portales, New Mexico; this tabulated the courses on science fiction offered in American universities, colleges, and a few high schools, in some cases with reading lists and course outlines. Unfortunately it is now out of print.

Detailed work on the history of pulp science fiction really begins with the indefatigable Sam Moskowitz. Sam was a fan,

with a fan's misssionary zeal; we are all in debt for his pioneering work. In particular his essay introducing a collection of all-
but-forgotten tales from the late Victorian era, *Science Fiction
by Gaslight* (Cleveland: World, 1968), is of great value, as is his
essay on the "pre-history" of pulp science fiction in the Mun-
sey general adventure magazines, *Under the Moons of Mars*
(New York: Holt, Rinehart, & Winston, 1970). Especially
noteworthy as an interpretation of pulp science fiction's history is the series of essays by Alexei and Cory Panshin that
appeared in the magazine *Fantastic* in 1972–73: "Mastery of
Space and Time, 1926–1935" (21, August 1972); "The
Domestication of the Future, 1936–1946" (22, December
1972); "The Search for Mystery, 1958–1967" (April 1973);
and "The Search For Renewal" (July 1973). The Panshins'
point of view, as another of their essays makes clear ("Metaphor, Analogy, Symbol and Myth," *Fantastic:* 21, February
1972), is almost diametrically opposite to my own. For that
very reason I urge all persons interested in science fiction to
read and consider the Panshins' work seriously. I have benefited from it, even where I disagree.

The history of science fiction, the Panshins note in a more
recent review (*Fantasy and Science Fiction:* 51, July 1976), is a
subject whose time is now. As with the old magazine illustrations, so with the words; "publishers seem to be convinced that
we want to see the face of yesterday's tomorrow once again."
As examples of this current interest in science fiction's history,
the reviewers cited *Alternate Worlds: The Illustrated History of
Science Fiction,* by James E. Gunn (New York: Prentice-Hall,
1976), and *Billion Year Spree,* by Brian Aldiss (Garden City, N.
Y.: Doubleday, 1973). They commented astutely on the
strengths and limitations of both books. Historical information can also be found in such books as Sam J. Lundwall,
Science Fiction: What It's All About (New York: Ace Books,
1971).

Lundwall's study, first published in Sweden in 1969,
reminds us, for example, that the first periodical in the world

that can be classified as a science fiction magazine was not an American but a Swedish creation, *Hugin* (1916); this is one of those necessary cautions against treating science fiction glibly as if it were but a reflex of American—or, at most, Anglo-American—culture. Another such corrective is the scholarly commentary by Darko Suvin on work being done in the Soviet Union and in Eastern Europe, in his anthology of science fiction from the socialist countries titled *Other Worlds, Other Seas* (New York: Random House, 1970). The Latin countries have also shown interest in this subject; a student at the University of Arizona, Roger Davis, has directed my attention to a Brazilian study, *Introdução ao Estudo da "Science-Fiction"* by André Carneiro (Sao Paulo, 1967).

Persons from completely outside the science fiction field— who have neither the specialist scholar's interest, like Clareson and Suvin, nor the hobbyist's enjoyment, like Moskowitz and Forrest Ackerman—commonly comment on science fiction only in the form of a pot shot, followed by a quick retreat to the conventional. One can nevertheless learn from such diatribes; one of the most significant is Bernard DeVoto, "Doom Beyond Jupiter" (*Harper's:* 179, September 1939). Far more comprehensive, as an example of a study of science fiction by someone whose primary intellectual interests lie elsewhere, is *Voyages to the Moon*, a book that wears its deep erudition with grace and readability, by the distinguished Renaissance scholar Marjorie Nicolson (New York: Macmillan, 1948).

ACKNOWLEDGMENTS

It is not possible to conclude this essay on science fiction in the library without venturing outside the stacks and reading rooms for a breath of air. I gleaned information and viewpoints that went into this manuscript from what was said and heard at two World Science Fiction Conventions; from correspondence with editors who published my own fiction, notably John W. Campbell, August Derleth, and Anthony Boucher;

and from letters of Ray Bradbury, Jack Williamson, and Donald Menzel of the Harvard College Observatory, all three of whom commented helpfully upon my treatment of their own work. I have been privileged to visit in the home of the late William A. P. White (Anthony Boucher's real, or rather private, name) in Berkeley, and at the headquarters of the Los Angeles Science Fantasy Society.

Mrs. John W. Campbell, Jr., and Mr. Albert I. Berger have kindly allowed me to quote from the taped interview Berger secured from Mr. Campbell in his *Analog* office on January 28, 1971. An early version of chapter 1 was read to my colleagues in the Department of History at Northern Illinois University in 1970; I benefited from their suggestions. A revised version appeared in the *Journal of Popular Culture*, 5 (Spring, 1972), with the title "'Extravagant Fiction Today— Cold Fact Tomorrow': A Rationale for the First American Science Fiction Magazines." Still further revised, it appears in this book by the kind permission of the *Journal of Popular Culture*. Chapter 2, similarly, originated as "Rockets to the Moon, 1919–1944: A Dialogue Between Fiction and Reality," *American Studies*, 15 (Spring, 1974), 31–46. It appears here by kind permission of *American Studies*. Other chapters in rough draft were inflicted upon some of my classes in the University of Arizona, and I profited from the feedback. Most of the manuscript was read, in five-minute chunks, over the University's radio station, in a twice-weekly program "Science Fiction Scrapbook," and I am indebted to Bob Ritter and Pat McQuown of KUAT-AM for the opportunity. Hearing these programs on the air prompted some rewriting, thereby somewhat lightening the task of my excellent editor at Columbia University Press, Mr. Leslie Bialler.

Conversations with three writers who visited the University of Arizona in 1975, during and after a panel I was asked to chair by the organizers of DesertCon III, an annual science fiction and fantasy film festival in Tucson, have influenced this manuscript at a number of crucial points. To Edmond Hamilton, Leigh Brackett, and Poul Anderson, I therefore owe a special debt, and I truly hope I have discharged it by not misrepresenting their views in this study. To my wife, Julie Raffety Carter, who bore through the writing of this somewhat uncongenial study with patience and critical acumen, the debt is incalculable.

Index

(Citations to pictures reprinted in this book are in boldface type.)

Picture Credits